Managing
For Mission

Managing For Mission

Pursuing the Magis in Jesuit Schools

Jack Peterson

To Mary,
my companion and inspiration
in the great adventure of life

Table of Contents

Introduction: Management vs. Leadership

It happened in the middle of summer. I had been selected earlier that spring to succeed a great school president, but on a warm Monday, July 1, 1996, I actually sat in his chair for the first time. Fr. Dan Weber SJ had served as the school's president for 20 years, bringing it through tumultuous times to a place of stability and strength. I had assisted him for 15 of those years, conscious that I had been learning at the feet of a master but nonetheless teeming with ideas and goals and convinced I could make our school even better. But when I actually sat in that chair, suddenly my perspective shifted. It dawned on me that simply having good ideas and a vision of what a Jesuit school should be would not be enough. I began to realize that it wasn't about my vision or ideas anyway. The Holy Spirit was making its vision known through hundreds of people in and around this school. I had to learn how we could take a vision and translate it into the many decisions we would make each day.

Many books and articles have distinguished true leadership from mere management. Leadership is visionary, inspiring. It stirs the souls of those working in Jesuit schools to create an education which goes beyond the ordinary to have an extraordinary impact on their students. Using an ancient Latin word, we call this the *magis*, which means simply the "more." It comes from the question asked by St. Ignatius of Loyola in the *Spiritual Exercises*, "What more can I do for Christ?" While I agree that the *magis* which Jesuit schools seek requires inspired and inspiring leadership, that's not what this book is about. This book is about management.

If leadership is the visible crest of a wave that brings the water crashing to the shore, management is the steady tide that brings the rest of the ocean with it. Both the highly visible waves and the steady tide are needed to advance our schools toward the *magis*. My hope is that this book will offer leaders in Jesuit schools management tools that can help them harness powerful and steady forces to produce continuous improvement. Good management will help our jobs and the jobs of those we work with be more satisfying, even fun. Done right, it will lead to a surplus of leadership, at all levels of the school's organization.

The task of this book is to share the management tools and approaches that I have found helpful in three decades of administration in a Jesuit school. Admittedly these are based on one person's experiences, but they are fortified by my observations of other successful administrators. They also borrow heavily from management practices developed outside the field of education which I have found can be adapted successfully to the challenges we face.

My hope is that this book will be of use to people who are responsible for managing Jesuit schools toward their *magis*. For readers just beginning a career leading a Jesuit school, I hope the book will provide a framework for addressing a full range of questions they will face. Experienced administrators will find much which seems obvious, much they already know, some they disagree with, and hopefully a few new ways of looking at old problems. I hope the overall structure of the book will help even the seasoned administrator step back from the daily exigencies of running a school and reflect on how all the pieces function together.

This book will be useful to people other than chief administrators of Jesuit schools. Board members will find it helpful in understanding the governance challenges of the school. It will also help them in their role as supervisor and supporter of those who manage the school. Someone who wants to be a president or principal of a Jesuit school will find the book helpful for discerning such a call and preparing for it. Anyone working in a Jesuit school who simply wants to understand the range of issues involved in managing the school will find this book useful. And its usefulness should not be limited to those involved with Jesuit education. Although my experience outside of Jesuit education is far less than that within it, most of what is said here can easily be adapted to other Catholic schools and schools and non-profit organizations in general.

One word the reader will encounter often in these pages is model. A model is a distilled representation of a system showing assumptions, main components and how they interact to achieve their purpose, so that the system can be preserved, changed or replicated as needed. Architects build models of a building so that they and their clients can have a better feel, before the building is constructed, for how all the pieces will function together. Even blueprints (which of course aren't blue anymore) are models highlighting the functional elements of the building and how they work together as a system. Often we don't see the systemic nature of an organization's behavior because it doesn't seem to be based on consistent assumptions. But more often organizations are simply unaware of their assumptions and the patterns that shape what they do. If we can describe the organizational models we are actually working from and compare them to the models we'd like to be following, we can more quickly identify elements that are inconsistent with the goals of our school. For instance, if my goal as an administrator is to build a collaborative environment, yet I often find myself unwilling to share performance data with faculty because I'm afraid they might draw different conclusions, there is a serious disconnect between my goals and my behavior. I need to articulate a model that brings out the essential elements of a collaborative environment, and then compare that honestly to what I am doing. Only then will it become clear what new assumptions I need to make, what components need to be in place and how they need to interact to accomplish my school's goals.

The structure of this book is based on the recognition that there are actually four functional models that shape what we do as Jesuit schools: an *apostolic model* with the purpose of accomplishing the mission entrusted to us by Christ; a *pedagogical model* with the purpose of achieving our educational objectives; a *community model* with the purpose of fostering healthy relationships within and around our institutions; and a *business model* with the purpose of ensuring that our schools can be sustained financially. Each of these models must be functional (as opposed to dysfunctional) if our schools are to flourish and accomplish their full mission. We will be looking at each individually, but also considering how they impact each other and how that mutual impact can be harnessed in the way we manage our schools.

The reader will note that the analysis becomes progressively more detailed and more concretely prescriptive as each successive model is described. For instance, the description of the first, the apostolic model, will have fewer practical recommendations than the last, the business model. There are two reasons for this. First, to make practical recommendations for the first two models requires a better understanding of the latter two, so some of the practical recommendations that support earlier models will actually appear in the latter two. Second, there is already a plethora of written and oral tradition with practical advice relating to our apostolic and pedagogical models. I also find that many of my colleagues are at least as skilled if not more skilled than I in these models. What I can offer them is a different way of looking at them that will bring greater clarity to how decisions are made, particularly how decisions for one model will impact the others.

I hope the reader will see a coherent, unifying philosophy underlying the approach to all the models. This philosophy follows the contours of Catholic Christianity and ways of proceeding based on Ignatian spirituality, and features four values that must be applied to each model: purpose, freedom, growth and trust. Applying this underlying philosophy consistently to all models will help the reader find new and sometimes surprising approaches to old and seemingly intractable management challenges. It is possible to move beyond school silos and resolve the institutional dissonance between the different sectors of our schools.

As detailed as the book may seem at points, there are still many elements of the strategies described which simply could not be included without making it unwieldy. It is my personal goal to make all this information available to whoever will find it useful. How to best do that is a continually evolving project. But at points in the book where more information is available from me, I indicate this and suggest the reader use the contact information at the end of the book to let me know what they need. I will, within my own limitations, try to find the best way to make that information available.

At times I use common words in specific ways, and when I do so, I try to offer the reader the precise definition I am using. I find that the very discipline of defining terms can yield new insights and ways of dealing with previously intractable problems. I have compiled these terms and their definitions into a glossary in the back of the book to make it easier to reference them at a later point.

Finally, I need to acknowledge that very few of the insights in this book originated with me. While everything that is said is grounded in my own experience, the insights I offer are based on what I have learned working with remarkable colleagues at my own school, observing and learning from colleagues at other schools, and listening to and reading the insights of many wise people inside and outside of Jesuit education. I have tried to name some of them in the *Acknowledgments* at the end of his book, but I could not include them all, and I cannot thank them adequately for the grace they have been to me.

Chapter I: Mission

While each Jesuit school has its own unique mission, we also all have one in common. We are called to be companions in Christ's mission and to invite our students to be companions in that mission as well. Before the cannonball blasted Ignatius' leg in the battle of Pamplona, God had already formed him as a brave, intelligent, disciplined and passionate man. What emerged from the pain and boredom of his convalescence at Loyola was a man now desirous of committing all that ardor and skill to something that really mattered, the only thing that mattered, bringing his soul and the souls of other people back into the arms of God who loves us. The mission of each Jesuit school is to replicate in ourselves and our students the transformation experienced by Ignatius after Pamplona. But we do it by a particular means, and in particular times and places.

We are schools, and so we are about the business of strengthening the minds, bodies and characters of our students. Since the Renaissance, western culture has believed that schools are necessary for the development of young people to meet the adult challenges of an increasingly complex society. Ignatius saw the need for this in his own life and spent years designing and pursuing his own education because he saw it as necessary for the mission God was calling him to. Where Jesuit schools differ from other schools is that we prepare students not for their own sake, nor even to simply contribute to the maintenance of society as we know it, but so that they can be truly transformational people, as Ignatius was, and as

Christ is. Perhaps this could be said of any faith-based school. What distinguishes Jesuit schools? I think it is the *magis*.

As Ignatius lay on his recovery bed, reading *Lives of the Saints* (not by choice, but because it was one of only two books available), he was captivated by the heroism of St. Francis and St. Dominic. Harnessing Ignatius' ego, God inspired him to say, "I can do great things like Francis and Dominic." And indeed he could, and did. Along the way, Ignatius learned that it was only by God's grace that he accomplished anything. He learned humility. But humility for Ignatius never meant doing the lesser; it always meant doing the "more," the *magis* in Latin. God's desires for us are huge. The desires God has planted deep inside us are also huge. Ignatius felt that his response to God must always be heroically generous. His *Prayer for Generosity* captures this spirit:

> Lord, teach me to be generous.
> Teach me to serve you as you deserve,
> to give and not to count the cost,
> to fight and not to heed the wounds,
> to labor and not to seek for rest,
> to toil and not to ask for reward,
> except to know that I do your will.

We can be a school and not ask this of ourselves or our students. We can be a good school without going this far. But we cannot be a Jesuit school.

Much has changed since Ignatius' time. At the time of his birth, all of western Christendom was nominally united under the Roman pontiff. Even as the Reformation fragmented Christendom, it could still be said that Christianity was the coin of the land. But today our neighbors, and our students, may be Jewish, Muslim, Buddhist or Scientologist. And actually most of the folks around us don't practice much religion at all. Does calling people to be companions of Jesus make much sense in such a world?

I don't want to give a simplistic yes to this question, because like the Jesuits throughout their history, we are confronting assumptions about Christianity, about Jesus and about religion that make it difficult to speak with clarity. I remember offering a prayer for a civic organization based on the quotation from Pierre Teilhard de Chardin that when humanity realizes that love is the power that runs the universe, we will, for a second time, have discovered fire. I thought this was a pretty Christian prayer, though I never mentioned Christ or even God. I felt pretty good when a woman came up to me afterwards and thanked me for such an inclusive prayer. She said, "I am a Jewish woman, and I am offended when people pray as if everyone in the audience is a Christian." I replied, that "I am a Christian man and I sympathize." My point was that even though I don't have her minority experience, I can understand how compromising that could feel, and I try to avoid putting people of other faiths in that spot. She misunderstood me, however, and thought I was saying that as a Christian man I sympathized with her being Jewish, as if that were something to be regretted. We finally got it straightened out, but it reminded me how difficult it is to speak clearly when there are so many misunderstandings, hurts and suspicions around religion.

Like Ignatius and the many Jesuits who brought their amped-up message of God's love to the uneducated poor, the apostate rich and the unevangelized peoples of other lands, we must be respectful and strategic in how we bring Christ to our own culture. Our mission is our greatest asset, more valuable than our endowment or our campus or our curriculum. But an inspirational mission alone will not make us the transformational institutions we aspire to be. We must be thoughtful and realistic as we go about our task. I think Jesus realized this when he sent the apostles into a hostile world, saying, "You must be as clever as snakes and as innocent as doves" (Mt 10:16). Simply raising the banner of Christ and charging bravely against the "infidels" or choosing to have nothing to do with the prevailing culture will only deepen the chasm that separates us from the people God sent us to love. This was not how Jesus himself did his work, nor Ignatius after him.

So if our common mission is to serve as companions of Christ and to call our students to be companions of Christ in mission, how do we as schools best go about accomplishing that mission?

A. One Institution, Four Models

Jesuit schools are unique, or at least that's what those of us who have worked in them feel. This sense of our uniqueness can lead to a couple of fallacies, however. One is that our unique mission makes it impossible to analyze our methodologies or outcomes in relation to any other organizations. The fact is that many organizations—other schools, other non-profits and even for-profit businesses—do some things better than we do. The other fallacy is that the identity of the school as a whole is a kind of mystery and the individuals working in it can grasp only the aspect of its identity that pertains to their job or department. As a result they will, consciously or unconsciously, be using a model to understand the school that is limited to their area of focus. Actually, Jesuit schools require four major models to describe who they are and how they work. So let's take a closer look at these models.

In the first place we can say that Jesuit schools are apostolates, because they carry on the ministry of teaching which Jesus entrusted to the apostles, and which the Church entrusts to the Jesuits and other orders and Church-sponsored institutions. Without this apostolic identity, a Jesuit school is just another school, perhaps more academically rigorous than some, perhaps better endowed than some, but just another private school. As an apostolate we are charged with helping our students discover through their studies and relationships just how much God loves them. Further we invite them to respond by becoming part of the loving, creative presence of God in the world. In this way, Jesuit schools are like parishes, spirituality centers and other apostolates, which are all trying to help people experience and respond to God's love for them. In this sense, they have an apostolic model.

But because we are schools we do this apostolic work in a particular way that is different from parishes and spirituality centers. As a school, we have a responsibility to help students grow intellectually, physically, emotionally and spiritually. We are governed by state laws and mandates concerning what students should know, and we have a responsibility to prepare students for higher education, which means we conform in great degree to the expectations of colleges and universities. We cannot ignore the demands of being a good school by claiming that we are an apostolate. Nor do we. Jesuit schools seek to be among the premier academic institutions in their regions. It is fundamental to who we are. And to be that, we need a pedagogical model that functions effectively.

But apostolate and school don't completely capture who we are. At my school and many other Jesuit schools (maybe every one), if you asked students, alumni, faculty and parents what one word captures who we are, the word most commonly heard will be "community." How does one experience God's love if not through community? How does one have the courage to learn new ideas, try new skills, and see things from different perspectives unless there is a loving, supportive and sometimes challenging community? In this sense, our schools are like families, or religious communities, or parishes. This doesn't happen by accident. We work hard to foster a healthy community, and the specific ways we do this can be called in aggregate our community model.

Apostolate, school, community. Does that about cover it? A word rarely heard to describe our schools is "business." This is odd if you think about it, because if we don't garner revenues that consistently cover all our expenses, we will soon not exist. People expect us to pay our bills, we have a payroll to meet every month, we have to carry insurance, borrow money from banks, market ourselves and do just about everything any other business does. But when we refer to ourselves as a business, a shudder runs down our spine as if we're about to sell our soul to the devil. We are reluctant to admit that being a school, even being a Jesuit school, also makes us an economic enterprise. We'd like to feel that our school parents are not making an economic decision to send their children to our schools. But the fact is, they are paying hard earned money to send their children to us and even if they don't admit it to themselves, they are making a consumer decision. They will not pay one penny more than they perceive it to be worth to them. How they judge its worth may differ vastly than the way they judge other purchases, but it must still be worth what they spend, and it must compete with all the other things they have to spend money on. We can be healthy from a purely apostolic, scholastic and community perspective, but if we don't also have a healthy business model, all the other aspects of the school will suffer, if not collapse entirely.

I will wager that anyone reading this book will have no trouble with anything I've said in the preceding paragraph. But how comfortable are you talking with your colleagues on the faculty and staff about your school as a business? How comfortable are they about engaging in such a conversation? Comfortable enough to want to learn more about how "our" business works and how all of us can make it work better, the way we all work together to strengthen the apostolic, pedagogical and community aspects of the school?

Effective management of a Jesuit school requires that leaders attend to each of these models—apostolic, pedagogical, community and business—and ensure that they are healthy. Figure 1 below graphically illustrates just how interrelated these models are, even though the boxes around the circle, and the connecting lines among them show only a small portion of the elements in each model and how they relate to each other. Even in this simplified form, it may be difficult to make sense out of the diagram. Rather than trying to comprehend it all at once, pick a box and follow a series of connections. The darkened arrows show one such series. Begin with Student Formation in the Apostolate quadrant. An essential element of student formation is Catholic social teaching, so we see an arrow coming from Social Justice box to Student Formation. But it's difficult to teach about social justice if it isn't reflected in the make-up of the student body, so Diversity, in the Community Model must reflect what is taught in class. Diversity is difficult to achieve without Financial Aid, which is impossible without Endowment, in the Business Model, which requires Marketing to attract donations, which requires a strong College Prep program to attract support. You might want to follow a few lines on your own, just to get a feel for just how much the four models making up the school's overall model interrelate. With that in mind, the ensuing chapters will explore each of these models in greater detail.

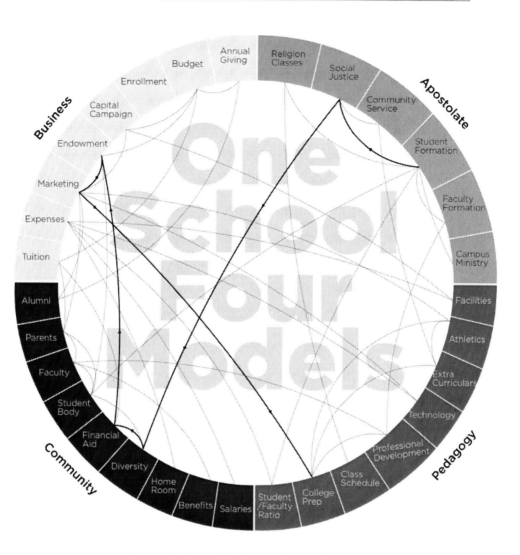

Figure 1: Four Models within a Jesuit School

Chapter II: Apostolic Model

Each Jesuit school was founded by a particular group of people with a particular purpose in mind. Furthermore, to continue to refer to itself as Jesuit and as Catholic, a Jesuit school must continue to accomplish a fairly specific mission. It is not enough to be a school or even a college preparatory school, training people to use their minds and bodies well. While education of the mind and body is in itself valuable and contributes to the well being of God's people, the Jesuit school has a further end in mind. In some way, this end must be captured in the mission statement of each Jesuit school.

In the document, *What Makes a Jesuit School Jesuit?*, the provincials of the United States, quoting the Society's Complementary Norms, say,

> All apostolates of the Society can be defined as a "service of faith, of which the promotion of justice is an absolute requirement." The service of faith is the aim of every Jesuit mission while faith "directed toward the justice of the Kingdom" is its integrating principle.

The provincials use the word "apostolate," in the belief that Jesuit works continue to carry on the mission established by Jesus himself, and then passed on to the apostles. Jesus described his mission when he began his public ministry, by reading in a synagogue in Nazareth from the Book of Isaiah:

"The Spirit of the Lord is upon me, because he has anointed me to bring glad tidings to the poor. He has sent me to proclaim liberty to captives and recovery of sight to the blind, to let the oppressed go free, and to proclaim a year acceptable to the Lord." Lk 4:18

This passage contains both elements of the essential Jesuit mission: helping the world believe in a God who loves us and wants us to be happy, and working to remove the obstacles in human society that prevent us from achieving happiness with God.

Jesuit schools consider themselves apostolates, because they carry on this essential mission which Jesus entrusted to his apostles. It is the same mission which God entrusted to Ignatius at La Storta when God "placed him with his Son," and Jesus invited him into companionship as he carried his cross.

The world has changed in many ways since the time of Jesus and the time of Ignatius. Our schools produce skilled, successful graduates and generally have strong balance sheets. They are well regarded even by people who have no idea what Jesus announced in that synagogue in Nazareth. Yet, if we do not carry on that same mission of faith that seeks justice, we cease to exist, at least as Jesuit schools. This is why we call ourselves apostolates, and why it is crucial that in managing a Jesuit school we pay attention to the health of our apostolic model. Like the pedagogical, communal and business models, it has to work, and it has to work well.

We use the word formation to describe the special dimension of our education that proclaims God's love for us and the consequent vocation to carry this love to others. This word can be a little off-putting to someone hearing it for the first time in an educational context. It can imply forcing the student into the shape or form we want her to take. Like many terms used by the Church, our sense of the word is the opposite of how it would be interpreted in the modern context. Formation means helping the student grow into the form that best expresses her potential. In his Principle and

Foundation at the beginning of the *Exercises*, Ignatius says that we were "created to praise, reverence and serve God, and by this means to save our souls." But many influences in our world can deform us and prevent us from reaching this goal and the happiness it will bring. In the story of the Prodigal Son, the father says to the older brother, "You are with me always and all I have is yours" Lk 15:31. Yet the brother's misunderstanding of his relationship with his father leads him to bitterness and resentment. All of us have similar misunderstandings to overcome in our journey back to God. By teaching, discipline, and encouragement in the responsible use of freedom, Jesuit education helps the student to become what she was created to be, a loved and loving child of God.

Formation, though, is really the middle step in a three step process toward our mission. The first step is *information*. This is actually as far as most education goes, just giving people a lot of information, or knowledge, but stopping well short of wisdom. *Formation*, rather, uses information to engage the whole person. It doesn't make artificial divisions between faith and reason, the spiritual and the physical, the moral and the social, history and our personal struggle. All these dimensions of our selves must grow together if we are to be fully formed. *Formation* is the education of the "whole person." But there is a third step, because formation leads to *transformation*. The fully formed person is one who feels whole, who feels loved, even cherished by God and others. Such a person cannot help but pour this back out into the world and begin to transform it. Love transforms him into a new being. As St. Paul says, "I live! Not I, but Christ lives in me!" Gal 2:20. And this transformed person in turn becomes a transformative influence in the world.

There are more complete elucidations of what *formation* means than I can provide here. My task is to take up the question of how we manage a school which has formation as its mission. Management and formation are not often used in the same sentence, but the formational mission of the school is not somehow insulated from the management of the school. It behooves us to give thought to how formation can be managed and management can be formed.

Management is "the direction leaders give to align the decisions and actions of all participants toward desired organizational

outcomes." Can formational objectives be achieved without leaders
giving intentional direction to the various activities and decisions of
those involved? It doesn't sound likely, but I think there is a
tendency not to apply management principles to the apostolic model
of our schools. In fact, I think we are reluctant to even consider the
apostolic dimension of the school as having a "model." There are
some good reasons for this. Management principles have for the
most part been developed in other contexts—manufacturing,
business administration, government agencies and yes, even the
military. These are all contexts where the outcomes are fairly
concrete. Applying assembly line process improvement to, for
instance, our retreat program, just doesn't sit well with us. The
reason is that assembly line production is dealing for the most part
with inanimate objects, where the correlation between inputs and
outputs is fairly constant and predictable. But the formation of a
person, and particularly that person's spirit, is anything but
predictable. Programming a person's spirit is a contradiction in
terms. If you could take away people's freedom, you would direct
them like machines. And that's been tried. But you can't really take
away human freedom, you can only deform it, which is precisely
what formation is intended to undo. Remember, Jesus' mission
proclaimed in the Nazarean synagogue was bringing greater
freedom, not less.

Management of an apostolic model is managing for greater
freedom, primarily, though not exclusively, that of our students.
How do we do that? A way of answering that question is to ask what
happens when our apostolic model fails, or at least when it falls short
of our hopes. What would that look like for you? Would you see
students flunking religion classes, not participating in liturgies or
retreats? Would there be a lack of civility in the way students treat
one another? Would students denigrate Church teaching, or simply
ignore it when making important choices? Probably if any one of the
foregoing reached a certain point, we would be concerned about the
effectiveness of our apostolic model. And rightly so. Somehow the
school's administrators would have to pull together and figure out
how to guide toward desired results the various decisions and
activities that constitute the formation program. That's management.

But what if we don't see any of these manifestations reaching alarming levels? Would we just relax as leaders and say we have nothing to do? Or would we say we want to put in place some assurance that the apostolic model won't deteriorate in the future? Or maybe we would want to find ways to improve on an already acceptable situation. That's what is meant by the *magis*. That is also what we mean by management.

The first step in managing the apostolic model is to define for ourselves what it is. I imagine that few schools have ever articulated their apostolic model, but whether it has been written down or not, they are following one. Articulating it helps us to be more intentional about it. It helps us determine, not only whether it is producing the results we want, but whether it is even the right model to begin with. It will also help us go from having many different models used by various participants in the formation process to a common model that all are managing together.

An apostolic model has five major components: Outcomes, messages, deliverers, receivers and methods.

A. Apostolic Outcomes

To understand the apostolic model one must first articulate the outcomes it should be producing. As discussed earlier, we have rich resources in Jesuit literature to guide us, from the *Complementary Norms'* "service of faith and promotion of justice," to Fr Arrupe's call for Jesuit alumni to be "men [and women] for others," to the profile of the "graduate at graduation" as a student "open to growth, intellectually competent, religious, loving and committed to justice." Our own school's mission statement will delineate what these phrases mean for our particular school. So the first place to look for the outcomes of our apostolic model is our school mission statement.

For instance, the school's mission may be "graduating students who will give their lives to proclaiming Christ's message of love and working to create a more just society." This gives us the general direction, but the apostolic model must also identify the concrete outcomes implied by the mission.

Based on this mission, the school's apostolic model might include the following outcomes: 1) an encounter with Jesus as a person with whom students can have a personal relationship; 2) catechesis that leads students to understand fundamental Church teachings; 3) experience of prayer forms and an understanding of how they can help students realize God's hopes for them; 4) an appreciation of other faiths; 5) hands-on activities that alleviate suffering and injustice in the world; and 6) a community that actively celebrates and evidences God's presence within it.

Do these outcomes of the apostolic model address the formational dimension articulated in the mission above? If they are effective, will they lead students to "give their lives to proclaiming Christ's message of love?" Will they lead to their "working to create a more just society?" Is anything missing? Is anything extraneous? Agreement on these outcomes will form the foundation of the apostolic model, the means by which the school accomplishes the mission given to it by the Jesuits, the Church, and ultimately Christ himself.

The first component of the apostolic model, then, consists of the outcomes of our mission to spread the Gospel message Christ has entrusted to us.

B. Message

The second component of the apostolic model is the message itself. Again, for a Jesuit school, the message comes from Jesus, by way of the Church, Ignatius and the current members of the Society of Jesus and their co-workers. At its root, it is the message from Isaiah that Jesus quoted: God's love for us and His desire for us to be free to enjoy that love. But how that gets played out in the human struggle, especially as it evolves over time, requires that more be said. For instance, it is critical that our students understand the role and meaning of the Eucharist in God's relationship with them. Another example is the importance to their own freedom and destiny of their choices relating to sexual expression. Without trying to outline all these messages, let us simply say that the Church has been working on getting them right for 2000 years and the Jesuits have given much to the Church in how best to convey them. With the help of the Church and the Society of Jesus, we must identify the key messages that should be conveyed to high school-aged students and the key experiences we should expect them to have on their journey to a deeper relationship with God.

The Catholic Bishops of the United States have undertaken an ambitious effort to define what needs to be taught in Catholic schools. *The Curriculum Framework for the Development of Catechetical Materials* is a helpful outline for the ground to be covered if a high school student is to be conversant in the full range of teachings the Church considers important. But it doesn't answer the crucial questions of how to lead students to a deep understanding of these teachings, which contain centuries of complexity and nuance, let alone how to foster the change of heart needed to freely embrace them. The *Framework* is a good start, but each school must be strategic about what messages it incorporates into its four-year religion curriculum, its campus ministry program, and the overall culture of the school. To do this effectively, it must understand well who it is who will be receiving this message, and that is the next component of the apostolic model.

C. Receivers of the Message

This component seems easy to define. The receivers of the message in our apostolic model are the students, of course. But having said this, we have said very little. Educators make many assumptions about their students, and if we don't examine those assumptions, it can lead us into trouble. For instance, our job would be a lot easier if we could assume all our students already have a foundation in Catholic catechesis. We know this not to be the case. Not only does a growing percentage of most Catholic schools consist of students of other faiths, but even the ones identifying themselves as Catholic may not have attended Catholic schools previously. Or their parents may not have continued to cultivate a relationship with the Church, let alone take up their role as their children's primary religious educators. Even if the students have knowledge of the faith, as they enter high school they will generally need to be re-converted to a more sophisticated and challenging faith than they embraced prior to adolescence.

The school's apostolic model must include an understanding of who it is we are evangelizing. It is not a question of one model fits all. An inner-city Nativity School will have a different challenge than a traditional college prep school in a historically Catholic city or a traditional college prep school in an "unchurched" region. Nor is it simply a matter of the students' religious background. Their poverty or affluence, the education level and academic expectations of their families, their ethnic background, the vitality of the local church, the trends in youth culture and the political landscape will all greatly impact how the Gospel message must be relayed in order to be heard. As Jesuit missionaries like Xavier, de Nobili and Ricci knew, the model changes based on whom you're trying to reach. I think our teachers and administrators understand this already. My point is that it needs to be talked about explicitly as part of the school's apostolic model.

One characteristic of our students that Ignatius would want us to make explicit in our apostolic model is that they have free will. Not everyone believes in free will. Even people who say they believe in free will, including many educators, seem actually to be behaviorists because they seem interested only in controlling students' behavior. Catholic teaching and Jesuit spirituality are firmly committed to the principle of free will. But even if we believe in the concept of free will, the open-endedness of it frightens us.

I remember one year having the responsibility of night supervision for a group of 160 high school seniors, boys and girls, on a camp-out retreat. In exchange for taking on this responsibility, I had asked the campus minister that all the girls' tents be set up as far away from the boys' tents as possible. All I had to do was keep the students out of the vast no-man's land in the middle. All the other adults had gone to bed and I patrolled around the tents with my flashlight overhearing and quashing the plots students were hatching to "meet in the middle." I had a high need for control at this moment and exercised all the authority I could muster. Then all of a sudden, coordinating their movements with 2-way radios, all the students flooded out of their tents at once, the girls from their side and the boys from theirs. They were screaming and running around and laughing at my powerlessness. After about 15 minutes, I climbed up on a tree stump, shined a flashlight on myself and whistled. When I got their attention, I said, "Okay, you win. I have no power to get you to go to your tents. But I am asking you, because we adults are tired, we worked all day so that you could have this experience, and we need to get some sleep." Some students started chanting, "Hell no, we won't go. Hell no, we won't go." I was not feeling good about the implications of free will at that point. But then one of the students said, "He's right. C'mon you guys, we accomplished what we wanted." Others students added to his voice, and in about 10 minutes they had all gone back to their tents and settled down. It was the most impressive demonstration of the responsible use of free will I have experienced. The next year, wiser administrators than I decided to mix the girls' tents and the boys' tents in the same area, and the supervision has never been a problem since.

What my colleagues realized is that students will exercise their free will. My authoritarian approach only challenged them. But when we gave them back the responsibility for how to use their freedom, they accepted it. I am not arguing that we don't need JUG or dress codes or other rules. But all of these must be used with a keen awareness of the irreducible gift of free will which God has given to human beings. Our task is to help our students learn how to use that free will responsibly. As Pope Benedict has repeated on a number of occasions, the Church is to "propose but not impose faith in Christ who is the way, the truth and the life."[1]

The other Ignatian assumption which goes hand-in-hand with teaching the responsible use of freedom is that our students' deepest desires will lead them toward the good. This is not a universal assumption, not among believers and not even among Christians. Ignatius believed that "God can be found in all things" and his *Spiritual Exercises* is built around God's using our deepest desires to call us to Himself. This was a bold approach, especially for someone like Ignatius, whose desires in his early life, for glory, the favor of a woman, drinking and fighting, had consistently led him away from God. Though these were strong desires, he began to realize on his bed in Loyola recovering from a cannonball wound, that these were not his deepest desires. This is where it takes some courage to be an Ignatian educator. Shallow desires can be a bad thing, but deep desires are a good thing. If you've ever rappelled down the side of a mountain, you will know a similar feeling. Minimizing your dependence on the rappel rope will have you leaning forward trying to stay upright. As a result, you will bang your body on the rocks all the way down. It could kill you. But if you lean back into the void, trusting the rope, you can simply walk backwards down the mountain. It's much easier, but it doesn't feel like it!

As Ignatian educators, rather than suppressing our students' desires, we need to inflame them. Rather than teaching students not to be greedy, teach them that greed for mere money is a cruel form of self denial. Help them be greedy for the universe, to want nothing less than God Himself. If that doesn't sound a little scary to you, you're thinking about it too abstractly.

I encourage you to reflect on the assumptions your apostolic model makes about who your students are. Ask how seriously it accounts for their freedom and the power of their deepest desires to lead them to God.

The first component of the apostolic model was the outcomes we seek for and from our students, and the second was the message that conveys the fullness of the Gospel that is integrated into our curriculum. This third component has been focused on the students who receive the message and the next will focus on those who deliver it.

D. Deliverers of the Message

This component also seems temptingly easy to define. Our teachers are the deliverers of the message, right? But again let's take a closer look. First of all we have to ask which teachers we are relying on to deliver the message. In some schools, people assume it's up to the religion teachers and the campus ministry folks, who are often the same people. In other schools, the math teachers have a clear understanding of how they support the school's apostolic model, not just outside their classrooms, but in them as well. In some schools, some of the administrators don't see themselves as having any evangelizing role, and in others it is clearly a constitutive element of being an administrator. In some schools, the facilities staff, the office staff, the lunchroom staff and the security staff are explicitly engaged, directly or indirectly, in formation. The question is what your school believes would best support the apostolic model. Most would agree that the more members of the adult community who understand, model and can speak to the school's formational goals, the stronger that formation will be. When students see a custodian pause in his work during a morning prayer over the PA, he can impress them more powerfully than a teacher, who is expected to.

I suspect we can all imagine a preternatural school in which everyone is modeling Catholic teachings, values and practice. The reality is that it is not just our students who are on a journey to deeper faith and more consistent practice. It is also our faculty, our support staff and even our administrators. This means they are imperfect deliverers of the message. That's an uncomfortable place to be, and they know it. It makes sense that they often hope that someone else will be the role model, that someone else will figure out how to convince teenagers to embrace the often difficult, counter-cultural and counter-intuitive teachings of the Church. Some people, particularly those not directly involved in education, believe that if we just hired faithful people, if we just held our faculty, staff and administrators accountable in their practice and their teaching of the faith, then we could be assured of our students receiving in a compelling way the true teachings of the Church.

This was the model used by the Puritans when they migrated to the American colonies. Scandalized by the growing religious pluralism and laxity of England and afraid of the impact it would have on their children, they banded together and moved to where they could all live by, and raise their children by, a strict and binding covenant. It worked well for a while, but communities change. Children see things differently than their parents, people join the community who turn out not to be quite so faithful, and even the most zealous proponents of the covenant can lose their way. So the puritans of New England went from Covenant, to "Half-way

Covenant," to the disestablishmentarian principle that now governs our land.

Given the tendency of all humans toward both decline and redemption, and the importance of the faith and practice of those who are passing on the faith to our students, this component of the apostolic model may be the most difficult of all. It cannot be simply reduced to accountability and careful hiring, though these, if we respect their limitations, are crucial elements. The model must also include an ongoing process to evangelize and catechize the evangelizers. More will be said about that in Chapter IV Community Model, under Apostolic Formation

Here it is important to remember what was said above about our students. First, our employees have free will. Though we may be tempted to think otherwise, because they are employees, we cannot impose that faith on them any more than we can on our students. We can help them realize when their level of commitment is not a good match for teaching in a Jesuit school. We will sometimes even have to come to that conclusion for them and not renew their contract because they are not able to acknowledge the contradiction themselves. The best Ignatian educator is one who is honestly following her deepest desires to grow closer to God and drawing others with her. Unfortunately, that simply cannot be imposed from the outside. Even someone who has a genuine faith can be turned off from her deeper desires when they are framed by authorities as "have-to's."

But the tricky part of managing people in a Jesuit school is that growing in the spiritual life and sincerely supporting the teachings of the Church really are "have-to's." Yet using the angle of accountability as the primary approach will kill or at least ward off the kind of genuine desire that makes all the difference in our students' experience of a relationship with Christ through their teachers. The other challenge is that it is sometimes hard to predict who will flower in their faith, given the right opportunity. I have seen religious people become shallow, judgmental and pietistic, and I have seen people who had no time for church, religion or spirituality develop a lively and whole-hearted faith.

How, then, do we evangelize our teachers in ways that prepare them to be the evangelizers? In Chapter IV on the school's Community Model, in the section on Professional Development and Apostolic Formation, I will address ways of working with freedom and desire in managing employees toward greater effectiveness as educators and evangelizers.

The first component of the apostolic model was the outcomes we seek based on our apostolic mission, the second was the Christian message that shapes those outcomes and the third was the students who are the receivers of that message. This fourth component has dealt with the deliverers of the message, primarily but not exclusively our teachers. The final component will address the methods we use to deliver that message in a compelling way.

E. Methods of Delivery

The fifth component of the apostolic model is probably the one we give the most attention to. Since we are schools, our apostolic model's delivery method encompasses curriculum, lesson plans, textbooks, liturgies, retreats, and prayer experiences throughout the program. My intention is not to try to add to the marvelous methodologies that educators in Jesuit schools have developed. I would rather focus on the bigger question of how these pedagogical methods function in the apostolic model. The next chapter, on the pedagogical model, will focus more on pedagogical method related to the whole school program.

In discussing above assumptions about our students I emphasized the importance of the use of freedom and desire in Ignatian formation. Ignatian pedagogy assumes that there is a dynamic to learning that parallels the natural dynamic of spiritual growth, which Ignatius captured in the Spiritual Exercises. We call this natural dynamic of learning the "Ignatian Pedagogical Paradigm" (IPP), which has five steps, *context, experience, reflection, action* and *evaluation*. I will discuss the IPP in greater depth in Chapter III, Pedagogical Model, under Methodologies, but for now I want to explore the three core steps, which are *experience, reflection* and *action*. Our apostolic model, just as our educational model, must build upon the student's need to experience, reflect and act if he is to grow in the spiritual life.

Unless the student *experiences* God's love for him, the message we proclaim will seem shallow at best. We believe that the student will experience God's love for him most fully in the context of a relationship with the person Jesus. But how does that happen? Reading scripture? Yes. Reading about saints like Ignatius, whose lives were inflamed by Jesus? Yes. Studying theological questions designed to uncover who Jesus was and is? Yes. But it will be highly unlikely that a person will experience the love of Jesus unless he experiences it in his relationships—with his family, his classmates and with his teachers. It is critical to our apostolic mission that our model provide opportunities like retreats, liturgies, and time in class and extra-curriculars for students to experience the loving presence of God in their lives. The bad news is that with all the distractions and pressures on everyone in the school community, it is challenging to design and sustain these opportunities. They often feel like an add-on to what we're supposed to be doing as a school. The good news is that it is difficult to stifle the Spirit. God truly can be found in all things, and all people, and all relationships. This doesn't mean that all experiences are equal in terms of revealing God to our students. But we don't need to coax God out of hiding to present Him to our students. They have a surprising capacity to see God in the irascible teacher, the boring homily, the poorly organized retreat. Especially if we help them learn how.

This leads us to the second of the core steps of the IPP, *reflection*. The apostolic model must not only provide opportunities where God's love can be experienced, but give students the tools to reflect on what they experience. In some sense, the entire religion curriculum is designed to help students reflect on the experience of God's people through history. We are giving them the benefit of God's self-revelation in Scripture and the wisdom of the Church, which is also based on experience and the inspiration of the Holy Spirit. But the student's faith cannot be second-hand. At some point, they have to reflect on their own experience in light of the tradition that has been handed down to them. An excellent example of this is the student talks at the upper level Kairos and Encounter retreats offered by Jesuit schools. The students generally talk about a significant and often painful experience in their life—the loss of a parent, addiction to drugs, a serious illness. What seemed hopeless at the time became an occasion for great grace in their lives. These student talks follow the pattern of Ignatius, who had many experiences in his young life, but only being hit with a cannonball could cause him to stop and begin reflecting on them. When he did, he began to hear Christ's call in his life. When finally healed, he was ready to do something about what he had learned.

This brings us to the third core step of the IPP, *action*. The apostolic model has to provide ways for students to put what they have learned into action. We all know that we haven't really learned something until we use it. I can have one of my kids show me how to change a function on my cell phone three times, but I won't remember it until I actually do it on my own. But formation is more than just remembering some bit of knowledge. We're helping our students make a fundamental choice in their lives. I remember being frightened at various times as a parent at how selfish my teenage children could be. And I have observed in the students I have worked with that adolescents can be amazingly selfish and self-absorbed. And yet, I have also been struck by how generous and self-giving they can be. Unfortunately, parents of teenagers generally get a lot more of the narcissistic side and we as educators see more the altruistic side. Young people are in the process of building themselves. They are receiving our love and support, and they need lots of it. But adolescents are also yearning to be like the people who love them, to be givers and not just receivers. Just about every junior on a junior retreat looks forward to when they can be one of the seniors giving that retreat. Kids this age want to make a difference in the world and they have a capacious idealism. Unfortunately, for the vast majority of adolescents in this country the opportunity to express that generosity never really comes. If they are not given the opportunity to act on their desire to be generous, it goes away, and it may take a long time to come back, if it ever does. This is why our community service and peer ministry programs are so critical. They allow students to take what they've experienced, reflect on it, and do something with it. In the process, they learn the deep joy of cooperating with Jesus, and being a channel of God's love to the world.

My point in the foregoing discussion is not to exhaust the topic of how Jesuit schools do or should be doing formation. This is, after all, a book about management, not religious formation. But managing for mission requires that we understand the model, either explicit or implicit, by which we accomplish our apostolic mission, because it will require the whole school, everyone, to make that model work. Remember the definition of management we're using: "The direction leaders give to align the decisions and actions of **all participants** toward desired organizational outcomes."

F. Managing Formation

To get a more complete picture of the model and begin shaping it more intentionally, we need to consider how all these components work together. The description of how the apostolic model functions could be quite complex and will vary from school to school. But let me offer a simple narrative to suggest how the apostolic model might work.

Drawing on its mission, a school might decide that its most important apostolic *outcome* is that students develop a vital and life-long relationship with Christ.

Based on this outcome, the school identifies the key ways that God invites students into this relationship so that it can help students hear God's message of love. These messages might include Jesus' words about God's love for His people; Jesus himself as the Word; Jesus coming to us in the Eucharist; Jesus coming to us in prayer; and Jesus coming to us in our neighbor.

How these messages are conveyed to the student will be determined in large part by who the school thinks the students are, as *receivers* of Jesus' invitation into relationship. The school might in this case determine that developmentally and culturally most of its students are not already invested in religious practice and need both catechesis and conversion. Acknowledging both their free will and that their deepest desires tend toward goodness, the school will design curriculum and experiences that give students ample opportunity to explore how those desires can be fulfilled in Christ.

It takes special people to create these opportunities. As deliverers of God's message, teachers must emulate Christ himself, who not only spoke the message, but embodied it. The school's apostolic model relies on people whose own faith and relationship with Jesus can ignite a desire for something similar in their students. But in this age (and perhaps all ages), teachers themselves are in need of conversion and catechesis. All of us are. So the apostolic model must provide for evangelizing the evangelizers and constantly supporting them on their faith journey. Far from being a weakness, the model uses this as a strength. Teachers and students to some extent journey along together. As the teacher experiences ever deeper conversion, the energy of this experience radiates out to students. This is one reason why among Jesuits in a school, regents in formation have such a powerful influence on the faith of their students. Through them, students witness the effects of ongoing Ignatian formation in the life of a trusted adult.

The apostolic model relies on a *method of delivery* that not only elucidates scripture and the teaching of the Church, but provides first-hand *experience* of Christ's invitation through relationships in the school community. On retreats, in classes and in informal conversations with teachers and peers, students *reflect* on the knowledge they are being given. Then through involvement in campus ministry, in Christian service and in school activities they *act* on the invitation to follow Christ in His ministry.

This, in far too brief a summary, is an example of how the model is designed to lead students to a vital and life-long relationship with Christ. But it is just an example. Even within the Jesuit framework there are many variations on this model. The idea is to intentionally develop an effective apostolic model.

If the foregoing outlines our basic apostolic model, how do we manage it? Is management even a word we should use in connection with formation? The alternative is to believe that we simply make formational opportunities available and out of them will emerge students who have a living relationship with Christ. This might happen. And it might not. Our role as leaders in the school is to align the decisions and actions of all participants toward desired outcomes (again, my working definition of management). Let's turn our attention to the rudiments of how we do that.

The first step toward managing our apostolic model would be to understand what we want the outcomes to be. We have already discussed above how the outcomes of our apostolic model are based on the school's mission statement. But to manage to those outcomes, we need even greater specificity. All the participants need to share an understanding of what those outcomes will look like. Otherwise we will not know when we've achieved them, or when we haven't. To know whether we are achieving our outcomes we need some sort of evidence we can rely on.

Ultimately there are three types of evidence, and they form a three-legged stool such that none is sufficiently reliable by itself. We can gauge our effectiveness intuitively, anecdotally or statistically. An example of an intuitive evaluation of apostolic outcomes might be, "I feel good about our apostolic model because we have a veteran religious studies faculty and a terrific campus minister who has the most extensive retreat program in the province." Of course, that doesn't mean that the students are being transformed by what they experience, just that our intuition suggests that our programs should lead to that result. An example of anecdotal evidence might be, "We must be reaching kids because we have several recent grads who have followed vocations to religious life." That's pretty good evidence that the formation program can impact some students at a deep level, but what does it say about the rest of the students? An example of statistical evidence might be, "The apostolic model must be working because our average scores on the religious questions for the JSEA Student Profile Survey increase by 15% from freshman to senior year." This reflects a breadth of change but not necessarily a depth of change. Maybe senior religion teachers just do a good job of preparing their students to take the SPS.

Each kind of evidence has inherent weaknesses, so it is important to use all three as checks and balances to each other. But the point here is that we want some method of evaluating our apostolic model. We want the measurement to be **accurate** so we don't, for instance, discontinue a program that is actually effective;

we want it to be **timely** so that we can respond quickly to what we're doing and not doing well; and we want it to be **relevant**, so that it guides actual decision-making (it doesn't do much good to know, for instance, that 85% of the students don't like the current pastor of their parish if that's something we have no control over).

I won't go into detail here about how to formulate performance metrics [to get more on this see *Contact the Author* at the end of the book], but it is instructive to recall Tom Peters' statement, "What gets measured gets done." It is as true for formation work as for the manufacture of widgets. The difference is the complexity of measuring formational outcomes. Peters' statement implies both that if we measure the right things, the right things get done, and if we measure the wrong things, the wrong things get done. We understand this intuitively, and the risk makes us avoid measuring formational outcomes altogether. But that is just as dangerous. Every member of the apostolic team is measuring outcomes by some yardstick. Unless we are explicit about our methods, everyone will be using their own metrics, and these will tend to be self-confirming. Let's consider some examples.

The first is a school that ostensibly doesn't use metrics to measure formational outcomes. This school has hired excellent faculty, including religion teachers with advanced degrees. It has made a substantial investment in providing retreats and other formational activities. It has taken seriously the fifth characteristic of the *Graduate at Graduation* and provided ambitious opportunities for students to address social justice issues. As good as all these inputs are, a problem develops for this school. A group of parents and faculty challenges the school's social justice efforts and makes the claim that the school has forsaken Catholic teaching to pursue a political agenda. The controversy swells to a point where others in the local Catholic community are withdrawing support because they feel the school is failing what they see as its primary formational objective. Even among the faculty there is an undercurrent of tension, which has undermined participation in faculty formation activities.

What has happened here is that different people are using their own yardsticks to measure the school's outcomes, and they are highly influenced by their own ideologies and perspectives. The school may be passing on the full range of Catholic teaching to its students, but if this is not measured, the school is pressured to make changes by people using their own, often subjective, metrics. This negatively impacts the school's ability to sail a straight course in pursuit of its mission.

The second example is a school that has established metrics for its formation outcomes, but has over-relied on statistical measures. This school has decided to measure program effectiveness by the number of students attending the voluntary, weekly mass offered during lunchtime in the school's spacious chapel. Since this is the only measure, the campus ministry department and the faculty as a whole focus their efforts on achieving a goal of 90% attendance. Nothing else is allowed to be scheduled during this time, the choral teacher invests time in preparing excellent music for the liturgies, and religion classes devote time to teaching about the mass and reminding students that the Eucharist is the source and summit of Catholic worship. Taking these steps the school sees mass attendance go from 30% up to 75% of the student body. Great. But at what cost? The statistical metric needs to be checked against anecdotal and intuitive evidence. Are other elements of the religion program, or the music program, being shortchanged? Does student attendance at mass coincide with deeper relationships with Christ or an embracing of Catholic values?

Continuing to look at this example, let's say that it is a source of frustration that, despite the increase in mass attendance, the campus minister or the school administration is bothered that the goal of 90% hasn't been reached, and only 75% of the student body is attending. So the school begins making PA announcements with implicit criticism of students who elect not to go to mass; teachers begin giving extra credit for mass attendance; the admissions committee takes fewer risks with students who aren't Catholic, or come from disrupted homes where mass attendance gets lost in the chaos. These responses are extreme, but they illustrate how over-reliance on one statistical measure, even a good one, can lead to trade-offs that ultimately undermine the mission.

The third example is a school which selects several measures that might include mass and retreat participation, growth as measured by the JSEA's Student Profile Survey, grades in religion classes, and surveys of alumni. The school establishes base-lines that show beginning levels, against which progress will be measured. It regularly reviews the results and shares them with the faculty, the board and parents. Progress on the metrics is used to make adjustments to policies and programs but the metrics themselves are reviewed in light of anecdotal evidence from teachers, students and parents and the intuitive judgments of experienced educators.

In this example, parents, and teachers as well, will continue to question the school's methodologies or emphases when they diverge from their own assumptions about how programs should be shaped. But with the statistical evidence, the school can show them objective reasoning behind its decisions and use their input to test and refine the model, rather than being locked in a power struggle over whose assumptions are more valid. By creating a feedback loop, the statistical evidence helps to build consensus about what the school is accomplishing and where to put efforts to improve its apostolic success.

G. Relationship to the Other Models

The other models will be discussed in the ensuing chapters, but it might be helpful to suggest how the apostolic model supports and is supported by the other three models.

Pedagogical Model

The apostolic and pedagogical models are closely related, so closely that it almost seems artificial to treat them separately. Both deal directly with student outcomes, but pedagogical outcomes comprise what we want them to know and be able to do, where apostolic outcomes are what we want them to become. The apostolic model relies on a pedagogical model that encourages students to be open to growth, gives them the skills needed for inquiry and reflection, and engenders the ability to engage the imagination. Conversely, the apostolic model supports the pedagogical model by providing a teleological grounding for the learning process. What is the purpose of education? By helping students experience God's love for them, and inviting them to become part of that love, our apostolic model gives a meaningful answer to that question. A key reason for our students' academic success is that they have some sense of why they are going through all this effort of gaining knowledge and skills. They have a sense of well-being and a purpose in their lives. Teachers who fail to access the graces of the school's apostolic model and do not strengthen the apostolic model through their teaching are running their race on one leg.

Community Model

While God has a personal relationship with each of us, that relationship is never solely between us and God. The apostolic model requires a healthy community for liturgies, retreats, religion classes and the encouragement and challenge we need from others on our journey toward a deeper relationship with God. If students are to experience God's love in our schools, they will do so primarily through their relationships with other students and their teachers. Conversely, the Gospel message conveyed by the apostolic model engenders the sense of well-being and abundance that leads to trust that is the *sine qua non* of a vibrant, life-giving community. It could even be said that in Jesuit schools the community model is a component of the apostolic model and the apostolic model is a component of the community model.

Business Model

The relationship between the apostolic and business models is not as apparent as the other two, so I want to spend a little more time exploring it. For a Jesuit school to remain viable it must function successfully as a business. People must be willing to spend money for its "product" and the amount they are willing to spend, either in tuition or in donations, must be sufficient to fund what it costs to produce the product. Put another way, the business model must support the apostolic model. But it also works the other way. Fortunately, or more probably thanks to God's design, the apostolic model of a Jesuit school will also strengthen its business model. This happens in two primary ways, and neither of them is that the needed money will miraculously appear because we are doing the Lord's work, although that has been known to happen. The two ways I have in mind are more mundane.

The first is that people really do want what our mission offers. They may not know that what they want for their children is a "faith that seeks justice." But they know that they don't want children who are cynical, selfish people. They may not be familiar with the *Profile of a Graduate of a Jesuit High School* or use its words, "open to growth, intellectually competent, religious, loving and committed to justice," to describe their aspirations for their children. But I have explained these characteristics one-on-one to hundreds of parents and when I finish, they tell me that's exactly what they want. People need what we have been created to offer. We have to explain it in terms they understand, in terms that connect with what they already think they need, but there is a real and felt need for what our apostolic mission impels us to do. That is an enviable foundation for a business model.

The second way the apostolic model supports the business model has to do with the concept of branding. Branding is a big word in business these days. It means developing an identity for your company or product that will somehow stand out from the infinite array of products competing for people's attention. The idea is to become recognized, or better, remembered, or better yet, trusted. Apple Computer has done this, especially with its iPod, iPhone and iPad products. Each one of them has been the "thing." Not only does everyone know what they are, but they are cultural icons and they are considered trustworthy, powerful products guaranteed to increase one's happiness.

Branding not only helps your product stand out, but gives people a basis for believing your claims about your product. If you say your school offers excellent education, don't be offended by the yawns in response. Every school claims that, from elite private boarding schools to struggling public schools. Even if you say you offer faith-based education, well we've all seen faith-based schools that aren't much to write home about. Somehow we have to differentiate ourselves, give people a reason why our claim (or *value proposition*) is credible. We are fortunate that as Catholic schools and Jesuit schools, we start with a brand that people identify as effective.

If we understand our apostolic model, measure its effectiveness and connect it to people's understanding of their needs, we have the basis for a healthy business model. Conversely, if we are unclear ourselves about what our model is, or can't explain it to potential customers in terms of what they need, why would they invest substantial money when free alternatives are available? And if we can't show them measures of our effectiveness, they will rely on anecdotal evidence or their own intuitions, which can make the same institution look very different to different people. That may be enough for some schools to survive, but not enough for them to achieve their apostolic potential.

H. Our Relationship to the Catholic Church

When I was growing up in the 1960's, my dad was the director of admissions for a Catholic university. When I went to college on the other side of the country, I met a young man who said he remembered my dad coming to his high school to talk about his university. I asked my friend how my dad did. He said, "He must have done pretty well, because I didn't know it was a Catholic university." Dad's probably rolling over in his grave as I relate this story. It would not be representative of his later work and the university's subsequent development. But I think it is indicative of the times he was living in. I can't pass judgment on his generation for deciding that in order for Catholic institutions to survive, they had to downplay their relationship with the Catholic Church. But I don't think this is the winning approach today.

Firstly, as discussed in the previous section, *Catholic* is part of our identity, our brand. Why would anyone think we have anything to offer if we were just another private school? Our connection with the Catholic Church is fundamental to who we are. Minimizing our Catholic identity would be like reducing the root system that provides life to a tree.

One of the ways we may have minimized our Catholic identity in decades past is by stressing our Jesuit identity. Although the Jesuits haven't always been more popular than the Church in the public eye, in our times, it seems that *Jesuit* has been less challenging for many people than *Catholic*. We have tended to respond to this public perception by stressing the more well-received identity. In some cases, I believe we have done this in order to give ourselves some independence from a Church, local or universal, that can seem at times backward looking and self-defeating.

Fortunately, we have come to see the short-sightedness of this. When I was a teenager, there were times when I didn't want to be associated with my parents, their styles, their values or their decisions. As I grew older, I didn't always agree with them, but I realized how foolish it would be to cut myself off from their love, their support and their guidance. I think Jesuit schools, Jesuit ministries and especially the Society itself have come to a similar realization. This was captured most explicitly in the experience of the 35th General Congregation in 2008. The Society has always acknowledged its charism of serving the Church in those areas of greatest need identified by the Holy Father. Pope Benedict XVI in his allocution to the Congregation appealed to this commitment. He touched them personally by showing his trust for the Jesuits and appreciation for their unique contributions.

> In his address, Pope Benedict XVI openly revealed his confidence...spiritual closeness & esteem, in words that touched our hearts, stirring & inspiring our desire to serve the Church in this contemporary world..."
> GC35, Decree 1

Pope Benedict, perhaps more than any other pontiff before him, acknowledged the historical work of the Society, which has brought it to cultural, intellectual and theological frontiers. He challenged the Jesuits to continue to work at the frontiers but also to live at the heart of the Church.

Therein lies our own identity as Jesuit, Catholic schools. If we simply stay at the margins of the Church, our relationship with it will attenuate, which is not consistent with being Jesuit. Yet we must also serve the Church by working at cultural, intellectual and pastoral frontiers. I substituted "pastoral" for "theological" when

talking about our mission as Jesuit schools, because we don't have
the competence that a Jesuit university would have to contribute
directly to the Church's theological development. But we can
contribute by sharing with the Church what we have learned as we
apply Church teachings pastorally in our work. It is not our role, for
instance, to formulate an alternate moral theology relating to
sexuality. But it is our role to relay back to the Church our experience
as we work with young people struggling with their sexual identity
and Church teaching. This is what Fr General Peter-Hans
Kolvenbach's phrase, "creative fidelity" means to me. We retain a
filial loyalty and devotion to the Church which connects us
historically and sacramentally to Christ, and we connect the Church
to its people, especially the young, and their experience.

We are entering a time which is bringing further complexity to
this already nuanced challenge. Given the upheaval caused by
Vatican II, the decline in religious vocations, declining enrollment
and other factors, Catholic schools are coming through a time of
instability. As suggested in my story that began this section, many of
these schools have not remained grounded in their Catholic identity.
This can be reflected in their hiring practices, expectations of
students, interactions with the local church, even mission statements
and public articulations from the schools. I think most Catholic
schools have found or are finding their bearings in a new
environment, but the specter of mission drift has evoked a response
from bishops across America, to "regain control of our Catholic
schools." This response has its roots in the changes to the Code of
Canon Law approved in 1983. These changes brought home to
bishops their responsibilities for holding Catholic schools
accountable and gave them expanded authority, even for order-
sponsored schools, to do so. Prior to this, the Catholicity of order-
sponsored schools was warranted by the order. While the order
needed the local bishop's permission to operate an institution in his
diocese, the bishop did not give direct supervision. Here are a couple
of excerpts that illustrate the change (emphasis mine):

Can. 804 §1. The Catholic religious instruction and
education which are imparted in any schools

whatsoever or are provided through the various instruments of social communication are subject to the authority of the Church. It is for the conference of bishops to issue general norms about this field of action and for the diocesan bishop to regulate and watch over it.

Can. 806 §1. The diocesan bishop has the right to watch over and visit the Catholic schools in his territory, even those which members of religious institutes have founded or direct. He also issues prescripts which pertain to the general regulation of Catholic schools; these prescripts are valid also for schools which these religious direct, without prejudice, however, to their autonomy regarding the internal direction of their schools.

The bishops' concerns over the catholicity of schools in their dioceses has led the US Conference of Catholic Bishops to formulate the document, *Doctrinal Elements of a Curriculum Framework for the Development of Catechetical Materials for Young People of High School Age.*

My sense is that many Jesuit schools while respecting the authority and responsibility of the bishops consider these developments problematic for satisfying their obligations to their sponsoring order. Given the current economic challenges to Catholic education, local bishops are struggling to manage and direct the schools they own or sponsor themselves. If to this is added the monitoring of religion curricula and instructors for order-sponsored schools, it will be difficult for them to do more than simply require these schools to function as diocesan schools. Rather than thoroughly understand and evaluate faculty formation programs from the perspective of the order's traditions, it will be more expedient to simply require them to participate in the programs offered by the diocese for their schools, whether they are more appropriate or not. In many respects order schools bring resources both in terms of charism and expertise that not only can serve students but can also provide a benefit to the local church. This is a contribution that needs to be welcomed.

Navigating the relationship with the local church will be a management challenge for Jesuit school administrators in the years ahead. The only way forward other than abandoning our unique identity within the Catholic education system, is to be able to explain the school's apostolic model and show compelling evidence of its effectiveness.

I. Conclusion

There are many challenges to face as Jesuit schools pursue their apostolic mission. Since the time of Adam and Eve, human openness to God's invitation has ebbed and flowed. In our own culture, we see both healthy currents and currents that pull not only our students, but their parents and ourselves as well, away from Christ's message. Amidst this, we grapple with financial limitations, the life struggles of our students and colleagues and the sheer depth, complexity and challenge of the tradition we have inherited. We must be more intentional than ever about strengthening our apostolic model to respond to these challenges. And we can. We can be clearer about the relationship with God that we envision for our students. The apostolic outcomes we seek are truly Good News. What we are holding out to our students, what lies at the very center of our tradition, is nothing less than the Gospel message of God's freeing love for them. By reflecting on who our students are and what they bring with them to the education process, we can feed their spiritual hunger and quiet the cultural noise that distracts them from satisfying it. We can better prepare the school's adult community for the challenge of passing on this rich tradition. Finally, we can learn from the experience of our students, our colleagues and other schools what methods work best in evangelizing the students who come to us today. This is how we accomplish our mission, and help students understand their own mission in the world. In the next chapter, Pedagogical Model, we will examine how we give students the tools to respond to that mission.

Chapter III:
Pedagogical Model

One question that haunts us as educators is why some students do well in schools while others do not. We can point to some schools or school systems plagued by obvious dysfunctionality and identify reasons why students aren't succeeding. But even in well-run and well-resourced Jesuit schools, some students just don't achieve the success we know they are capable of. Though the public may consider Jesuit schools homogeneous bastions of privilege, its students are still subject to poverty, turbulent home life, mental health issues, addiction, learning disabilities and cultural differences. These are just some of the factors that will affect the outcome of a child's education. Some students, even when those factors are not present, will not reach their potential, and other students, even when they are present, will achieve at a high level.

Sometimes in education, we wish we were producing widgets, for which the inputs are uniform and outcomes predictable. That is certainly not our world. Our work in education brings us to the very core of who human beings are. Ignatius would tell us that our students have free will and are engaged in a great struggle between good and evil, life and death, God and ego, and their lives are the battlefield. We join our students in this struggle by offering an education that will make sense of their lives and give them tools to live lives of purpose. In the face of human freedom, we must not exaggerate the control we have over outcomes, but neither should we resign ourselves to assuming the outcomes are random. What we need is a model that takes into account who our students really are and works toward the hopes for them expressed in our mission statement. Just as our schools have an apostolic model, implicit or explicit, they also have a pedagogical model. School management will be more effective if the pedagogical model is explicit.

The pedagogical model has five major components, which are analogous to those of the apostolic model: outcomes, curriculum, learners, teachers and methods. We make many assumptions about these five components, and when we name the assumptions we begin to see how the components support one another. We also see how the school team can better collaborate around them, and how the pedagogical model can support the apostolic model, as well as the community model and the business model, and vice versa. Let's consider each component.

A. Pedagogical Outcomes

As Jesuit schools, the ultimate outcome of our teaching is that students become companions of Christ, as Ignatius was, and engaged in the service of faith and the promotion of justice. If our apostolic model is intended to enlist them in this mission, our pedagogical model equips them with the tools to carry it out. For over 30 years, Jesuit education has clearly articulated a specific set of outcomes for its program. We call it the *Profile of a Graduate of a Jesuit High School at Graduation* or, simply, the *Grad at Grad*. By the time they graduate from our schools, students should be well on their way to becoming men and women who are open to growth, intellectually competent, religious, loving and committed to justice.

Open to Growth

This characteristic is first because our whole enterprise succeeds or fails here. If a student is open to growth, if he is willing to take on new challenges, see things in new ways, take risks and stretch himself, he will ultimately succeed, by any definition of success we want to use. Conversely, if he is not open to growth, unwilling to accept the vulnerability that growth involves, there is little we as educators can do to move that student toward his potential. The fact is that he has free will. We can incentivize him, but we can't make him do anything. Our pedagogical model can, however, create an environment that is conducive to growth. Everything in the school, from classes to activities to relationships with students, teachers and coaches, creates a current flowing in a particular direction. As in a river, a student stands in the midst of these influences—the senior that urges him to try out for the play, the teacher who suggests he could take an honors course, the student leading a campus retreat. He can resist this virtuous current, but that actually takes more energy.

Intellectually Competent

Of course you would expect intellectual competence to be an outcome of any school, and particularly one that calls itself college preparatory. The difference for our schools is that, as important as intellectual competence is for us, it is not an end in itself. It is a means to a bigger end: students living a life of purpose, becoming the persons God created them to be. I believe that Ignatius desired, above all, that students in a Jesuit school experience the loving, creative presence of God in their world. Not just hear about it, or read about it, but experience God's love for them. As they experience being loved by God, through relationships with their classmates and their teachers, they not only feel safe to stretch themselves and be more open to growth, but they hear an invitation to become part of the loving, creative presence of God in the world. They are given the opportunity to do community service, or lead others on a retreat, or tutor a friend. For adolescents, this may be the first time they realize that the world needs them and needs them to be their best. They realize that to respond effectively they will need knowledge, skills and self-discipline, and they will need to be able to express themselves—all of which will require a college education. All these attributes that we as parents and educators desire for them, they now desire for themselves, to become the persons they desire to be, the person God created them to be. Once they embrace these for themselves, their intellectual growth takes off. This is the great secret of Jesuit academic success. The school is more effective in fostering intellectual competence precisely because it is not an end in itself. It is a means to a bigger end, to become companions of Christ engaged in the great struggle of our time, fostering faith and promoting justice.

Religious

What does it mean to be religious? The word is at once shallow and fraught with many meanings. We have witnessed over the last half-century a huge change in the religious preparedness of our students and the religious commitment of their parents. Some would say that the erosion of faith in our culture has made our job more difficult. I think it is safer to say that we are challenged by the diversity of expectations around what being religious means. When we say we want our students to be religious, we intend it on three levels. The first is that of the individual spirituality of the students, their own personal relationship with God. Jesuit education benefits greatly from a spiritual tradition adept at leading people at many points on their faith journey to a deeper relationship with God. As secular as our world has become in one sense, people are remarkably open to the influence of Ignatian spirituality on their children. So they are comfortable with this first level, that of personal spirituality.

But for us there is a second level. As Catholics, though this is not unique to Catholics, we believe that the journey to a deeper relationship with God is never one we do on our own. We need others to encourage us and to challenge us. Our schools have developed powerful experiences of the communal dimension of spirituality: our retreats, our liturgies, even prayer experiences in the classrooms or on sports teams. I have found even non-religious students and parents, once they participate in these communal religious experiences are also comfortable with the second level.

We also mean religious on a third level, and this is the most challenging. We want our students to commit themselves to a faith community that will accompany them on the journey for the rest of their lives. For our Catholic students, we want them to understand and value their Catholic tradition, receive the sacraments and land in a parish that will continue to nurture them. For our non-Catholic students, we want the same outcome, at least analogously. If God is calling them to a deeper relationship through another tradition, we want them to understand how important this is. At this third level, we are fighting both developmental and cultural trends that are suspicious of institutional religion. The students will soon be off to college, and most will find themselves cut off from the roots that connected them to religious practice. But if our pedagogical model is effective, we will have given them knowledge that can act like seed for a lifelong faith. Even if they experience a prolonged dry period, their roots can eventually stretch down deeper to where faith can nourish them once again.

Loving

This is what it's all about, the Great Commandment. Beneath everything our students learn, we want them to see how loved they are, proximately by others and ultimately by God. We also want them to become loving people. Both of these are complicated by the developmental challenge for adolescents to learn to love themselves. When they begin high school they are generally unsure of where they fit in the world. They want to be like everyone else, yet they want to have their own identity. Our job for the next four years is to help them come to accept themselves for who they are, with both strengths and weaknesses. As they develop a more authentic acceptance of themselves, they can have more authentic, loving relationships with their peers, with their families. This authentic love extends out, then, to people who aren't in their circle, who don't have the same interests, outward to people who don't look like them or live in the same part of town, or the same part of the country or the same part of the world. Our hope is that their embrace of love can become so broad that it leads to the final characteristic, that they be committed to justice.

Committed to Justice

This is the acid test of a Jesuit education. As Ignatius says, love should show itself more in deeds than in words. By justice, we do not mean subscribing to a particular ideology. Foisting an ideology on our students would dishonor our role as educators, and particularly as Ignatian educators. What we mean is that the student will have the ability to ask whether something is fair. And we don't just mean fair to themselves. From what I can tell, everybody is already an expert on that. We want them to be able to put their own interests aside long enough to ask, "Is this fair to the other person? The other gender, socio-economic group, race or nation?" If we've done a good job fostering the other four characteristics—if they are truly open to growth and able to challenge their own perceptions; if they are intellectually competent, which means they are fearlessly seeking the truth; if they are listening to what their religious tradition is telling them, certainly the Catholic tradition but others as well; and if they are truly loving people—they will be able to understand and respond to the needs of others rather than simply cling to privileges they aren't even aware they have.

The first component of our pedagogical model is the ultimate outcomes we desire for our students—who they were created to be. Before outcome-based education became a common trend, the *Grad at Grad* defined the ultimate outcomes sought by Jesuit schools. We turn now to the second component of the apostolic model, the learners for whom these outcomes are intended.

B. Learners

In all our focus on pedagogy, we sometimes forget that education, after all, is about learning. We forget that each of us acquired the most difficult skills we will ever learn without school or any systematic program of instruction. In order to begin using language we not only had to memorize a vast vocabulary for which we had no definitions, and orchestrate the movement of lips, tongue and vocal chords in extremely complex ways, but we had to figure out on our own what language even was and why it was important. When we first go to school, the model shifts dramatically. Now we are no longer responsible for figuring out how to learn things or what things we should learn. We have professionals who are now responsible for what we are to learn and how we are to do it. And learning slows way down. It becomes, in some cases, a battle between the teacher who wants the student to learn something, and the student who wants to avoid learning it.

I am not arguing that education is unnecessary or even counter-productive for learning (although I think that's a question which educators should regularly consider). But one of our challenges is that education interferes with a process that happened naturally up to school-age, and in some ways would continue naturally if we were just left to ourselves. But at about the age school starts, the nature of what needs to be learned changes. Up to that point the things we need to learn have an immediate pay-off. As we get older, however, the knowledge and skills we need are of less immediate use. We begin learning things we don't even know we need to know. Other people are now deciding what we should know. Why do we need to know how to read when we can watch TV and just tell mom and dad when we need something? Okay, there are lots of things we want that are easier to get if we can read. But why do we need to know that 2 and 2 are 4? Okay, we can see some situations where it's pretty handy to be able to do simple arithmetic. But we begin to suspect that the nose of a very big the camel is now under the tent. It's not long before adults are telling us we need to know how to figure out when two trains traveling toward each other at different speeds will pass in the night, or what caused the Spanish American War, or where on the periodic chart we find elements that haven't even been discovered yet. Except for the most precocious or the most compliant of us, education soon seems to radically diverge from what we desire in life. I'm not surprised when I encounter unmotivated students today. Under these circumstances, I'm amazed how many are motivated at all.

Again, I am not making some Rousseauvian argument that education is counterproductive. The fact is that for us as individuals and for us as a human race to achieve our full potential, we do need to learn a lot of things, the uses of which are not immediately obvious. That's where education comes in. It's designed to take us to the next stage just when the pay-off for getting there seems dramatically reduced.

The point here is that we need to be aware of who our learners are, what they need and what they think they need. As supple and absorptive as the human brain is, our students are not warehouses into which we can just forklift the information we know they'll need.

Of course, we all know that, but we still make assumptions that suggest we don't. The week I was writing this section a parent told me a story about her freshman son. In his health class, an outside speaker was giving a presentation about substance abuse, including video clips about drinking and driving. One clip showed a driver under the influence who killed a person and was sentenced to six months in jail. The student raised his hand and asked what color the driver was. The teacher immediately stepped in and told the student this was an inappropriate question. The presentation was about substance abuse, not race. He told the student to refrain from asking any questions if he couldn't ask appropriate ones. The teacher was right that the young man's question had nothing to do with what the school wanted to teach him at that moment. But the student, an African American, one of the 8% attending the school, had an uncle who was in prison for six years for possession of narcotics. Recently, the student and his father, for no reason he could figure out, were pulled over and ordered at gunpoint to get out of their car. I could see why the puzzling part of the presentation for him was why a man who killed someone while on drugs got a lighter sentence than his uncle, who was merely in possession. So when does he get his question answered?

Understanding who our learners are takes place on four levels. First, we have to know who human beings are in general. Second, we have to know what kind of students come to our particular school. Third, we need to know the subgroups within the student body. And fourth, we need to acknowledge the uniqueness of the individual student.

On the first level, one of the salient characteristics of human beings for us as Jesuit educators is free will. We need to understand at the beginning of the education process that we will not make our students do anything. Of course we believe in free will, and none of us likes to think we use coercive methods. But any of us who have responsibility for other human beings as educators, parents or bosses, when confronted with resistance, look for ways to make people do what we want. We feel vulnerable being responsible for the growth or performance of someone free to choose whether they cooperate or not. Yet that is precisely how God deals with us. If anyone has the right and the power to make people be good, it is God. Yet God has given us free will and, from what I have observed, absolutely refuses to take it back. If, as Ignatian educators, we are called to work with God in the formation of his children, we must be willing to accept that same lack of control.

One of Ignatius' great insights was that rather than suppressing our deepest desires, God chooses to work with them. God uses those desires to lead us to Himself. As educators, we must also acknowledge free will and work with the innate desires that would lead students to be open to growth, intellectually competent, religious, loving and committed to justice. We may have to help them dig a little to find those desires. They finished the high pay-off learning that satisfied their immediate desires eight years ago. If they are precocious they may have figured out that what we are teaching will be useful for them later. If they are compliant, the reward of our approval or the avoidance of sanctions may be sufficient motivation to get them from one requirement to another. But there is no way we can program our students to be educated in the fullest sense. They have to want it.

To borrow from Ignatius, we have to bring our students in their door if we hope to bring them out ours. The more we know about them, the better we can help them use their education to meet needs that are real, or will become real, for them. We can begin with an understanding of young people in general today. How have youth culture, social media like Facebook, prevailing values and other factors unique to their generation shaped them? All these factors present challenges to our pedagogy, but they also present opportunities. Beneath all of the cultural influences are their own deep desires, which, properly understood and nourished, will lead them to everything God has in store for them. If we understand their desires and challenges, we can think about how our curriculum, and how we teach each lesson, will support their own choices to grow and become the person God created them to be.

The other critical belief for Iganatian educators is the essential goodness of human beings. If we believe that God can be found in all things, we surely believe that God is present in all people. We might paraphrase the advice St Ignatius gives to the retreat director in the beginning of the *Spiritual Exercises* like this: "...it is to be presupposed that every teacher ought to be more inclined to give a good interpretation to a student's statements and actions rather than to condemn them" (Annotation 22). We like to believe we do this, but it is easier to be judgmental, to attribute problematic behavior to bad will, moral turpitude, laziness or spite. I got a good lesson in this watching a group of freshmen eating lunch outside my office window one day. One of the students kept walking over to the end of the porch, reaching his hand over a short wall and dropping his garbage into the garden. After watching for a few minutes, I'd finally had enough. I stormed out of my office and onto the porch to confront the student. I angrily asked him why he was throwing his garbage into the garden. He looked at me with what could only be feigned innocence and stammered that he was throwing it into a garbage can. "Don't play dumb with me. I've been watching you from my window throwing your garbage over that wall." He managed to squeak out, "There's a garbage can there." "No there isn't!" I went to show him and, sure enough, there below the wall in a garden where it had no business being, was one of our school's official garbage cans. This student had found it there and was conscientiously disposing of his garbage even when he thought no one was watching. He was being good. I apologized.

Every time I go on a retreat with our students and spend time in a cabin listening to how things look from their perspective, I am reminded of how they are working overtime to do the right thing, as they see it. I don't always agree with their take on life, or the choices they make, but it's helpful to know that they are trying to live out the goodness of God within them.

If the first level of understanding who our students are is knowing what we believe about humans in general, the second level is knowing the specific characteristics of the students who come to our school. As much as we value diversity of all kinds, our schools are not intended to be all things to all people. If we are college preparatory, we attract students who desire to continue their education beyond high school. If we charge tuition, we attract students whose parents are either affluent or willing to sacrifice to pay tuition and apply for financial aid. If we are in the inner-city, we attract students who are not intimidated by the urban environment. Who we are and how we carry out our admissions process leads to a narrower slice of humanity that has its own set of characteristics. How are our students different than students at other schools? Are they wealthier, more driven, more materialistic, more cosmopolitan? How many are coming from Catholic grade schools? Are they more catechized, more religiously open, or on the other hand, feeling "burnt out" on religious education? Do many of them need additional help with math, or writing or study skills to be in a college prep environment? How we answer such questions will have a significant impact on our pedagogical model.

The third level of knowing who our learners are requires disaggregating them into subgroups that have specific needs and making sure the school has program elements in place to meet those needs. Within the school, a student from an ethnic minority will have a different perspective and different needs than majority students. The same applies to students who are on financial aid, or struggling with issues of sexual identity, or are non-Catholic, or have physical challenges. We accept students with diverse backgrounds, skill sets and life experiences because we want to give them an equal chance at the opportunities we have to offer and we recognize that they bring a richness to our classrooms and community. We want to simply open our doors and treat everyone who comes to us the same. But we also accept responsibility to acknowledge their differences and meet their needs. It's wonderful to accept a promising public school student born in Vietnam. But how will her experience be different than our traditional student? Who will communicate with her parents? Will financial aid be needed? Will it be enough? If we accept a student with a learning disability, do we have the resources to support him in a college prep environment? Our pedagogical model must include an understanding of our commitments to different subgroups within the student body as a whole.

The final level is that of the individual student. We know that each student who comes to us is unique. As early as the 19th century we became aware that there were sometimes differences in how students' brains were wired that prevented them from seeing letters and words the way "normal" students do. The more we studied the differences, the more we realized that there is a spectrum of learning differences along which all students can be found. Then we realized it was more complex than a continuum because there are a variety of learning styles. Different individual students follow different paths to understanding and not all those paths are equally encouraged or supported in the traditional educational environment. Former JSEA President, Ralph Metts SJ, has surveyed the research on learning differences in his book, *Ignatius Knew*. This book can be a great help as we evaluate the ability of our pedagogical model to meet the needs of individual students.

Students' needs will vary because of other factors as well. Issues in the student's life, like addiction, physical or mental illness or issues at home, such as poverty, family turmoil, illness or tragedy for a family member will profoundly influence a student's ability to learn. Not only will these factors vary from student to student, but for each student they can vary from day to day. Unfortunately, the most careful lesson planning and preparation on the teacher's part can be easily undone by an obstruction to learning experienced by the student. It is impossible to know what all of these might be, but I have seen skilled teachers pick up on their students' issues and make adjustments that allow the students to stay engaged in the learning process.

The more we know about our learners, the better we can support them in their task of learning. We all know that. But we also know that there is only so much time in a day. If a teacher has 120 students in her classes, not to mention extra-curriculars, how can she know each one's personal story and give personal attention to each? There is a limit to what we can do. The bad news is that we simply cannot as educators be aware of and make allowance for the individual needs, challenges and gifts of all our students. The good news is that we don't have to. Education is primarily about learning, not teaching. Teachers are facilitating, not controlling, a learning process. Just as the first imperative for a physician is "Do no harm," and the first responsibility of the Retreat Director is to "Let God work directly with the retreatant," the first imperative of an educator is, "Don't obstruct the learning." Even minimal awareness of our students' desires, gifts and challenges can bring huge gains in their ability to learn and grow. Our pedagogical model must therefore help us understand and adjust our assumptions about the learners in our schools.

The first component of the pedagogical model was the outcomes we are seeking, and this second one consists of the learners for whom those outcomes are sought. We turn now to the third component, the teachers who lead the learning process.

C. Teachers

If we reflect on a time in our own schooling when we achieved a new level of success, gained a key insight or experienced an intellectual growth spurt, most of us will associate that moment with a teacher. Teachers, especially great teachers, loom important in our lives because they have such an impact on them. But what makes a great teacher great? Certainly there are skills and methods that can be learned, but when I think of the effective teachers in my life, I am struck more by their qualities, who they were as people. That might suggest that teachers are either effective or not and there isn't anything they can do about it. The good news is that qualities can also be learned, but they can only be learned by being changed— changed by the Holy Spirit, by our students and by their colleagues. We would much rather learn a new technique than a new way of being in the world, but no one working in a school inspired by the *Spiritual Exercises* should be surprised to learn that it is the latter to which we are called.

I want to focus for a moment on the role of the teacher in the pedagogical model. Let's briefly consider the various roles of a teacher in a Jesuit school: teacher as Guide, teacher as Model, teacher as Learner, teacher as Collaborator and finally, teacher as *Alter Christus*, a mediator for Christ.

Teacher as Guide

The virtue of seeing teachers as guides is that it acknowledges that the journey belongs to the student. The teacher is there to help her on her way. The teacher is not there simply to answer questions. It would be easier for both the student and the teacher if that were the teacher's role, and so often both get trapped in such a relationship. The teacher must resist this temptation steadfastly. His role is to help the student learn what the questions are, what her questions are, and help her to find answers. At times, the teacher's experience and knowledge will be helpful to this process, again not as a substitute for the student's experience but as a navigation beacon against which the student can check her own perceptions. At other times, the teacher's superior knowledge must set boundaries to assure safety for the student. But ultimately the teacher must let go of the results and let the student take ownership of them.

Teacher as model

In *The Insecurity of Freedom*, Hassidic scholar Rabbi Abraham Joshua Heschel wrote this about teachers:

> Everything depends on the person who stands in the front of the classroom. The teacher is not an automatic fountain from which intellectual beverages may be obtained. He is either a witness or a stranger. To guide a pupil into the Promised Land, he must have been there himself. When asking himself: Do I stand for what I teach? Do I believe what I say? he must be able to answer in the affirmative. What we need more than anything else is not textbooks but textpeople. It is the personality of the teacher which is the text that the pupils read; the text that they will never forget.

Most of us experience some discomfort at the thought that students pay more attention to who we are than what we teach. I know I do. I would much rather believe that my students or my own children will do as I say and not as I do. My ego likes that fantasy because it gives me a sense of control. All I have to do is keep track of my words, which is a lot easier than keeping track of who I am. Twelve-step programs like Al-Anon, for the families and friends of alcoholics, have exposed the fallacy of this kind of thinking. No amount of nagging, preaching or arguing will cure the alcoholic. Al-Anon members learn that the best thing we can do for an unhealthy person is to be healthy ourselves. Not be healthy so we can lord it over them; just be healthy. Just as an unhealthy person can negatively influence the health of those around him, a person committed to her own health can positively influence the health of those around her. So it is with teachers. If you want your students to be disciplined and organized, be disciplined and organized; if you want your students to write well, write well; if you want your students to be respectful; be respectful; if you want your students to be life-long learners, be a lifelong leaner. It doesn't mean they will be, but it's the best way a teacher can influence them to make that choice for themselves.

Teacher as learner

It seems that the operating definition of adulthood for many adults is that, at last, they can stop learning. I wish I could say this is not true of people working in education, but in my experience it's almost as common as in the general adult population. The very teacher who insists that a fourteen year old brain learn how to prove that the sides of congruent triangles are proportional in length, will try to avoid learning how to use on-line tools before she retires. If we think that students will be learners if teachers are not, or that teachers will be learners if administrators are not, we are simply kidding ourselves. The business world has figured this out. Peter Senge and others have written that in the current dynamic environment every business needs to become a learning organization. Ironically, the education world has been slower to see the importance of learning to its own effectiveness. We as educators must be most open to learning that helps us crest new horizons in our subject area and become better teaching professionals.

Teacher as collaborator

The foregoing suggests that a lot is expected of teachers in a Jesuit school. How can that be sustained? It comes back to what my colleague told me, "It's all about relationships." It's important that teachers be supported by their administrators and that teachers support one another. Sharing ideas, giving honest feedback, comparing outcomes of specific lessons, consoling each other in times of hardship and challenging each other in times of complacency, these are what strengthen our teaching more than anything I know. Teachers know this, but collaboration often doesn't happen for two main reasons. The first is time. It's challenging to find room in the hectic school schedule to collaborate. If we take time from the class schedule, we feel like we are cheating our students. If we simply tack it onto the day, we risk putting an unfair burden on those teachers who are already stretched as far as they can go.

The second obstacle to collaboration is ego. I'm not referring to people who simply don't believe there is anything they can learn from others. It's more subtle than that. One of the attractions of teaching is being able to close the door to your classroom and have a world where you can do meaningful work, without a lot of interference. The students have to do what you say, and if someone with the authority to tell you what to do comes into your classroom once a year, that's a lot. It can be lonely, and teachers often crave more professional interaction and support, even from the administration. But to live in a truly collaborative environment means giving up some autonomy and being more vulnerable to others' needs and expectations. Managing for mission requires that school administrators work resolutely and sensitively to remove these obstacles. For instance, the observation and evaluation process must be consistent, supportive and formative. The school should also commit to a proven collaboration model like Professional Learning Communities. These two approaches are discussed in the Chapter IV on the community model. Other ways of supporting collaboration include strengthening the role of department heads as mentors, identifying others as mentor teachers, building schedules and work spaces that allow for teacher collaboration and providing funding for collaborative work outside the school year.

Teacher as *Alter Christus*

Our lives are a journey back to God. When we are first born, God's immense love for us is mediated through our parents. Completely vulnerable and unable to do anything for ourselves, we are held in their loving arms and through them we have our first palpable experience of God's love. From that moment forward, we become more and more autonomous and our parents' role as the sole intermediaries for God's love declines. Our journey to a direct relationship with God requires both taking more responsibility for ourselves and learning to put our trust in God. This is a painful journey for both the child and the parent, because it involves giving up security for the former and control for the latter. Not only has God sent His Son to lead us on our journey, but God has sent us many people to be Christ for us, the first of which were our parents.

As a child grows older, teachers will become his Alteri Christi, or "Other Christs." This is why the US Bishops called their groundbreaking document on Catholic Education, published in 1972, "To Teach as Jesus Did." How did Jesus teach? We know he taught in parables, that he walked among the people, that he knew who they were and what they desired, that he didn't judge them, that he was willing to bend the rules to put people first, and that he taught by example. Our students don't have the opportunity to experience Jesus preaching on the mount, from a fishing boat or on the plain. They won't meet him at the well, or have him call to them in the Sycamore tree. If they are to encounter Christ, it will be through the adults in their lives, and for adolescents this will happen in a pre-eminent way with their teachers. The thought that we must be Christ for others and particularly for impressionable young people, is a frightening one for most of us. As discussed earlier under the apostolic model, we are all on a journey of faith ourselves and even the best of us are stained glass windows with panes missing or in need of stronger color. Not to worry; Christ shines through us. We don't have to be perfect for that to happen, and ultimately, we can't even prevent it from happening. But we can cooperate with the light that shines through us so that students encounter Christ more readily. We can use parables, stories or experiences to make learning more accessible. We can walk among our students in the cafeteria, on their retreats, at their games. We can listen to them and learn what their desires, gifts and challenges are. We can refrain from judging them. We can bend our rules when appropriate to make space for them to grow. And, most important of all, we can exemplify what we want to teach them.

Good teaching requires many skills—communication, knowledge of subject area, organization—but great teaching, the kind we expect in Jesuit schools, requires a total donation of self. Great teachers must be willing to listen—both to their students and their colleagues, to attend to their own learning and growth, and to trust the learner to take over where even the best teaching must finally leave off.

The first component of the pedagogical model was the outcome we desire for our students and the second was the students themselves. In this component, the teacher, our pedagogical model must help us see, reflect on and adjust our assumptions about those who are leading the learners on their journey to God.

D. Curriculum (including "extra-curriculars")

If the *Grad at Grad* characteristics tell us the ultimate outcomes we desire for our students, the curriculum spells out what we believe students will have to know, and know how to do, to achieve those overall outcomes. Curriculum also addresses the *how* of student learning, but I want to deal with that in the next section on methods. In this section I want to focus on the *what* of the curriculum.

Backward Design

Much of education focuses on giving students the knowledge and skills they will need in life. If students know important facts and have basic skills like reading, computation, composition and use of technology, we can say on one level that they are educated. Knowledge and skills are important, but Jesuit education must aim for a deeper goal if it is to honor its underlying mission of serving faith and promoting justice. It must aim for *understanding*. Certainly understanding is the goal of all education systems, but true understanding is not easy to achieve. True understanding requires more than just knowing about a subject, it requires knowing the subject in itself, its inner workings, its meaning, its significance, its intelligibility. Perfect understanding would be like the understanding God has of us, characterized in Psalm 139: "O, Lord, you have probed me and you know me. You know when I sit and when I stand." While we cannot understand in the way God does, our understanding should lead us out of ourselves to experience the other in itself. This is, after all, what the education means. The Latin *e-ducare* means to lead out, out from ourselves, out from narrow, limited and purely utilitarian knowledge to transcendent knowledge.

Grant Wiggins and Jay McTighe, in their book, *Understanding by Design*, published by the Association for Supervision and Curriculum Development in 1998, break understanding down into six facets. They say that students who understand subject matter:

- "Can *explain*: provide thorough, supported, and justifiable accounts of phenomena, facts, and data.
- "Can *interpret*: tell meaningful stories; offer apt translations; provide a revealing historical or personal dimension to ideas and events; make it personal or accessible through images, anecdotes, analogies, and models.
- "Can *apply*: effectively use and adapt what we know in diverse contexts.
- "Have *perspective*: see and hear points of view through critical eyes and ears; see the big picture.
- "Can *empathize*: find value in what others might find odd, alien, or implausible; perceive sensitively on the basis of prior direct experience.
- "Have *self-knowledge*: perceive the personal style, prejudices, projections, and habits of mind that both shape and impede our own understanding; we are aware of what we do not understand and why understanding is so hard."

This sets a high standard for what curriculum should achieve. There is no way we can cover the material we are expected to cover and have students appropriate it at this deep level. Wiggins and McTighe agree and point out the irony of the term we use when we say we are "covering the material." They remind us that education is about "uncovering" the subject, exposing it to daylight so that it can be understood. They contend that when our objective becomes simply to "cover" the material we do exactly that. Not only do we bore our students to death, but we obscure what they are studying and actually make it more difficult to understand at any level worthy of the term. More effective curriculum trades broad but shallow surveys of knowledge for narrower but more focused lessons that address the six facets of understanding. This is consistent with a Jesuit pedagogical model, which seeks depth over breadth. The old Latin phrase is *non multa, sed multum*. "Not many, but much."

Designing curriculum, for Wiggins and McTighe, begins with outcomes and works backward to the inputs that lead the student to this understanding. We begin with understanding, but understanding is not in itself measurable. So we next need to identify what students should be able to do if they understand the subject. These are the six facets. If we want students to understand Shakespeare, then we want them to be able to explain *Macbeth*, interpret it, apply what they learn, see through Shakespeare's perspective, empathize with the characters and learn more about themselves through their experience of the play. Knowing that these are what we hope to see from our students, we can then think about what knowledge, what skills and what experiences will prepare them for each of the demonstrable facets of understanding. Here we have a range of options: Read the play, watch it on film, perform it, explain it to younger children, write their own version in a modern context, etc. We would select from these choices based on what best brings students to understand the play as evidenced by the six facets.

Backward design makes sense, but is nevertheless counterintuitive. We tend to start with the inputs, the lessons, presentations and activities that we feel good about and then trust that they will produce the desired outcomes. But as with every other aspect of the school, we are dealing with a scarce resource. In the case of curriculum, the scarce resource is time—the students' time, their attention span, our time with them in class. When resources are scarce, we must keep our outcomes clearly in mind and select and align only the inputs most likely to lead to those outcomes.

Integration

Any process as complex as education we tend to break down into smaller units. So the curriculum is broken down into departments, departments are broken down into classes, classes into units and units into lessons. We can sometimes forget that the student himself is not fragmented in this way. In so doing we can miss a tremendous opportunity. If the student is actively engaged in his learning, he is trying to integrate all the fragmented knowledge he is being exposed to. If we make this too difficult for him, he will conclude that it is more expedient to keep the different subject areas compartmentalized. As educators, we must stop and think about the individual students and how the mosaic of learning from different classes and departments is becoming an intelligible picture for them. Certainly, we expect the principal and the vice principal responsible for academics to be keeping track of this. But in the pressure of working with all the building blocks and scheduling all the required classes, this doesn't happen without making intentional choices. And who within the departments is thinking about how students are integrating their knowledge? And who between departments? These questions can't just be left to the academic administrators. The entire team of educators must keep an eye on how the curriculum is integrated for the student. They must have the time to think about this and the time and means to learn from students how they are integrating all the knowledge they are gaining. They also must help the students to find time in their busy schedules to integrate fragmented knowledge.

What offers even greater potential, as well as increased challenge and complexity, is how the curriculum relates to the student's extra-curricular activities. Does a student working on set crew for the play use the Pythagorean Theorem to calculate a plywood cut? How does the point guard reconcile the Sermon on the Mount which she studied in religion class with her desire to compete at the top of her abilities? Sports, clubs and activities offer enormous opportunities for converting knowledge into true understanding because they are practical, they are both individual and communal, and they are voluntary. Of course we give a lot of thought to how all the curricular and extra-curricular elements produce a strong program, but are we thinking through how we can help the individual students pull all this together for themselves? This is a critical piece of our pedagogical model, but unless we focus on it intentionally, its effects will be well below what they should be.

The first component of the pedagogical model was the outcomes for students, the second was the students themselves and the third was the teachers. In this fourth component we've focused the curriculum, what it is we want students to know, to understand and be able to do. The last component, methodologies, deals with how we produce those outcomes.

E. Methodologies

The final element of the pedagogical model is the methodologies used to foster learning. This element addresses the question of how learning happens, and how our teaching can be structured to assist the process. Drawing on both Ignatian spirituality and educational research, Jesuit schools believe there is a consistent and natural dynamic to the learning process, which we work with as educators using what we call the Ignatian Pedagogical Paradigm (IPP). The IPP consists of five stages of learning: *context, experience, reflection, action* and *evaluation*. To understand why this is called the *Ignatian Pedagogical Paradigm*, let's trace the roots of the IPP in the spirituality of St Ignatius.

Ignatian Pedagogical Paradigm (IPP)

The goal of the *Spiritual Exercises* is to help the person receiving them to encounter Christ as directly as possible. If we think learning is difficult, cultivating a vital, continuous and palpable relationship with the unseen God can seem impossible. Today, if we believe in mystical experiences at all, we believe they are the privilege of a few who are disposed by personality or divine providence to receive them. Based on the improbability of his own conversion, Ignatius believed that anyone could develop a relationship with Christ. And so he documented his experiences on that journey and developed them into a series of exercises to strength the spiritual capacity we all possess. Without re-capitulating all of the *Spiritual Exercises*, I want to highlight a few elements that relate to education.

Ignatius realized that no one could have a relationship with Christ simply by reading or hearing about him. Any vital relationship must be based on experiencing the love of the other, and experience comes through the senses. Yet God is not present to us as other people are. So we tend to treat God, even the person of Jesus, as abstract. Ignatius felt however that if we use our imaginations we can give Christ a way to be present to our senses. So the retreatant is shown how to enter a Gospel passage, carefully using all her senses to imagine herself present within the story. So instead of simply reading the story of the Nativity, she asks herself: What did it look like, where was the light coming from? What did Mary's or Joseph's voice sound like as they talked to the baby? Did I smell hay, or manure? Was I wearing rough clothes? Did I touch the baby's hand? Did I taste the dust of traveling to see him? It takes a lot of concentration and undisturbed time to apply all the senses to the scene, but once we do this, a strange thing happens. It becomes no longer an effort. The characters of the Gospel story, including Jesus, take over our imaginations and can speak for themselves. We move beyond abstraction to experience and from experience to relationship.

After we experience the Gospel story with enlivened and empowered imaginations, Ignatius then invites us to have a conversation with Mary, with Jesus, even with God the Father. In these colloquies we can ask questions about the Gospel story, or about our own lives, and let Mary, Jesus, the saints or whoever we encounter in our imaginative space, speak to us and help us reflect on the meaning of what we have experienced. "By reflecting on it and reasoning about it...we can thus discover something that will bring better understanding or more personalized concept of the history," as Ignatius says in the introductory explanations (Annotation 2).

I said that Ignatius' purpose in the *Exercises* is to help us come to a relationship with Christ, and this is true. But he has a further purpose in mind. The imaginative meditation described above helps us to experience God's love for us and engenders in us a deeper love for God. But Ignatius points out that love ought to express itself in deeds. And so the *Exercises* is geared to making an election, or a decision, about how we will use our lives. One contemplation has us standing before the cross and asking ourselves what we have done for Christ, what we are doing for Christ and what more we may do for Christ. It is this apostolic openness which characterizes the Jesuits as contemplatives in action.

Choices and action then generate further experiences, which themselves are to be reflected upon and lead to further decisions and actions.

Experience, reflection and *action* are also the core movements of the learning process. The student experiences something, perhaps something unusual that causes her to question its meaning or intelligibility. Or perhaps she experiences something quite ordinary and only on reflection does she wonder for the first time what it might mean. When she reaches an adequate explanation for what she experienced, she naturally wants to test that in real life when she has the opportunity. This action will produce a new experience, which fosters further reflection and refinement of the explanation. The new understanding leads to revised actions and the cycle continues in a process we call life-long learning. Let's look at a couple examples.

Experience: A student watching his backyard bird-feeder notices that his feeder gets much less traffic than his friend's. *Reflection*: Wondering why this might be so, he also notices that there are no trees near his feeder, as there are at his friend's. He also notices that whenever he approaches an active feeder the birds scatter to the nearby trees. So he reasons that the birds will favor a feeder where trees are near enough to flee to when threatened. *Action*: He then moves his feeder to another area of the yard and keeps track of activity to see if his explanation is correct. *Experience*: He observes the activity at the feeder and starts to keep a more detailed log. Etc.

Experience: A student enjoys reading magazines to keep up with current fashions and news. She looks at the ads, but doesn't give them much thought. *Reflection*: Her philosophy teacher gives her an assignment to review the ads in a magazine and ask what implicit assumptions those who produce the ads are making about the people who read them. The student becomes aware that while the ads make their products look attractive, she resents some of the stereotypes they reinforce. *Action*: The student begins viewing the ads differently, more aware of how they might be reinforcing negative or restrictive images of herself and others. She even begins to see the ads as warnings to help her not fall into the patterns they promote.

The IPP assumes that learning naturally follows this cycle of experience-reflection-action. It is how, for instance, we learned to speak a language before we ever went to school. The IPP also assumes that learning cannot take place without these three stages. If we skip the *experience* step and just give the explanation, it is difficult for the student to understand what the explanation explains. If we skip the *reflection* step, the student has only meaningless data. If we skip the *action* step, the student will not know whether he has the right explanation. Learning never skips these steps. Unfortunately teaching often does. Even though we know better, in the pressure of covering all the material and meeting various state and college requirements, we have a tendency to cut to the chase. Curriculum which is highly dependent on textbooks is particularly prone to this. Textbooks are a terrific invention. As a response to the challenge of teaching a staggering quantity of material, they are usually well-written and capture, organize and explain vast amounts of information. They've done all the work for the teacher, and unfortunately for the student as well. It's a little like having a machine chew your food for you. You could hardly call that eating, just as you could hardly call digesting text books learning.

I have focused on the core dynamic of the IPP, experience-reflection-action, but there are two other steps which are pedagogically important. At the beginning of the cycle is *Context*. Ignatius gave instructions about how each prayer period should begin. He has us place ourselves in the presence of God, to imagine God beholding us. We also pray for the grace we seek during our prayer. These preliminaries prepare us for what we will experience. Just so, the IPP encourages the teacher to prepare students for each learning experience. Attending to *context* includes reflecting on who the students are who are about to experience a lesson. Will we be reading a story with images, like a dial telephone, that were ubiquitous in our lifetime but not theirs? What background information will they need? It also means helping the students see how the discreet lesson fits into a bigger picture, especially because each lesson tends to be like a piece of a mosaic. In isolation, it is sterile and meaningless. Students need to know that the pieces will produce a meaningful picture. If we skip the *context* step we are asking our students to do the impossible, to take an interest in and make sense of dissociated packets of information.

At the other end of the dynamic is *Evaluation*. *Evaluation* is what bridges us back from *action* to *experience*, so that the process can continue to spiral toward greater understanding. We do a lot of evaluating of our students and what they know. But if these are only summative assessments, used to determine a grade, they will not lead to greater learning. We must also include formative assessments to encourage them to refine their own understanding of the subject.

Describing assessments as formative or summative was introduced in 1967 by British-born philosopher Michael Scriven and applied widely in education. Essentially, formative assessments are intended to provide feedback that leads to improvement during a process. For instance, a teacher may ask if the students have understood a concept he has just presented. The students may think they understand it, but when asked to solve a problem based on the concept, they realize that they need to learn more. This testing determines whether additional study of the concept is necessary. Programmed learning uses this model of testing the participant and moving them on when they have mastered a concept and looping them back to additional lessons if they have not.

Summative evaluation is designed to measure outcomes. Although summative evaluations can also be used to improve processes, their primary purpose is to determine if an objective has been achieved. Even if they come after any adjustments can be made to the process (e.g. final grades for a semester), they foster improvement by holding participants accountable for the outcome.

Though it is difficult, our *evaluation* steps should as much as possible correspond to the real world. Getting an answer right on a Spanish test is an abstraction. Having to communicate with someone who speaks only Spanish gives us much greater incentive to use the language effectively as a tool. This then becomes the new *context* for student learning and provides new *experiences* that begin the cycle of learning anew.

Modes of delivery

The IPP is an abstract construct. It is helpful in making visible the steps that learning must go through to achieve understanding. But how do we design a program which fosters this learning dynamic? Traditional education since the Renaissance has been built around the assumption that to be productive adults, young people must acquire a prescribed body of knowledge and set of skills. Unless this repertoire is mastered by adulthood, it is believed, people will not be able to navigate within, and contribute to, our complex culture.

Based on this reasonable assumption, education breaks down this body of knowledge into subjects, prescribes a canon for what should be known and assigns experts in each field to impart the prescribed knowledge to the students. At the end of the process, the student will emerge as informed, to one degree or another, about all the subjects. This is the warehouse model of education. The idea is to view the brains of our students as storage facilities and our goal, while they are in school, is to fill that warehouse with as much of the knowledge they will need later as possible. Thus, when they need to know how to titrate liquids later in life, they can go into their mental warehouse, to the chemistry section, and retrieve the information.

I had an English teacher in my sophomore year of high school who realized he was running out of time for covering the material, and resolved to have us at least be "conversant" with the range of English literature. He had us memorize the names of famous authors and drilled us weekly on their major works and one idea each had put forward. This may sound hopelessly shallow, but his theory was that if we at least knew these names, we would engage in conversations or recognize them in articles we read, which might lead us to deeper knowledge. He was hoping we would have a framework to which understanding could precipitate out of the culture like crystals from salt water. He wasn't entirely wrong. We do need some store of knowledge on which to build continuous learning. Our education system, however, tends to overestimate how much people can truly learn this way. We do so because students are able to learn the material long enough to pass a test. We are able to point to a few outliers, students sufficiently motivated by a desire to please or by the prospect of future rewards to keep their knowledge warehouses well-stocked. And there are those with a personality disorder from which I suffer, a desire to learn for learning's sake, like eating food whether I need to or not. But how many people ever really achieve and retain an understanding of the subjects studied under this regime?

My children are all experts on the music from the 1920's to the present minute. They know more about the music from "my era" than I do. They know about the musicians, the song-writers and the history of how one genre has influenced another. A couple of them took classes about contemporary music, yet I am certain that these classes had little to do with their current understanding. I know this because the ones who took them know no more than the ones who didn't. And the ones who never took a class on contemporary music know far more about it than about subjects in which they took several classes. And it's not just my children. This wide-ranging knowledge seems fairly common among their generation. How did they become experts? The answer: iPods and the internet technology that puts thousands of songs in their vest pockets.

Two things have changed that should cause us to rethink our delivery model for education. The first is that the body of knowledge young people need to master so that they can navigate and contribute to our culture has outstripped the effectiveness of this model. We can't possibly stock their warehouse with enough information, even if they could retain it. Even if a motivated student read all the Great Books, her education would be incomplete for not having read the *Autobiography of Malcolm X*, or little known authors emerging from the Third World, or the *Q'ran*. The solution is not to expand the literary canon, nor even to revise it. There is simply too much for that approach to work. Certainly students must read and understand great literature. But even the most scholarly will only be able to survey a small sampling of it. And random sampling won't do. They will need to identify the threads that lead them to a deeper understanding of their own mission. This is not a quantity-of-information challenge; it's a navigational challenge. We have to help them care more about the world around them and equip them to find more and more adequate understandings of that world. It goes back to Ignatius: we need to help them experience the loving, creative presence of God in their world, and respond to the invitation to be part of that loving, creative presence. With this rudder they can navigate through the sea of knowledge and come to understand the world, their mission in it, and how to go about accomplishing that mission.

If the first change causing us to rethink our delivery model is that we can't sufficiently stock the warehouse anymore, the second change is that we don't have to. One of the great insights which the Japanese discovered as they revolutionized their manufacturing process after World War II is that they didn't need to maintain a huge warehouse for all the parts they might need to assemble their products. By working with the other links in their supply chain they could develop "just-in-time" inventories, where materials arrived at the warehouse just as they were needed. This freed up enormous amounts of capital which could then be reinvested in improving the manufacturing process.

With a comprehensive, easily accessible and searchable database on the internet we no longer need to stock our mental warehouses with the kind of knowledge we once did. When I was younger and read a book, I realized that if I didn't memorize or write down information I thought might be helpful, I would never have access to it again. First of all, I probably wouldn't remember that I'd even read it, and if I did, I wouldn't remember where I read it. Now, as I write this book and dimly recall references that might be helpful, or even if I realize that my knowledge of a certain area needs to be bolstered, I don't even have to leave my chair. I simply click on the little "e" with a circle around it at the bottom of my screen and Google around till I track down what I'm looking for.

The internet doesn't mean our warehouses can be empty. But it certainly changes our strategy for storing knowledge and when we need to learn things. Now we can spend more time learning how to synthesize ideas rather than just maintaining facts. This is a boon for the IPP, as it allows us to move quickly from an experience to reflection to action. We don't have to spend most of our first 16 years of education in context mode, just gathering enough knowledge to begin answering questions that are important to us.

How useful knowledge is produced is also being changed by the Internet. A generation ago, education began exploring the role of cooperative learning. Many of us questioned the merits of this approach, because it is so contrary to the ideal of the well-educated (read: "knowledgeable") individual. As one of the conscientious students, I was always a little skeptical myself, seeing it as a way the lazy could ride on the coat-tails of the studious. But now I see a powerful encyclopedia written daily by a community of people who don't even know each other. I know we are impatient with students who think all the research they have to do is cut and paste from Wikipedia, but we'd be crazy not to recognize what a boon this is to learning. It has topics that would not otherwise appear anywhere, even if you could find them. It is kept up to date. Its accuracy is challenged by readers. Even the subjectivity of some of the articles brings a great dimension to education, because a student can track the editing process and follow real-life debates among passionate, informed (and sometimes uninformed) contributors.

Cooperative knowledge bases, like Wikipedia, aren't just a new warehouse that someone else stocks for our students to save them the effort. They are a way to take field trips to the frontiers of knowledge so that they can learn sooner in their education why all that knowledge we've been trying to give them is important. They also uncover for us what has always been true. Learning, in the sense of knowledge formation, is always a group process. Just as technology has made it easier for communities of people to form and verify knowledge, it can also help our students take their place in the discernment process engaged in by the whole human race. That is at the core of our mission as Jesuit schools.

This book is not about educational reform. There are people far more qualified to tell us how to improve teaching, learning, curriculum and all that goes into an effective education program. This book is about how to manage the educational process to serve our unique mission. I want to turn our attention to how we manage our pedagogical model for continuous improvement that incorporates new approaches and evolves with available tools.

F. Managing the Pedagogical Model

Having identified and defined the components of our pedagogical model—outcomes, teachers, learners, curriculum and methodologies—we can manage these components to support the school's mission. Management, again, is the direction leaders give to align the decisions and actions of all participants toward desired organizational outcomes.

Outcomes

We discussed outcomes earlier in terms of the *Grad at Grad* characteristics—Open to Growth, Intellectually Competent, Religious, Loving and Committed to Justice. Managing our schools for mission means helping the school community come to a common understanding of what these mean, how they support our mission and how the curricular and extra-curricular program supports these outcomes.

What does it mean to be *open to growth*, not just in general, but for our mission as a Jesuit school? Does *intellectually competent* mean more than being knowledgeable? Does it require critical thinking skills? Does it require creativity? Eloquence? Empathy? If we feel that all of the characteristics of the *Grad at Grad* are important, there must be in the curriculum particular opportunities for fostering them and the ability to assess whether the opportunities are getting results.

"What gets measured gets done," to quote Tom Peters again. Conversely, what doesn't get measured gets done only sporadically. If our mission is important to us and to the world, that's not good enough. We need to figure out ways to measure our outcomes. At the level of the individual student taking a particular subject, we do this with great rigor. An economics teacher will know with some certainty which students understand what components are included Gross Domestic Product calculations. As we try to measure the bigger and more important outcomes, like whether the student understands how the calculation of GDP effects policy formation around environmental issues, or whether this understanding has shaped her commitment to justice, it becomes more difficult. So we have a tendency to keep our assessments at the granular level, assuming that success at that level will lead to understanding, which will in turn produce the *Grad at Grad*.

In 1985 the JSEA developed the first Student Profile Survey (SPS) to measure on a school-wide basis student progress on the characteristics of the *Grad at Grad*. The SPS was revised in 2003 and in 2009-10 was administered to freshmen by 30 of the Jesuit schools across the country and to seniors by 21. According to a presentation by Ralph Metts SJ, who managed the development of the SPS II, Jesuit schools as a whole have actually seen declines in some of areas of the profile between freshman and senior years, based on student self-perceptions. One can conjecture why this would be so—greater honesty or self-awareness of seniors vs. freshmen; developmental or cultural trends which Jesuit education can only slow but not reverse; or, God forbid, the inability of our programs to accomplish our mission. I don't know the answer, but I do know that the question is too important to dismiss.

We need to use the SPS II or some other means to honestly measure how successful we are at achieving the mission-centered outcomes to which we have dedicated so many resources, not to mention our professional lives. Lacking any statistical measures, we will rely solely on intuition and anecdotal evidence. As discussed in the previous chapter, these are valid but insufficient methods for evaluating our success. Intuition can only make assumptions about what outcomes will be and anecdotal evidence can only suggest that results happen, not that they happen broadly. Statistical measures, which are also insufficient by themselves but get at outcomes and the breadth of results, are the third leg of the three-legged stool.

Once we have established our outcomes, we can then review the curricular and extra-curricular program to see where and how these are supported. This is a mission-driven, top-down approach. I realize that it often works the other way, from the bottom up. We begin with some form of curriculum mapping and determine the outcomes the current program supports. But we still need to identify what outcomes are called for by the mission and re-align the curriculum to produce those results. And we need to measure how well it is working and make adjustments to continually do it better.

This is only a cursory treatment of outcome-based curriculum to suggest how it fits into the overall pedagogical model of a Jesuit school. For a more complete treatment of how to design outcome-based curriculum, see the work of Lorraine Ozar PhD, Director of the Center for Catholic School Effectiveness at Loyola University Chicago, such as her *Creating a Curriculum That Works: a Guide to Outcomes-Centered Curriculum Decision Making* (NCEA, 1994).

Assessments

We assess our students a lot. Hardly a week goes by when a student isn't assessed more than once, in each course, about what he has learned or what he has done. As educators, especially Ignatian educators, we have some qualms about how often we judge the work of our students. We feel this when we see their exaggerated concern about grades. Who can blame them? Generally, the results of these assessments will affect their final grade, which will affect their GPA, which will affect the college they get into, which will, or so it seems, shape the sort of life they will lead.

There are two challenges to assessing student learning. The first is the impact assessment has on learning and the second is how to measure what we really want to know.

The first challenge, the impact assessment has on the student, is something like Heisenberg's *Uncertainty Principle* in quantum physics. German physicist Werner Heisenberg (1901-1976) realized that you could determine either the motion or the position of a subatomic particle, but not both. The decision you make, therefore, determines the outcomes you will observe. Analogously, if we use multiple choice tests as our sole assessment tool, students will work to acquire knowledge in discreet packets that efficiently prepare them to check the correct boxes. If we use only essay tests, students will identify the big picture theses the teacher feels are important and acquire only the knowledge necessary to support each thesis in the short time-frame of the exam.

The second challenge is how to measure what we really want to know. If I am teaching a poetry class, what is it I really want for my students? That they can identify the meter or rhyme scheme? That's helpful, but pretty superficial. That they can identify the point of view of the poem? Good... That they can also see how I or some recognized poetry critic arrives at their interpretation? Better... That they can articulate their interpretation of what the poem means? Better still... That they can tell the difference between a less adequate and a more adequate interpretation and move toward the more adequate? Even better... That they have enough skill and understanding to read, appreciate and be inspired by poetry? Best. But difficult to measure. As we move our goals from good, to better to best, from knowledge to understanding, it becomes increasingly difficult to assess outcomes.

These two challenges can make us diffident about how we assess student learning. Tests that measure knowledge are objective and easy to administer, but don't tell us if we are fostering the intellectual growth called for in the *Grad at Grad*. Tests that measure the understanding characteristic of true intellectual growth are difficult to administer and are subjective.

I don't have an easy answer for this conundrum, and it is not the intent of this book to give an in-depth treatment of student assessments. My task is to identify the importance of student assessment to the school's pedagogical model, to encourage administrators to address it explicitly as they manage for mission, and to offer some direction on how that can be done.

Assessment is like interpreting poetry. There is no single way to interpret a poem, and there is no single way to assess a student's level of understanding, especially if we consider all six facets of understanding put forth by Wiggins and McTighe, cited earlier. And just as the reading of poetry benefits from using different interpretative methods, evaluating student learning benefits from a mix of assessment tools. So the first management imperative is to make sure teachers are skilled with and using a variety of assessment tools.

Just as in poetry there are less adequate interpretations and more adequate interpretations, so there are less and more adequate assessments of student understanding. The second management imperative in the area of student assessment is to make sure teachers are moving from less adequate tools to more adequate tools. This requires that teachers get feedback on the tools they are using, in other words, assessing the assessments. Certainly the administrator will draw on his experience and intuition and advise teachers on their assessment methods. But this subjective feedback must be grounded in relevant data. This should be done in three ways.

First the administrator should provide the faculty as a whole with data on how students are progressing toward the integrated vision of the *Grad at Grad*, as discussed above, under *Outcomes*. If that data points to specific areas that need to be strengthened, individual teachers can gear assessments to support institutional goals to strengthen areas of student learning or growth.

Second, the administrator should encourage teachers to use different types of assessments and then reflect on any variations they observe. What does variation tell them about the assessments? Are they measuring what they really want students to learn? What is the effect of learning styles and the consequent assessment-taking strengths of their students? How do the six facets of understanding converge with or diverge from each other in the assessments?

Finally, the administrator should have teachers collaborate with each other, sharing their rich collective professional experience. She should have them compare assessment methods and results with colleagues teaching different sections of the same course to see which are most effective. She should have them collaborate with teachers of other courses, both within their department and in other departments, to see if what they are assessing will both complement and integrate with the learning expectations the student will encounter throughout the school.

Collaboration

The foregoing discussion of how teachers develop assessments that support the educational outcomes of the school, points out the importance of collaboration to the school's pedagogical model. Beyond developing assessments, faculty collaboration is key to steering the model as a whole.

Tying mission to program is a top-down process, because it means going from principles to implementation. But it is not top-down in the sense that the administration is simply imposing it upon the teachers. The whole process, from identifying outcomes, to designing curriculum, to formulating metrics to making curriculum adjustments, should be done collaboratively by the faculty with the leadership of the administration. The teachers are the experts and the ones who will implement the decisions. We need to take advantage of their collective intelligence and insight.

The other advantage of collaboration in shaping the pedagogical model is the empowerment it gives to all the participants. Teachers need to be proprietors of the vision, but if they are not involved in shaping it, they feel like mere hirelings. Collaboration to shape the pedagogical model is the best antidote for the cynicism that can creep into a faculty when they feel that the direction of the school is at odds with their personal inclinations. Of everything I have observed the most successful way to move teachers to taking responsibility for the big picture of the school is having them work together with other professionals on a project centered on their common mission. In these collaborative settings, either within the building, or with professionals from other schools with a similar mission, idiosyncratic approaches have to yield to something shared, something more encompassing and compelling. Take the example of the art teacher who in his own classroom can concentrate on his particular genre, say drawing. But in collaboration with the other teachers in the department, he must now think about how drawing would influence a student's learning of other forms of expression. With colleagues outside the department, he has to consider how, for an individual, student art interacts with what she is learning in social studies, math or religion. With colleagues from another Jesuit school, he must consider how what he teaches accomplishes the same mission that gave birth to both and sustains their shared form of education.

To be a functioning element of the pedagogical model, collaboration must be more than a buzzword. We must underestimate neither its necessity for moving our mission forward, nor the complexity of embedding meaningful collaboration in the culture of our schools. How to do this will be discussed in greater detail in the next chapter on the community model.

Collaboration takes time, and that is true in two ways. First, administrators must strategize how time will be made available in the school day and the school year for collaboration. Second, they must be patient, and encourage the teachers to be patient, as the flywheel of continuous improvement is agonizingly slow at first. But that initial momentum, almost imperceptible, will yield huge rewards if it is sustained.

Technology

Sometimes we fear technology as a virus that will undermine our humanistic education, and other times we see it as the panacea for the many limitations we encounter. One thing is certain, at this point in history, our pedagogical model must explicitly address the role technology will play.

Computers allow access to interactive learning tools; but they also distract students for hours with addictive role-play games. The internet gives students access to vast knowledge-bases; but it also helps them plagiarize and exposes them to violence and pornography. The democracy of the World Wide Web has encouraged collaborative knowledge acquisition on a global scale via sites like Wikipedia. Others have produced vast amounts of information ranging from the maliciously false to the banal. In my school, any student caught using a cell-phone in class, even in the hallways, will have it confiscated. We know that students use them to cheat, or distract themselves or others during class, even engage in inappropriate behavior outside our supervision, like "sexting," or harassment. But when students no longer wear watches because they keep track of time on their cell phone, when the distinction between cell phone, PDA and computer is fast disappearing, it is clear that we need a new relationship to this technology. When our IT Director substituted in a class, he surprised the students by telling them to take out their cell phones. As he presented the lesson, he asked them questions to test their understanding, instructing them to text their answers to a website. He projected the website with a graph of their responses as he went, so that he and they could tell where he needed to loop back and clarify.

I realize we have to be careful about the consequences, both foreseen and unforeseen, of adopting new technologies, but we cannot simply deny ourselves and our students the power such technologies can offer. We must develop as part of our pedagogical model a vision for the role technology will play. I am reluctant to be too specific about how this should look, both because it is beyond the scope of a book on school management and because anything I write will seem laughably anachronistic in a matter of months. But a few touchpoints will be helpful.

1. Technology and brain development.

There is much research being done on the impact of new technologies on child brain development. Although it is too early to draw conclusions, much of it seems to be suggesting that the brains of upcoming generations are being rewired. My colleagues are observing that incoming students have shorter attention spans, prefer multitasking, and are less able to write in prose English because of their extensive exposure to image-based communications and word-based vehicles that require extreme brevity like Twitter and text-messaging.

But there is also research emerging that suggests that this is not a new phenomenon. For instance, our brains haven't been able to sustain oral traditions the way we used to before writing became widespread. We now think of writing as the only way of remembering important things. One member of the Swinomish tribe in Washington, which still maintains an oral tradition, once told me that they believe the opposite is true. "If something is important to us," he said, "we remember it. White people write things down so they can forget them." The research further suggests that though brains may be "re-wired" by technology, it is not permanent and they can be rewired again as they adapt to their environment. Some teachers feel they can only LOL as a growing number of students use texting jargon in their written assignments. Others say they simply tell the students it is not acceptable and they quickly make the adjustment.

My reason for referring to this research is to suggest that we will lose the battle if our strategy is to preserve a pre-technology educational environment. Again, Ignatius tells us to bring students in their door so that we can bring them out ours. But it is more than simply accommodating ourselves to the inevitable. Our pedagogical model should take advantage of opportunities which only technology can make available

2. Distance learning

I agree with Harvard's Clayton Christiansen that by 2019 over half of all high school courses will be delivered on line. In fact, I think he may be conservative in his estimate. What does that mean for us? Will a significant portion of our courses be accessed on line? Will they come from other providers? Distance learning could allow us to offer Arabic in our schools, even if only three students were interested. Or a fifth year of French. Distance learning could enrich current classes or leverage teachers who may only need to meet with their class once a week. Or provide for greater flexibility in student schedules. These are all huge opportunities, which should not be dismissed because of the comparatively primitive quality of current on-line courses. Envisioning today's computer-aided classroom instruction required similar imagination when all we had were Radio Shack TRS-80's. Even with current technology, distance learning can greatly enrich the curriculum. In the next ten years it will revolutionize it.

3. Digital Textbooks

I can't figure out why we still have expensive, clumsy, environmentally wasteful, inert textbooks. Perhaps when you read this we won't. Again, don't judge what can be done by looking at your Kindle. Amazon is just skimming a market with a primitive early technology. Think of full-color, full functioning, lightweight, inexpensive, interactive digital notepads that can function simultaneously as textbook readers, internet access devices, writing pads, laptop computers and more. The school's pedagogical model must take into account the replacement of textbooks with devices that have much more functionality. Think about how much textbooks shape curriculum. In some schools, textbooks are the curriculum. Because they are expensive and inert, we over-rely on them to shape our courses. New media will push us beyond the regimentation of the textbook.

4. Wiki environments

The most promising and most difficult technological change for me to understand is wikis. Four years ago I had no idea what "wiki" meant, other than as the first two syllables of "Wikipedia." Apparently, it is originally a Hawaiian word that means "quick." But in the accelerated etymological evolution associated with all things technological, it has come to mean "created by a community." Who would have believed that a community of people who have never been in the same room with each other and who have not received any financial compensation could develop a free office software suite to compete with Microsoft? I still don't understand how it works, but it is clear that such collaborative environments, made possible by powerful communication technologies, are changing the way we work and relate to each other. The cooperative learning methods we use to help our students be better people are becoming the fundamental modality for relating to people in their business and personal lives. Our pedagogical model must not only incorporate those tools and knowledge-bases created by wiki communities but must prepare students to function effectively in a wiki environment themselves. It's not just a necessity, it is a tremendous apostolic opportunity for "serving the faith and promoting justice." The wiki environment is ideal for building community to bring about the Kingdom Jesus envisioned.

These are just four examples of how technology must be addressed in our pedagogical model. Admittedly, where technology will be and what opportunities and threats it will offer is a moving target. By making our assumptions about it explicit and doing so as a collaborative educational community, we can be more agile and poised for where technology goes in the future.

Beyond technology's direct role in educating our students, we must also consider how we use it to manage the school and communicate and collaborate with each other. The possibilities suggested above can be harnessed to increase our effectiveness as administrators. Not only will this help us better support the work of the classroom teachers, but it will help us learn more about how technology works and model its use for the teachers and students.

G. Relationship to the Other Models

The pedagogical model defines how the school functions as a school. But as we have discussed, Jesuit schools are also apostolates, communities and businesses, and the models that define how each of these identities is actuated don't operate independently. So before we leave this chapter on managing the school's educational program, let us look briefly at how the pedagogical model impacts and is impacted by the other three models.

Apostolic Model

The apostolic model defines how we carry out the mission entrusted to us by Christ. As a school, we must do this through our pedagogical model. You can have a school which is not apostolic, and you can have an apostolate which is not a school. But Jesuit schools are founded to proclaim the Gospel message in a particular and indispensable way: by helping students acquire knowledge and use that knowledge to reach a deep understanding of the world that God is creating out of love for them. All too often people seek our schools solely as rigorous academic preparation for college, and would be content to skip the faith and spirituality part. We would consider such an education shallow, and even from an intellectual perspective, incomplete. In rarer cases students, and even their parents, think that they can prescind from academic challenges as long as they have a strong faith. The classic case is the parent who doesn't understand why his daughter is being asked to leave because of failing classes when she is doing well in religion and participates in campus ministry. We are not parishes. Our path to a deeper relationship with God and to the service of faith and promotion of justice is through learning, and we expect students to commit themselves wholeheartedly to that path.

Community Model

The community model, to be discussed in the next chapter, defines the relationships that support the people involved in the school, both individually and as a group. The *who* of education is even more important than the *what*. Healthy relationships among students are a pre-condition, giving students the freedom required to learn. Trusting relationships with teachers, which mirror the empowering love of Christ, encourage students to seek help when they need it, take risks, stretch themselves and be open to new ways of looking at the world. In this way, the health of the school community strengthens the educational enterprise. Conversely, the educational program shapes the community. The way we teach can focus on individual achievement at the expense of community or it can help students see themselves as part of a greater whole. It is in classrooms, theaters and sports venues, where students spend most of their time, that they must *experience* community, *reflect* on its values and be invited to *act* in ways that support it.

Business Model

A school is a business and education is its product. The business model must generate sufficient resources to continue producing and improving that product. Quality education requires money for training, release time, incentives, technology and other tools. Resources for the pedagogical model are highly dependent on the business model, which will be discussed in a later chapter. Conversely, the pedagogical model must provide a product that will persuade prospective parents and donors to invest those resources. To do this, the pedagogical model must not only produce a compelling product, it must also generate the evidence needed to make the value proposition. A parent must be able to see some evidence that the school gives their children an advantage in the race for college, or faith that will lead to a virtuous life, or whatever it is they desire. Donors need evidence that the education is truly giving opportunities to scholarship recipients, before they part with hard-earned dollars. Tracking measurable outcomes not only leads to improvement of the program itself, but provides the information needed to market the product to the people who will make the financial decisions needed to support it.

Chapter IV: Community Model

At an open house for prospective parents at a Jesuit high school recently, the school's admissions director welcomed her audience with these words: "Someone asked me earlier this week to sum up what this school is in one word. I thought about it a few minutes and the best word I could use to describe who we are is 'community.' This school is an amazing community of teachers, students, support staff and administrators working together to create a really unique education."

The importance of community is probably being similarly proclaimed across the country in Jesuit and other Catholic schools. We see it in viewbooks and annual reports. We hear it from our alumni. It underscores the significance of relationships to learning and to the experience that people remember and value in our schools.

A colleague of mine, who has served for nearly three decades as principal of a Jesuit school and has a background in counseling, taught me the importance of relationships in education. "Get the relationships right and the learning will happen," he once told me, and has demonstrated the great fruits of paying attention to relationships among students, between students and teachers and among teachers. I certainly know that the converse is true: "Get relationships wrong and learning won't happen."

Our schools, therefore, need to understand not only their apostolic and pedagogical models, but their community model as well. This chapter is about the people that make up our institutions and how they relate to each other.

A. *Cura Personalis* and the Chain of Care.

The employees of a Jesuit school, like Jesus, come not to be served, but to serve. This does not mean, however, that they are simply resources to be consumed in the production of our educational product. Nor are they simply hirelings who exchange an honest day's work for a fair wage. They are the key link in a "chain of care."

After his conversion, Ignatius saw his personal mission as caring for souls. In addition to preaching and engaging in "spiritual conversations" he and his early companions also worked hands-on with the homeless, the diseased and the prostitutes. Fr. Joseph Tetlow points out that during the difficult year of 1537, they fed 10% percent of the poor in Rome, which had been wracked by famine and plague.[2] They realized that a precondition for people to hear about Christ's love for them was experiencing that love through human beings. Ignatius felt that "love ought to express itself more in deeds than in words." So every Jesuit ministry incorporates *cura personalis*, or care for the person, as a fundamental characteristic.

Ignatius desired that every person served by a Jesuit ministry experience the loving, creative presence of God in their lives. God's love is experienced first through relationships. Only then can God be found in all things, in astronomy, literature, botany and all the subjects we want our students to explore. From the foundation of authentic, loving relationships, students can see God's creative love in everything they study.

The student's first experience of *cura personalis* is within his family. When he is first born, nearly everything God desires for him is mediated through his parents. Through their love and care he first experiences God's love and care. As he becomes more autonomous, his parents are no longer the sole intermediaries of God's love.

Increasingly others refract God's love into his life. When he comes to our school, teachers become the mediators of God's love. The care we show protects him from the ravages of a world which he is not yet ready to fully engage. It also frees him and empowers him to grow, to take risks, to inquire into the purpose of his life and what God may desire to give the world through him.

Just as the student grows in the warmth of his teacher's care for him, the teachers themselves need to experience love. It will be impossible to give *cura personalis* unless the teacher experiences it in her own life. If she experiences love, care and respect from the administrators she works with, she will understand how important love is to the mission she is engaged in, she will have models for how to show love, and she will have a well of love to draw from. In order for an administrator to give *cura personalis*, he must experience it. If he feels unappreciated, or that *cura personalis* is just something to be somehow manufactured for the benefit of the teachers and students, he will not be able to model it or draw from his own well. To have a rich, sustained *cura personalis* for the student, therefore, there needs to be a chain of care from the student, back to the teacher, back to the administrator, back to the board, the sponsoring province and back to the Church itself. The *cura personalis* actually flows both ways, but it is more likely to first cascade down than up. So it is incumbent on us as leaders to understand how *cura personalis* works in our school's community model and have a strategy for tending to it.

The metaphor of a chain is instructive in another way, because each link must be anchored to the one before it. You can't skip links. Just so, an administrator's direct care for students, while important, cannot replace the care shown by teachers. The administrator's primary responsibility therefore is to support the teacher in her care for the student. He cannot exhaust his time or energy in direct care for the students and have too little left to support the teachers. Put another way, his best way to care for the students is to care for the teachers.

As important as community is to who we are, however, we are not just communities. Nor are we in existence just to be communities, even vital, loving, healthy communities. We are apostolic communities, which means we have been gathered together to accomplish a certain mission. If that mission ceases to exist, so does our primary reason for being a community. That we love and support one another, as important as that is, is not enough to justify our school's existence.

When the Jesuits were founded, they represented a radical departure from religious communities of the time, which were primarily monastic. A monastery creates community as an end in itself. Certainly it also has an outwardly directed mission, which includes prayer, hospitality and other important works. But monks, at least the vast majority in the Benedictine tradition, take a vow of stability, which means they are committed to remaining with a particular group of fellow monks. They don't anticipate God calling them off to some other setting in order to pursue their mission. In contrast, Ignatius wanted the Jesuits to be apostolic. While community was important to Ignatius and he paid great attention to what makes for a healthy community, it was primarily so that it would support the work of the members. The primacy of apostolic work was evidenced when Ignatius sent his closest friend, Francis Xavier, to the Far East, knowing he would probably never see him again.

This apostolic orientation of community is an important part of our heritage as Jesuit schools. Even as our mission has come to rely increasingly on lay people, whose availability for mission is conditioned by commitments to family and financial self-support, we must still maintain our apostolic orientation. To be truly Jesuit, we have to be people who are responsive to the call of Christ. We have come, not to be served, but to serve our students, and through them, the world. This becomes especially clear in how we use scarce resources. If our identity as a community were an end in itself, then available resources would be committed to sustaining that community before anything else. But while it is important to our mission to protect the jobs, incomes and working conditions of our employees, it is not in the end our mission.

B. Profile of a Jesuit School Educator

The *who* of a Jesuit school is more determinative than the *what*. No curriculum, facilities or materials can make up for having the wrong people leading the learning process. So who are the right people? A good framework for answering this question is the same profile we seek for our graduates.

Open to Growth

Not only must those who work in Jesuit schools model openness to growth, but the profession they have chosen and the school they have chosen to work in demand it. For many people, the very definition of adulthood is that now, finally, they don't have to grow anymore. It's human nature to desire stability, to find an acceptable steady-state and maintain it. That's why it is so inspiring to see the veteran teacher learning new technologies, or eagerly participating in the in-service or listening to her students' music to stay abreast of their world. The world changes. Our personal world changes as we age; the world of our schools changes as successive generations bring their own challenges; and the wide world changes as it is globalized, technologized, secularized and super-sized. The only way to stay effective is to be able to grow ourselves. We know this is true for our students. It is no less true of the people who teach them.

Intellectually Competent

One of the great joys of working in a school setting is the stimulating intellectual environment it offers. In some businesses it may be acceptable, even preferable, to have employees who are not critical, imaginative thinkers. But our job can't be done without them. Preparing young people from diverse backgrounds and with diverse gifts to become critical, imaginative thinkers is an intellectual challenge. It requires people who can model that in their own lives. Our teachers should be masters of their fields who can bring their students to the frontiers of knowledge where the wonders of human inquiry engender excitement and the creativity of God can be experienced. Breaking free of the textbook to accompany students to this frontier requires a commitment to the teacher's continuous intellectual growth.

Religious

As we asked under the student profile in the previous chapter, what does it mean to be religious? The word means different things to different people, and some people use it only in a pejorative sense. I remember snowshoeing up the flanks of Mt. Rainier on a glorious winter day. I was above the clouds of Puget Sound and the sun was glinting off Rainier's many glaciers. As I paused to take it in, I was passed by two men. One of them remarked, "What a beautiful day! I'm not much for religion, but a day like today sure makes me feel spiritual." I wish I had a dime for all the people who told me they were not religious but were spiritual. "Religious," for most people, refers to organized religion with all its human and organizational shortcomings. "Spiritual" refers to something mysterious, unbounded and transcendent. Being religious seems to mean formalism, routine and the distraction of supporting a structure from which the spirit often seems entirely absent. Pure spirituality, however, runs the risk of responding to feelings only. When they are present, we are spiritual. When they are not, we aren't. And most of the time we aren't. Teachers in Jesuit schools should be religious in a way that involves both feeling and the cultivation of feeling through personal and communal practice. Further they must experience, understand and be committed to our particular Ignatian spirituality and our particular Catholic religion.

This will play out differently for Catholic and non-Catholic teachers. Catholic teachers are expected to pursue a path to deeper communion with the Catholic Church. While they may not already know and believe everything the Church teaches, they can't live a double life of claiming to be Catholic and not continuously exploring what that means in their life. Non-Catholic teachers must be on a faith journey as well. This first of all calls them to steep themselves in their own tradition through which God is calling them into a deeper relationship. But they must also continue to increase their understanding of and appreciation for the Catholic faith. They must be able to uphold the mission of the school to present the Church's witness in a clear and compelling way. These two parts of their journey may come in conflict with each other, and if the conflict is serious enough, they may have to consider whether in conscience they can continue to teach in a Catholic school. But for the most part, they play an indispensable role in sharing the richness of their own tradition and an outsider's appreciation for a faith which many of our teachers and students were born into.

Loving

My wife was for many years a first grade teacher. What I noticed whenever I saw her with her students was how much she genuinely loved them. It might be more accurate to say that she was in love with them, because she delighted in their smiles, quirky expressions, and the unique way each one approached life. I could tell they knew this when they would say later that she was their favorite teacher. Adolescents are harder than six-year olds to love in the same way. They are autonomous, challenging and can engage in dangerous behaviors. But I am still moved when I listen to teachers in Jesuit schools talk about their students. Even as they correct them and hold them accountable, I can sense the love beneath it all. The students often don't see it at the time, but later it becomes clear to them what a gift of love they have been given. It would be difficult to teach in a Jesuit school if we weren't able to feel genuine love for our students. Not just a desire to serve them, not just an abstract love. But one that sees each as a unique creation, an outpouring of God's love on the earth, a love that takes personal delight in the beauty we see before us.

Committed to Justice

Teaching is itself an act of social justice. I have rarely encountered a teacher in a Jesuit school whose major reason for becoming a teacher was something other than a desire to improve the world. All people, including teachers, need livelihoods. But our teachers are intelligent, educated and self-disciplined enough to find work which is probably more remunerative than teaching in a Jesuit school. Further I find that they desire especially to teach the poor, to make sure their gifts are used to give opportunities to the people who need them most. They worry that our tuitions make it possible for only the wealthy to access our schools. They support our efforts to make sure that is not the case. They also want to make sure that those students who are privileged enough to attend our schools are sensitized to the majority of the human race who don't have such privileges. Ignatian teachers are also committed to the demands of justice in their own work environment. They desire collaboration, mutual respect, giving a good interpretation to each other's statements and actions, reaching out to a colleague who is suffering and being honest with each other. We fall far short of achieving these goals of justice on a daily basis, but the kind of people we want in our schools are those who desire them and are willing to dedicate their lives to making them more present in the world.

All the foregoing characteristics of the profile of a teacher in a Jesuit school must also be found in the administration and support staff. Administrators must be open to growth if they are to lead schools that grow; they must be intellectually competent to lead what the Jesuits call a "learned ministry;" they must be authentically religious, aware of their own need for faith and committed to the faith journey; they must be loving and delight in the beauty and grace of the people they lead; and they must be committed to justice, navigating the school through currents that flow against this commitment, and showing compassion and justice in exercising their authority over employees and students.

Support staff often have markedly different roles than teachers. Some rarely come in contact with students. But they have a unique opportunity to impact the school by embodying these characteristics when no one expects them to. When they do, teachers are encouraged by their example and students see that the characteristics they are being called to are modeled by the school from its skin to its marrow. I knew a maintenance superintendent who often felt unappreciated by the teaching staff. One day he ran across a picture created by a Jesuit brother. It was of hands over an altar lifting up the Eucharist. The caption read, "Ours are not the hands that consecrate the bread, but we provide the altar for the sacrament to take place." He posted this in his work area to remind himself of the dignity of his work in supporting the work of our teachers which he so admired. Those of us who saw his picture looked at our own work in a different light.

C. How Jesuit School Communities Work Together

We have looked at a profile of the individuals who make up our teaching communities, but how would we characterize those communities themselves? The ways we live and work together will shape our students' experience by creating an environment conducive to their learning and growth. Jesuit school communities should be student-centered, collaborative, and built on trust.

Student-centered

As important as community is to who we are, it is not in the end the reason we exist. We are an apostolic community called together to serve the world in a special way, by educating its next generation. Everything we do as a community should be seen in terms of its impact on the students. If we are collaborative, we do so because it helps us be better teachers and integrate the experience of the students. If the way we are collaborative distracts from student learning and growth, we need to change how we collaborate. The way we use technology, how we schedule in-services, how we compensate our employees, how we structure administrative authority, how we make decisions, everything we do must be evaluated through the lens of how it helps students learn and grow.

Collaborative

Collaboration has positive connotations. Who wouldn't support the idea of professionals working together, sharing ideas and supporting each other? But if most of us are honest, our actual experience of collaboration is filled with frustration and wasted effort. I rarely hear people, especially educators, say how much they like meetings. Most of us have probably felt, if not said, that if we want something done well, we have to do it ourselves. Why then do we want to collaborate? Because in any given school, the collective wisdom, experience and skill can accomplish goals beyond the reach of individuals. If this seems dubious or at best theoretical, consider collaboration from a different perspective. Consider two highly collaborative projects that you are probably participating in right now. One is to digitize old books which, because of their condition or antiquated graphical conventions, are impossible for even the most sophisticated digital readers to interpret. You didn't know you were involved in the project? When you order something on many websites, or download information, you may notice that you are asked to recognize and type into a box some strange looking alpha characters that have been distorted. This is done to prevent "robots" from routinely accessing these sites and misusing that access. But some clever people have come up with a second purpose for this process. In some cases, the graphics displayed are actually fragments from the old books in the digitizing project. A computer program distributes them to the security programs of the participating websites, and millions of bits of our brains are enlisted without our even knowing it to digitize the books. To date hundreds of thousands of pages have been digitized using the surplus intelligence of millions of unsuspecting collaborators.

The second project you are collaborating on is Google's audacious goal to "organize all the world's knowledge." I don't know how far they are toward that goal, but I know that I can type just about any question in a Google search box and it can find the answer to my question. But what amazes me more is it figures out from all the possible interpretations of my question which one I meant. It does so thanks to you. Every time you do a search on Google, you share some of your wisdom about what people doing searches for that kind of information are really looking for. Put another way, when we use Google, we are voting on how knowledge should be organized. The result is that millions of us, without expending any extra effort, are collaborating on no less complicated a project than organizing all the knowledge in the world. It is hard to overestimate either the significance of this or the elegance of how it is being done.

These examples may seem extreme and unrelated to collaboration about matters like writing across the curriculum in our school. The digitizing project and Google have in common that great care went into designing a process to harness people's wisdom. So much effort and cleverness went into the design of the collaborative process that the actual collaborators don't even know they're working on it. No one says, "I'm burnt out on collaborating with Google on organizing all the world's knowledge." Wouldn't that be great if no one ever said that about a department meeting? I don't know that we can design collaboration in our own buildings so well that people don't even feel they are expending energy on it (and I don't know that we can't), but I know we can do better than scheduling a meeting, putting together a six point agenda and letting people have at it.

Collaboration is valuable in many settings, but in schools it helps us solve one of the perennial problems: how to be student-centered when we have teachers isolated in classrooms, departments isolated by academic discipline, and even the extra-curricular program isolated from the school day. This isolation is efficient for defining and meeting the needs of those particular classes, departments or activities, but it makes it hard to remember that students have to somehow integrate all of this. They are being pulled, at times jerked, in many different directions, and most of them have difficulty making sense of it all. We have a responsibility to leave our silos and collaborate with our colleagues who like us are making demands of students to meet their personal or departmental goals. If we can create an integrated experience for our students we will significantly enhance their learning and growth. Given that this does not happen automatically, it behooves the administrators of the school to dedicate time and thought to shaping how collaboration will happen.

Collaboration is important not just among those who work directly with the students, but among the administrators who direct the different components of the program—academics, activities, sports, discipline, campus ministry. They need to model collaboration and they need to integrate the work of the teachers who, like their students, are being pulled in different directions. Collaboration must also occur with and among the administrators who are responsible for institutional health—the president, development director, CFO, technology director and facilities director. They must model collaboration and integrate their work to support the teachers and ultimately the students. They must also share the insights and wisdom of their various disciplines to solve challenging problems that face the school as a whole. For example, a school facing seismic safety issues needs to get accurate structural information and costing from the facilities director, a realistic sense of how much money can be raised and by when from the development director, possible financing scenarios from the CFO and how to keep from disrupting classes and improve program space as a result of the repairs from the principal. The more collaboratively they work on the project, the more creative and ultimately effective the approach can be. But they are busy people and face many forces that impede collaboration. How we design the collaborative process, discussed below under Decision-making Model, is a critical piece of managing for mission.

Trusting

The most important ingredient to successful collaboration is the trust of participants for each other. When a high trust level is present in a group, it's amazing how quickly things can be accomplished. Conversely, when trust is absent, everything has to be negotiated. The US found this out in its peace talks with North Vietnam in 1968. It took about eight months just to agree on the shape of the table. When people trust each other they are able to focus on common interests and develop creative solutions to meet those interests. This is why St. Ignatius gives the advice, referred to earlier, to the giver and the receiver of the *Spiritual Exercises*: "it should be presupposed that every good Christian ought to be more eager to put a good interpretation to a neighbor's statement than to condemn it. Further, if one cannot interpret it favorably, one should ask how the other means it. If that meaning is wrong, one should correct the person with love; and if that is not enough, one should search out every appropriate means through which, by understanding the statement in a good way, it may be saved" (Annotation 22, translation by George Ganss SJ). Often referred to as simply the *Presupposition*, this is practical advice not just for people taking or giving the *Exercises*, but for anyone who has to work in a trusting relationship with others. As president of a Jesuit school, I met with every new employee to discuss the school's mission and their role in it. At the end of the meeting, I gave each one a copy of the *Presupposition* and told them this is the kind of community we strive to be, despite often falling short of the ideal. I invited them to help us better live and practice this *Presupposition*.

Consistently giving favorable interpretations to our colleagues' action will raise the trust level significantly. But trust requires more of us. First it requires honesty. We know that, and I think most of us value honesty, in ourselves and in others. A few years ago, as part of a 12 Step program I was participating in, I did a "searching and fearless moral inventory" that took me about a year and a half to complete. The most surprising discovery for me was how dishonest I am. It's not that I intentionally lie to people. Rather, my dishonesty grows out of my sense of responsibility. I take responsibility for how people feel, for whether they are happy, for how they see our school, for how they see me. What I found is that I can't take this responsibility without cheating a little. To influence how people see or feel about things, I have to give everything a little spin. I'm doing it for their own good (at least for the most part), but it eats away at their trust for me. It even eats away at my trust for them, because I resent having to take responsibility for how they perceive things. What I realized from this is how hard it is for even well-intentioned people to trust each other. We all begin playing the game of figuring out why the other person said what she said. Since we can't really know, and don't want to ask because we now doubt that we will hear the true motives if we do, we jump to conclusions and begin looking for patterns. We connect the dots in ways that seem obvious to us, but often aren't accurate. In fact, if I reflect back on those times when I was able to find out how the dots really connected, I realize that every judgment I make is somewhat wrong, about half are mostly wrong and some, as with the student in the story earlier about dropping garbage, are completely wrong. This is not a good record. I need a better process for figuring out what people's motives are. That process is known as transparency. Transparency leads to trust, but transparency also requires trust. It's hard to be transparent if I feel others will misuse what they find out. Someone has to step out in trust, and I think that is the responsibility of the leader. The leader has to set a tone of honesty, even if it makes her vulnerable, and even if it makes others feel vulnerable.

I have increased my efforts to be honest since I took that moral inventory, and overall I like the results. It makes me happier and more integrated as a person. And I think it makes me more effective as a leader. But I have found that it's not always easy to tell the truth, even when you intend to. First, it requires knowing what the truth is. For most questions, the most truthful answer is "I don't know," because there is very little that we know for sure. When a teacher asks me what salaries will look like in the future, I may be pretty sure that salaries will match the state scale over the next five years, but how much weight I give to probabilities greatly influences my ability to tell the truth. The next challenge is speaking precisely. What does it mean to match? Just the base or all across the scale? How about extra pay for extra work? Was I saying that we would match for each of the next five years or that we'll reach parity by year five? I may think I was very clear, but others may be hanging on every interpretation of these words, and that brings up a third challenge. Even if I know the truth and speak precisely, I can't control how people will interpret what I say. Even if I say, "I don't know," which is almost always the most truthful response, they may be expecting a statement of what is probable and think I am being purposely opaque.

The bad news is that even if you are honest, it is hard to always speak the truth.

The good news is that if you speak the truth, even when it hurts, over time, the people you work with will begin to trust your commitment to honesty. Even if they can't find a favorable interpretation, they will do the next thing Ignatius suggests, they will ask you what you mean by it. I remember during one of the early years of my presidency one of our faculty coming to my office with a copy of a memo I had sent out. It was covered with red marks. He said, "I remembered the *Presupposition* and when I got your memo, I tried to give it the best interpretation, but I just couldn't come up with one. So I decided to come and talk to you about it." This was a watershed moment for me, and I knew that we were taking a positive step in communication built on trust.

Trust also requires mutual accountability, especially if the school is reaching for what Chris Lowney calls "Heroic Ambitions." High-performing teams need to know that they can count on each other. If the principal doesn't feel the development director is doing his job with as much skill and commitment as she is, she will be reluctant to cooperate with requests like a change in the school schedule to accommodate a fundraising event. If the CFO thinks the principal is not holding department heads accountable for their budgets, he will be less likely to support the principal's proposals for budget increases.

How accountability is handled can either increase or decrease trust. I had a development director whose greatest strength was not planning. When board members started pressing me on his results and plans for the ensuing years, I began pressing harder for his long-range development plan. He would give me what he thought were adequate plans, but I found them too vague. I finally made it a condition of his contract that he have a written plan meeting certain specifications to me by a certain date. He was hurt by my putting conditions on his contract and concluded that there was not sufficient trust between us for him to continue working at the school. I was disappointed because I had hoped he would rise to the challenge. I believe I was right about the importance of the plan to his work, but holding him accountable in the way I did undermined rather than increased the trust between us.

An example of increasing trust happened with our IT Department. During the early days of the department, the school lacked any clear standards for technology and as a result the fledgling department was struggling to meet a vast and unpredictable array of expectations for a mishmash of user-chosen technologies. People criticized the IT staff and felt that their own performance was being undermined by inadequate IT support. The IT staff resented the impossibility of the job they were given, which came out in how they responded. I was pretty sure we had the right people, but that we were fibrillated by trying to meet too many expectations. So the IT director and I hired a consulting firm which had national experience to evaluate our IT operation and give us a set of industry standards that we could measure them against. At first the IT director was afraid this would be one more stick to beat him with. But he was also smart enough to realize that meeting one agreed upon set of standards was better than trying to meet an endless array of ad hoc standards. We agreed to some benchmarks and set up some tools for measuring how they were doing each month.

We reported to the rest of the school how IT was doing on things like help desk response time, email filtering, and email uptime, with green numbers where the benchmarks were exceeded and red where they were not. They started out with a lot of red numbers, but people saw that we had some challenging industry standards and that their colleagues in IT were being evaluated against them. As the "customers" of IT, they were asked to help by completing an evaluation and making comments each time the help desk responded to a problem. Instead of mistrusting IT, their customers started sharing responsibility with them, helping them to be better and meet their marks. Today the IT staff not only regularly meets ever higher performance metrics, but the staff, and especially its director, are now sought as consultants and partners in curriculum design, construction, and the school's change process in general.

Moving at the speed of trust is an exhilarating experience. Building the trust takes time. It takes time to lay the foundation of giving the best interpretation, transparency and mutual accountability. It also takes time spent with each other. People who work together on high-performing teams need to know each other as people, not just as people who have a job to do. In actuality, the prerequisite of trust is love. There is a kind of trust that can happen without love. We can trust that people will do certain things in certain situations. That kind of trust does not require love. But to trust someone when a catastrophe strikes, or the chemistry of the team changes, or the rules of engagement have to change for any reason, that requires love.

One night I prayed that God would help me to be generous in serving people, so that they would trust me, so that I could love them as we are called to by Jesus. That's how I saw it: first service, then trust, then love. But later I had a dream in which Jesus came to me and said I had these in the wrong order. He said that I must first fall in love with people. He created them to be beautiful, to be lovable. Once I loved them, I could truly trust them. And when I trusted them, maybe, just maybe, I could serve them. But he said whether I served them would be less important than whether I loved and trusted them, because those are themselves the greatest gift I could give.

To love people, we have to get to know them. We have to spend time together, have fun, goof off. I have worked with an unusual and insightful CFO who insists that every major meeting needs to have a fun component. For some reason we all groan at the thought of doing something fun. First of all we're busy. Secondly, coming up with something fun for a diverse group of people is a challenge. But we've gone from toleration to support when she has us do some corny game so that we can laugh at ourselves and with each other. We have done drum circles, theater games, chowder cook-offs, mystery dinners, tree planting and Pictionary, to name a few. We also try to celebrate our achievements with our employees. This crashes right up against cynicism, especially the sort that resists celebrating while some of their discontentments remain unsatisfied. But the tide began to turn as we spent more time having fun together and celebrating our achievements. We did this in part for our own enjoyment, but also because it strengthened us to serve the students whose education gathered us together.

D. Decision-making Model

How decisions get made shapes the community. As an apostolic organization, as a school, we need to make a lot of decisions about how we go about our work. These decisions often have to be made quickly in response to developments around us. A good example is when your benefits broker tells you that rates for employee medical insurance are going up 25% and you need to consider moving to another carrier. These are some of the toughest decisions I've had to face. The dramatic rate increase means we simply have to change;

changing carriers means changes in providers for employees and a difficult adjustment for their families; even if you have time to get input on the decision, there is never enough time to have people feel their needs were taken into account; and no matter what you do, some group is going to be adversely affected. It is difficult to come through a decision like this without some damage to trust.

Authoritarian and Consensus Models

My experience working with various groups and organizations is that people in North America today have two models for decision-making in their heads and they tend to explain decisions that affect them in terms of these two models. The first is the authoritarian model. Businesses, especially those that are privately held, tend to operate on this model. Someone, often an owner, is vested with the power to make decisions. She may ask for input, but it is clear that ultimately she will be making the decision. We tend to be ambivalent about this. On one hand, it seems archaic, hearkening back to the Middle Ages and the divine right of kings. We chafe at the thought of one person or a few people having so much power over our lives. We see the waste caused by decisions that treat subordinates like robots and don't take advantage of the cumulative, on-the-ground wisdom of everyone in the organization. Even the military has moved beyond a purely hierarchical model, realizing the need for participation to achieve higher performance objectives.

As much as people complain about authoritarian decision-making, they also long for the security it brings. We see this in the political realm. Countries which overthrow authoritarian regimes often go back to them when they experience the messiness of democracy. This cycle may continue through many iterations until the culture becomes comfortable with a truly participative polity. The United States went through this cycle, especially during the presidencies of Washington, Adams and Jefferson, to get to the relative confidence with democracy that the US enjoys today. And schools go through these cycles. An authoritarian president will be replaced by one who is more laissez faire. The insecurity this causes for some will lead to his being replaced by a more directive president again. I remember a school with a loose discipline culture hiring an ex-Marine as the dean of discipline, and then realizing they got more than they bargained for.

The other model people have in their heads is the consensus model. What drives this is the belief that if you ask for my advice, I expect you to take it. A common complaint I hear about administrators, teachers and coaches is that they didn't listen to the person who is bringing me the complaint. When I ask them why they feel they weren't listened to, the answer is that the decision-maker didn't do what they asked. It's understandable. How else can we really know that someone has listened to us? There are other ways decision-makers can confirm to someone that their input has been heard and taken seriously. This both requires trust and helps build that trust.

No matter how many times I experience it, I am surprised by how easily people feel left out when their position on an issue doesn't win the day. This puts pressure on a leader and the group as a whole, to keep everyone happy by trying to achieve consensus. In some cases, when the group has the time required for consensus building and everyone's buy-in is crucial, this is entirely appropriate. But we rarely have that time and we rarely need everyone's buy-in to that level. Yet the expectation of consensus for all decisions can stall a school's progress or drive it back to an authoritarian model where people's input is simply not sought because of the expectations it creates.

Consultative Model

A third alternative is a consultative model. Consultative decision-making is a model where authority and responsibility for making decisions on behalf of the organization are vested in certain individuals or groups, with the requirement that they listen to and take into account the experience, insight and needs of those being affected by their decisions. It is the model used by the Society of Jesus in its own governance.

The Jesuits have essentially three levels of governance: the Superior General, the Provincial Superior and the Local Superior. In an organization where members take vows of obedience, the men holding these positions exercise enormous authority over their companions. But at each level there is a process in place to make sure the superior is listening to those under their authority. For instance, the Superior General appoints consultors for the Provincial, who represent diverse views to which the Provincial is obligated to give ear. The consultors do not vote or give binding advice. The Provincial has the sole responsibility for making the final decision, not on his own behalf, but on behalf of all the Jesuits in his care as well as those they serve.

The consultative model is more nuanced than either the authoritarian or consensus models, which can make it more difficult for people to grasp as a coherent decision-making paradigm. But it is the most appropriate model for most of the decision-making that happens in schools. Hundreds of decisions are being made by people every day. For most of them, we simply have to trust that the person making them is doing so in the best interests of the school as a whole. For their part they have to find ways to get an appropriate level of input on those decisions, both before and after they are made, from those who are affected. Some will require very little input, while others may require full consensus of the participants. In the consultative model, the judgment about level of input required is vested in the decision-maker, who even in this matter must be open to the wisdom of those affected, but must still make the final decision. Let's look at a couple illustrations of how the consultative model works.

Illustration A: An unexpected snowfall occurs overnight. The principal is charged with making the decision about delaying or closing school. She has to make the decision quickly, but it affects many people in different ways. She gives herself 1 hour before posting the decision on the internet and notifying the radio stations. In that time, she calls some of the administrators and two teachers in outlying areas to get their input. Based on the weather report, which says the snow will continue into the afternoon, the input from others and her own assessment of conditions at the school, she decides to close the school. As it turns out, the rain comes and the streets are clear by 9:00 am. Other nearby schools took a riskier approach, did not close and were able to hold class that day. Some people second-guess the principal's decision and say if they had been asked they would have given her the right advice. But there is a reason we vest the authority in one person to make that decision. It has to be made within narrow time constraints, which mean many complex factors can't even be considered. The principal not only must make the decision about whether to close the school, but even how much consultation can be done.

Illustration B: The school is building a new library wing. Up to this time contractors for major projects have been chosen by the traditional method of having an architect prepare bid documents and conducting a competitive bid process. This time the facilities director is suggesting a design-build approach in which the contractor is chosen before the project is designed so that they can help with value-engineering and give practical input on constructability. The president has the authority and responsibility for making this decision, but he must consult widely before he does so. He first meets with the chair of the board and they agree on a process of gathering board input. The chair confirms that the decision about how and when to hire the contractor is not a board decision, but they both agree that the board must be knowledgeable and supportive if there is any second-guessing in the community. The president also meets with the development staff and the campaign committee, knowing that a number of donors are also contractors and so he wants to hear how the decision might impact fundraising. One of the outcomes of this is a decision to have the president meet with a few contractor-donors and architect-donors to ask their opinions and advice, most of which is supportive of the design -build approach. He also meets with his administrative cabinet, which includes not only the facilities director and development director, but the principal, CFO and Jesuit superior as well, to hear any concerns or insights they might have. In each of these consultations, the president takes notes or has minutes taken, which he uses to confirm back to the groups what he heard from them. At that time or in a second communication, he reports on his decision and the reasons for the decision. He delegates to the facilities director and the Facilities Committee the authority and responsibility for the selection process and the choice of the contractor, subject to his final approval.

Ignatian Discernment

We are fortunate that the consultative model comes to us from our Jesuit roots. It works best when used in conjunction with another aspect of our Jesuit legacy: Ignatian discernment. The consultative model tells us how authority and responsibility should be structured to involve people appropriately in decisions that affect them. Ignatian discernment is a way of making decisions that uncovers God's desires for us as well as our deepest desires for ourselves, both individually and as organizations. It is at the level of those deepest desires that the power of our mission resides. The push and pull of everyday forces can keep us from tapping into this deeper current. Fr Pat Twohy SJ, who ministers to Native Americans in the northwest, compares our journey to that of the salmon. "It is the same sea of life that holds and sustains us all. Our Origin, Our Home, Our Destiny, is the same. And yet we find ourselves thrashing in the shallows and on the surface of the sea, where we are most clumsy and vulnerable. There we bruise and wound one another. There our common enemy overtakes us. It is only in the deeper waters that the swimming is smoother. There we find serenity. There is room for everyone. The deeper we are graced to swim in the sea of mystery…the more we have in common with our fellow travelers."

Ignatian discernment finds its roots in the *Spiritual Exercises*, where Ignatius provides the exercitant with guidance on making important life decisions. The first set of guidelines appear in the Second Week under methods for making a "good election," and then in the supplementary material after the fourth week under "Rules for the Discernment of Spirits." These are the product of his own discernment of the Holy Spirit acting in his life, beginning with his recovery from his leg wound in the Loyola castle. Ignatius realized that God was leading him through his thoughts, experiences and feelings. He began developing methods to become more attentive to the directions in which God was calling him. Eventually he realized that he could share these methods with others, which led to his writing the *Spiritual Exercises*.

The application of Ignatian discernment to the work of groups has been a subject of some dispute. Since everything in the *Exercises* is geared toward the individual, it is only by adaptation that one can apply Ignatius's guidance on discernment to the joint decision-making processes needed in organizations. Much has been written about group discernment, but the models described vary so widely, that it is difficult to find a common structure. At the risk of further confusing the issue, I want to offer the following guidelines which I have gleaned from my reading of these various sources and have found effective in my own work. These are not so much steps of a decision-making process as how the participants must dispose themselves in order to tap into the deeper currents of God's will for us and our own true desires.

Dispositions for Ignatian Discernment:

1. A desire that, above all, the outcome of the deliberation be in accord with God's will and a willingness to commit ourselves in prayer for that outcome

2. A willingness to listen deeply, to ourselves, to others and to God

3. A trust that others are speaking with good intentions and bringing information and perspectives important to the issue

4. A willingness to consider all sides of the issue

5. A detachment that seeks not to win the argument or pursue the interests of the individual, but seeks interior freedom to make the best decision for the organization as a whole

6. A willingness to work through and not avoid conflict and to make hard decisions

7. A willingness to grow in understanding by attending to the natural dynamics of human learning captured in the Ignatian Pedagogical Paradigm: context, experience, reflection, action and evaluation

I have tried to work with groups on a standard procedure for applying Ignatian discernment and have found them all to be too formalistic. But the above guidelines can be used as preparation for the board or a committee or team when it is trying to make an important and difficult decision. When decision processes seem to be going sideways, when participants aren't listening to each other and the deliberations are becoming divisive, this can be a good check-list to diagnose how the group needs to re-center itself. In such a case, however, resist the temptation to accuse participants of, for instance, not being willing to consider all sides of the issue. It might be good to take a time out and have a neutral party lead the group through a prayerful reflection on these seven dispositions.

E. Hiring

The next two sections are about how we bring people into our community, first those we hire for the educational team and second those we admit as students.

I can't emphasize enough the importance of the hiring process. If we refer to the profile of a teacher outlined at the beginning of this chapter, it is clear we have high aspirations for the people we want in our schools. They need to be growth-oriented, bright and thoughtful, spiritually alive, caring, and courageous in their generosity. If I were to say that nothing is more important for shaping our schools and determining how well we achieve our mission than those we bring onto the team, I would expect no one to disagree with me. And yet it is remarkable how often we try to minimize the efforts we put into hiring. Why is this? I think there are several forces that undermine the implementation of thorough hiring procedures. First, they take time, and since most hiring isn't calendared in advance, it means we're taking time from something that is. Who sits down in spring of one year and builds into the calendar for the following year time for hiring a mid-year teacher to replace someone who will become ill, or to replace the development director who will up and leave in May? We are assuming they will all be staying, except for those who are somewhere in the termination process, so why would we schedule time to replace them?

Second, hiring feels like such an unreliable process. Some do it better than others, but there are so many unknowns when we hire someone, that we are tempted to rely on our intuitions and God's providence. It's important to have good intuition, and to trust God, but if hiring is as important as we think it is, we need to give ourselves every advantage. I want to share some of the steps of the process that I have found offer the most potential for improvement.

Marketing

We will discuss marketing in several places in this book, but this is an area where it is sometimes forgotten. To hire the best person, we need to have lots of choices, which means we have to cast our net broadly. But it isn't just a matter of getting hundreds of resumes. We want the right people to apply, people who have the unique qualities we seek and who will be passionate about our unique mission. So when we put together our marketing plan, we need to think about how we are marketing ourselves to potential employees. What will they find when they visit the website, or visit campus? What will they see at job fairs, in the newspaper, or on diocesan job boards? Will they get a clear, compelling message about who we are? If they do, it will have two effects: it will excite talented people who want to be part of a high-performing team with a mission that reflects their own values, and it will dissuade others who don't match the school or the position from clogging our inbox with resumes.

Then there is the actual advertising for the position. I don't want to say a lot about this, because I suspect most of us know the websites and periodicals we need to advertise in and what needs to go into an ad. But I do want to say three things. First, make sure the ads are consistent with the overall marketing strategy of the school. Include your logo wherever possible, assuming your strategy is to continually reinforce this as the graphical identity of your school. It may cost extra, but it's generally worth it. The same thing applies to core marketing messages, like a tag-line that captures your mission. Keep building that identity. This is an important place to do it.

Secondly, understand the legal environment. The two most important words to know are "job related." In order to protect the school from lawsuits, what you say in your ad about who you are looking for and information you want from them must be job-related. There are some things that shouldn't be criteria, like someone's age or whether they are married, and you don't want to give the impression that they are. On the other hand, there are attributes that are job-related for us as Catholic schools which aren't for most businesses. I remember calling our local newspaper a number of years back to post a position for one of our offices. I wanted the ad to say that the school was a Christian environment, and the person taking the ad said they couldn't print that. I'm sure the paper's legal counsel had crafted a general policy to avoid lawsuits, and I couldn't convince her that it is job-related and therefore legal for a Catholic school to describe itself as a Christian environment. I'm not qualified to give legal advice, but given the over-reaction to legal issues regarding religion in the public square, I encourage you to work with your own counsel to craft clear, legal messages about who you are.

The third point about advertising has to do with the school's diversity goals. Most Jesuit schools could benefit from having a higher number of teachers, administrators and staff from under-represented ethnic minorities. The perception is that there just aren't many qualified candidates available. It is true that at least for some minorities, there is a smaller pool available, often exacerbated by our geography, religion and the make-up of our student bodies. But this can be a self-actuating assumption. It is in this first step, marketing the position, that we have to challenge ourselves to be most creative. It may involve looking at new and non-traditional ways of advertising, attending job fairs we would not otherwise, or developing personal relationships through involvement in organizations where minorities are better represented. Many people are re-thinking affirmative action, and its legality in publicly funded institutions has been challenged. While I understand some of the concerns, I think it is still appropriate for us to make an extra effort and even adjust our criteria when appropriate in order to build the diversity of our campuses. By putting extra effort into expanding the pool, we won't have to cut corners and put someone who is not a good match in an untenable position just to meet our diversity goals.

As we shift from marketing the position, where we want to be as inviting and positive as possible, to the selection process, we need to continue to market ourselves, but we also need to develop a healthy skepticism about the applicants. To some extent, applying for a job is an act of desperation. If someone doesn't have a job, they probably need one, and badly. If they have a job, the prospect of moving to your school is so compelling that they are willing to leave the security of their current circumstances. It feels like jumping off one ledge onto another across a frightening chasm. In such situations, people can be excused if they stretch the truth about as far as it will go in order to land safely on our ledge. They honestly believe that they can make it good once they are hired. While this is understandable, we owe it to ourselves, our school and them, to keep at least one eye jaundiced and searching dispassionately for the truth. It begins with the application process.

Applications

A resume is not an application. It is a marketing tool designed to hide the weaknesses and exaggerate the strengths of the applicant. In what they say and especially in what they don't say, resumes are almost all at least somewhat misleading. An applicant for a vice principal position who sat quietly on a committee reviewing dress code becomes "a leading member of a team that designed the school's innovative discipline program." An applicant for annual giving director who worked in a development office processing gifts and answering phones becomes "a key player in the school's successful $25 million capital campaign." If you've been in administration for any length of time, you've seen it and you've developed a fine sense of skepticism as you read resumes. Yet I am surprised how many people still treat them as applications, and use them as the sole basis for selecting which candidates they will interview.

The resumes should be used to select the candidates to whom you will send application forms. The application form is a legal document, signed by the applicant, which not only helps you identify those whom you will not hire, but lays the basis of an employment relationship with the one you do. Without describing the application in detail, here are some key elements it should include:

A place to list all employers for the last ten years, with the instructions that any gaps should be explained; a space for the names and contact information, if it is available, of direct supervisors; and a space for the salary the applicant received in each position. This is the most critical information of the entire form. Direct supervisors are the most important references, in fact the only references that really matter, because they have experienced the applicant in the relationship you are considering entering into with them. The salary information will be useful for negotiations, and it is also the most reliable metric of the responsibility level of the position.

A place to tell what they know about the institution and why they applied. Their impressions will tell you a lot about their fit for the job and the level of commitment you can expect.

A place to list applicable skills. Presumably they did this in the resume, but now they have to sign their name to what they claim and the document can be used later if they made false claims. It tends to bring things into sharper focus.

A place to give permission to contact references. Often the applicant has listed references in the resume, but I would look at these with only passing interest. They simply say that in my whole life, I am capable of finding five individuals who will speak well of me. Everyone but the most egregious sociopath could come up with five references. We already have the most important references, prior supervisors. We want the permission to contact the people they don't list as references (which will be explained more in the discussion of reference-checking, below). Of course, everyone has the right to prevent us from contacting people they don't want to know they are applying for a job. So we ask them to sign a statement giving us permission to contact anyone who could shed light on their candidacy except those they would like to list below the statement. This gives us freedom to contact people they might be hiding from us who have important information that would be adverse to their candidacy. For those they list for non-contact, it allows us to ask them why they would not want them contacted. In some cases, there are good reasons. For example they may not want their current employer to know they are applying for the job. In other cases, their reluctance will alert you to concerns you may want to explore more thoroughly with them.

Other permissions, disclaimers and notifications. The application form is also the place to get their permission to conduct background checks, to ask them if they require any accommodations in order to do the job and let them know of any workplace restrictions, like smoking bans or religious expectations, that will be requirements of the job. By addressing these up front, in the application, and having them sign their acknowledgment, you now have legal evidence of notification and their acceptance of these terms. This can eliminate a lot of misunderstanding later.

Not everyone who is sent an application will respond. This may be the first time they think seriously about what working for your school means, and some will, thankfully, take themselves out of the process at this point. Knowing this, select a large enough pool of invitees that you have a sufficient response to work from for the next steps, demonstrations and interviews. It is better to err on the side of inclusion. It takes very little work to send and review applications. Most of the work is done by the applicant, and they are generally happy to do it if it means they have a chance of being considered for the job.

Demonstrations

Having read the candidates' own assessment of their ability to do the job, we want to somehow see them in action and judge their skills for ourselves. How this is done will vary by job, and what kind of access we have to the candidates. In some cases we have to be creative. When hiring teachers, it is crucial to observe them teaching a class in our school. For development officers, having them write a solicitation letter and a phonathon script based on the case for our school will tell us not only how well they understand the fundamentals of asking and how well they write, but also what they understand about the school's mission. A CFO could be asked to evaluate the school's financial statements and create a hypothetical five-year plan, highlighting what questions she has and how she would go about getting answers to those questions. My administrative assistant, who is extraordinarily skilled in all aspects of office computer software, got tired of working with secretaries who claimed to have office skills that they didn't have, and developed her own test. Most have failed the test, some turning it in and saying they need to go take a tutorial before they apply for a job like this. But those we have hired from this test have had the requisite skills to be successful in our offices.

While some people are put off by having to do the extra work, I have found that the best candidates relish the opportunity to show what they can do. Some have told me that it increased their desire to work for the school because it showed how committed we were to our mission and the quality of our work. That's great marketing and it works best for the people we want most.

Interviews

How many applicants you interview and who interviews them will depend on the job. For an entry level custodial position, the facilities director may just keep interviewing candidates by himself until he finds the one he likes. Hiring a principal will require a search committee with board representation and a narrowing of candidates to a number which can fit the time availability of a group of busy people. In cases where a committee is involved, the person to whom the new hire will report should do preliminary interviews to help narrow the selection and get to know the candidates.

Interviews should be structured, with standard questions asked of all candidates. But there needs to be enough flexibility to ask questions, address concerns or explore opportunities that are unique to each candidate. The challenge is to have enough consistency to defend the process against possible allegations of prejudice yet flexible enough to get a 360° view of the candidate, which is in itself an element of fairness. Questions should be open-ended and include both what-if and how-have-you-handled scenarios that call forth a narrative from the respondent that suggests how she would handle certain situations. In some cases, it is appropriate to role play situations to see how candidates would handle them. A scoring system based on agreed upon, sometimes weighted categories should be used to increase the objectivity of what is nonetheless a subjective process. Like the resume, interviews can be misleading. A verbal, self-confident candidate may totally outshine an introverted, but highly capable candidate. The interview tells us only one thing for sure: how well the candidate interviews.

Remember that during the interview, while you are trying to eliminate those who are not the best candidates, you are also trying to attract the one who is. This would be easier if we knew which was which beforehand. Since we don't, it is important that, without neglecting our need to probe and find the truth, we do so in ways that put the interviewees at ease, reflect the good qualities of the school and let them know that the candidate hired will be welcomed into a caring, high-performing apostolic community. One way to do this is to assign to each of the interviewees someone who will call them before the interview to encourage them, see if they have any questions and let them know how much the school appreciates their participation in the application process. Good candidates have pulled themselves out of selection processes because those charged with hiring, in an attempt to be and appear objective, gave interviewees the feeling that they wouldn't be valued by the organization.

References

Reference checks can be done at several points in the process. Because it takes time to do them well, it is more efficient to wait until the process is down to two or three candidates. On the other hand, some reference checking might be helpful in choosing the candidates who make it to this point. Waiting also runs two risks. The first is that we won't have time to do them well and a looming deadline will cause us to cut out steps or limit the number of checks. The other is that as our commitment level to the candidates rises during the process we may not really want to hear any negatives. I have often found that people who call me for reference checks late in their process don't really want to hear bad news; their minds are made up and they just want confirmation.

A few pointers for reference checking. As mentioned earlier, you want as much as possible to talk to people who have supervised the applicant. They are the ones who have related to them in the way that mirrors how you would. They have the most knowledge about their performance, they have presumably done evaluations and they are the most likely to assess the candidates against job objectives, rather than whether they were their best bud in the department. Armed with the applicant's permission to talk to anyone (job-related) that they haven't asked you not to speak to, hunt around for different perspectives. When talking to one reference, ask whom they could recommend that might have a different perspective from theirs. Don't be disappointed if you come across someone with negative opinions of the applicant. Who doesn't have such people in their lives? But if you can find out why, it may give you a helpful parallaxis. I have found that some of the negative comments have actually increased a candidate's stock. For example, an administrator candidate whose decisiveness you worry about, might receive a comment about how she angered some of the faculty by making a difficult decision.

The most difficult part of reference checking is getting candid observations, and this is increasingly difficult. Employers are worried more about legal repercussions, and they really don't have much incentive to warn future employers about employees they are glad to be rid of. Many employers refuse to give any evaluative references. This is a terrific disservice to the people impacted by incompetent, dishonest or toxic employees. Even employees with professional boundary issues can cover their tracks unless employers are willing to share information. Recognizing this, some states are developing laws and policies to compel schools and districts to share information about abuse. It is difficult to balance accountability with privacy rights, but our job is to protect our institutions and our students as best we can. There are two strategies I find particularly helpful.

The first strategy for getting important information from reluctant references is to take a few moments to remind them of the importance of the process. Give a quick background on the school in ways that would make them not want to see it hurt. Explain that your job, in the interest of both the school and the prospective employee is to determine if there is a good match. If there isn't, it will only cause trouble for the candidate if he is chosen. Point out that the candidate has given you permission to contact people for references because he knows that will be a prerequisite for being considered for the job. Also say that you aren't expecting to find the perfect candidate and that while shortcomings are helpful to know about, they won't necessarily preclude the candidate from getting the job. I find this contexting makes the conversation less of a cat and mouse game.

The second strategy is to word questions in a way that allows you to draw inferences even if the reference doesn't want to say anything negative. For example, after asking for the candidate's strengths, we then ask about their weaknesses. If they are reluctant to offer a list, think about what important characteristics were missing from the list of strengths and ask specifically about those. If the answer is evasive, you have a clue that you can check in other ways. Asking whether they would hire the person again will give you a good sounding. If the reference is avoiding a negative response, you will still likely hear it in their tone or choice of words. They might say, for instance, "It would depend on the circumstance." If you ask them what those circumstances might be, and they are vague, it is another clue that something needs to be investigated further.

If there is a hiring committee, it is a good idea to divvy up the reference checks among various members, having different people doing checks on the same candidate in order to get different perspectives. Again, it is good to have standard questions as a basis, with the ability to follow up on issues that may be unique to a candidate. And then it is helpful to have a system for scoring the reference checks.

Orientation

The selection process is actually the beginning of the orientation process. The candidate who is eventually selected has been learning who your school is from the moment he saw your logo in the classified ads and logged onto your website to learn more. The materials you provide, how you communicate with your candidates and the quality and thoroughness of your process will say something about how important employees are to the school's mission, the professional standards you expect and the *cura personalis* that characterizes the school.

Large corporations have elaborate training and orientation processes, which include videos and standard classes conducted by human resource specialists. The informality of a small organization like a school can cause us to undershoot what people need to get off on the right foot as part of our apostolic team. While most schools have orientation programs for new faculty, many do not for staff and even administrative positions because such hires tend to be irregular in occurrence and timing. But a simple checklist should be developed to make sure the new employee gets all the information she needs as quickly as possible. For example, it should include the following: all the legal steps, like background checks, if those have not already been done; signing all employment documents; learning about and signing up for benefits; an organization chart including people's names; meeting key personnel; orientation on the school's computer network and protocols; getting keys, passwords, email account and voicemail; receiving and reviewing documents and manuals covering school policies; physical orientation to the campus. [To get a sample orientation checklist see *Contact the Author* at the end of the book] Beyond the initial orientation is an ongoing program for professional development and apostolic formation, which we will turn to now.

F. Professional Development and Apostolic Formation

Professional development and apostolic formation are two areas in which our employees need continuous growth if we are to accomplish our unique mission. Although they are intimately related, I will treat them separately so that the goals of each can be seen in relief.

Professional development

For teachers and administrators, the field of education has professional development built into it. Teaching requires professional degrees and certification, as well as continuing education and clock hour requisites. Most schools have pay scales that reward teachers for attaining ever higher levels of educational preparation and higher degrees. Many excellent training programs are offered by colleges, governmental and private agencies. Every school has its own in-services and programs of professional development. And just working with students who bring their own knowledge and questions encourages us to continue to grow and learn.

As much as one might assume that a college prep school would be teeming with adults who want to learn, to engage in spirited dialogue and travel to the frontiers of knowledge, there are several factors that militate against this. The first is the human tendency, alluded to earlier, to find a steady-state and maintain it. Educators are as prone to this as anyone. The second is the susceptibility of school staffs to either chronic or infectious cynicism. I don't know that this is any truer of schools than other types of organizations, but I've seen faculties get pulled into the black hole of negativity and it can be hard to get them back out. I remember hearing a provincial once talk about the difference between criticizing in order to make things better and just griping to get some immediate relief from one's general discontentment. Pathological cynicism, while it can be entertaining and even momentarily cathartic, is toxic to schools with our lofty mission.

The third counterforce to adult learning is the temptation to think that being a teacher means having to have all the answers. If we believe this, it will be difficult to live with open questions and be engaged in ongoing exploration with our students. And if teaching makes us vulnerable to this temptation, administrating can be even worse. Take technology for example, where the hierarchy of expertise is reversed. Students achieve mastery most easily because they don't have to give up old habits and ways of thinking. They are, so it seems, born into it. Teachers, because they learned their skill sets in a different technological environment, have to unlearn, as well as learn. But they will be pulled along by a need to catch up with their students. Administrators, tend to be older and have even more entrenched and anachronistic skill sets. They also have the opportunity, which too many indulge, to insulate themselves and avoid getting on that learning train altogether. Technology is just an example. We can have similar responses to learning new concepts, techniques and ways of looking at the world. Schools, especially Jesuit schools, should be places where we all push ourselves to learn new things, to be critical thinkers and to aim for high intellectual standards.

As with student learning, adult learning in our schools should aim not just for knowledge, but understanding. One of the dimensions of understanding discussed by Wiggins and McTighe is that people be able to apply what they learn. Just as it is not enough to expose students to scientific method, it is not enough to expose teachers to theories, for instance, about learning styles. If understanding learning styles is something the school feels is important to its pedagogical model, teachers have to have a deep enough understanding to add this to their tool belt, know when to use it, and apply it when appropriate. Professional development for our faculty requires the same components as our pedagogical model to be fully effective. Have we as school leaders thought through what outcomes we want for our professional development programs? Have we determined how we would assess whether those outcomes have been produced? Have we designed a curriculum, a step by step process to get to those learning outcomes? We need to look at our in-services and other elements of our professional development programs and think in terms of a scope and sequence designed to lead to the learning outcomes. An episodic approach in which we expose our faculties to good ideas currently circulating in the education world is not consistent with what we know about how learning happens. We also need formative assessments along the way, or summative assessments to determine whether the hoped-for outcomes were achieved.

In the business world, there has been an awakening to the need to become learning organizations. Businesses have discovered they must have processes for identifying new knowledge that will fuel innovation or shed light on current practices that make suboptimal use of the business's resources. In their 1998 book, *Professional Learning Communities at Work*, Richard Dufour and Robert Eaker of the Association for Supervision and Curriculum Development, cite Peter Drucker from his 1992 book Managing for the Future: the 1990's and beyond: "Every enterprise has to become a learning institution [and] a teaching institution. Organizations that build in continuous learning in jobs will dominate the twenty-first century." The importance of learning as a source of power should be no surprise to us as educators. Many of us are in education precisely to empower our students to become positive influencers of their world. If we didn't believe that learning leads to such efficacy, we would find another line of work. Yet, how have we incorporated this belief into our own lives both individually and as institutions? We are teaching organizations, but how good are we as learning organizations? Do we have effective processes for identifying new knowledge to fuel innovation or shed light on current practices that suboptimize the use of our resources? Dufour and Eaker, in the book previously cited, state that while a learning organization must learn from its external environment, most educators are not willing to [loc. 56]. They cite a 1996 survey by Seymour Sarason ("Revisiting the culture of the school and the problem of change"), which concludes that "school personnel are remarkably uninterested in issues outside of their daily routines.'It is as if they are only interested in what they do and are confronted with in the encapsulated classrooms in their encapsulated schools.'" We can hope that our schools and our faculties are not similarly afflicted with this disinterest, but it is part of the broader culture of education. We are influenced by that culture and must design thoughtful professional development programs to resist this tendency.

Collaborative learning

Becoming a learning institution requires a collaborative culture. While it is commendable for teachers to continue to develop their individual skills and knowledge, this doesn't necessarily translate into an organization that can learn and improve. For this to happen, teachers must share ideas, insights and best practices. They must experiment with new approaches to see which ones work and should be propagated and which ones don't and should be laid to rest.

Collaboration among educators helps schools become learning organizations in several ways. First, collaboration allows the school to survey a wide range of practices being used in education and beyond by having different teachers research different subjects or schools. Second, every faculty has a wide range of intelligences, experiences and skill sets residing in its teachers. Effective collaboration aggregates those into a formidable collective intelligence, experience and skill set. Third, collaboration leads to integration of knowledge at the level of the individual student, as opposed to each teacher operating as if he managed a separate compartment in the student's brain. Fourth, collaboration among the adult community models collaboration for students. As noted earlier, these students are entering a highly collaborative work environment brought on in part by powerful new technologies.

Dufour and Eakin have developed an excellent model for collaboration. Their concept of Professional Learning Communities is highly compatible with the kind of schools and communities Jesuit schools strive to be.

Apostolic formation

In addition to the professional competence of our teachers, we must also be strengthening their apostolic effectiveness through programs of spiritual formation and catechesis.

Fifty years ago, the faculties of Jesuit schools were nearly all Jesuit. This meant that nearly all teachers had been through 4 to 13 years of religious formation, had done a 30 day retreat and had made vows of poverty, chastity and obedience. Today's teachers bring great professional preparation, commitment and diversity of background. But they rarely have the formal religious training that Jesuits receive. Many are not Catholic. Even those who are may be struggling with what that means or whether they can accept everything the Church teaches. Their last systematic instruction in Catholic theology may have been 12th grade, or 8th grade, or their parish religious education program. Even if they have 16 years of

Catholic education, they may be uncomfortable leading prayer, or unsure of how to vitalize their own prayer life. We want to get the best, most effective teachers for our schools, but given the changing world around us, we often feel we can't always get both talented teachers and teachers who are already up to speed with our religious tradition.

We do benefit from some faculty members who bring exceptional Ignatian backgrounds, for example as Jesuit Volunteers or alums of Jesuit schools. At times, however, the lack of pre-formation in our specific religious heritage can cause us to wonder whether the religious dimension of our enterprise has much hope for the future. Rather than long for a past set of circumstances, we should recognize that in all times and places, God sends us people to carry on the work and wants us to work with them and incorporate them into the mission. The apostles themselves were an unlikely team for the huge teaching task Jesus could only begin. We should recognize that we have been given an opportunity. For what faculties in Jesuit schools today lack in pre-formation, they make up for in other attributes. First they generally have superior professional preparation for the vocation of teaching. Second, they bring a diversity of religious backgrounds that helps them prepare their students for the world they are entering. Third, their very lack of formation can give them an openness to the formation we want to give them. They are often not as jaded, or convinced that the catechesis they received in their youth will be sufficient for the rest of their lives.

The relative lack of formation before teachers arrive at our doors means that we have a greater responsibility to do that formation ourselves. Our schools have recognized this and have responded with effective programs at the local, regional and national level. The focus has been on inspiring our faculties with the Ignatian vision and helping them see how that vision will influence their teaching. Using experiences based on the *Spiritual Exercises*, teachers have been led to deeper relationships with Jesus and with each other. They have become powerful teams for inspiring their students to a deeper appreciation of their spiritual life and the call to be servants to a needy world. They have learned new ways of understanding

who their students are and who they can be when they are
"graduates at graduation" who balance personal achievement with
social responsibility. They have learned about the Ignatian
Pedagogical Paradigm and how to incorporate this understanding of
the natural learning dynamic into their lesson designs. I have seen
evidence of this remarkable strengthening of formation in every
Jesuit school I have visited.

There are still big challenges. In a recent survey of Jesuit
schools, I found two glaring gaps in most teacher formation
programs that schools are beginning to address. The first is that they
are not geared to the needs of teachers based on their years at the
school. Most formational activities are aimed at the entire faculty
with a one-size fits all approach. So if a faculty retreat focuses on the
theme of Ignatian discernment, or the life of Ignatius, everyone will
get it at once. The next year a new cohort of faculty may join the
school, and they will not have the benefit of that great retreat. It
doesn't make sense to repeat the same retreat theme every year, and
yet the themes are needed by the new teachers too.

In recognition of this problem, many schools are developing
sequential formation programs that continue beyond the orientation
given in the first year. Most of these schools have sequenced various
experiences or content out over the new hires' first three years. Some
have extended to five years. When one considers the complexity,
richness and uniqueness of Jesuit spirituality, it may take up to ten
years for a teacher to reach her full effectiveness as an Ignatian
educator. We would do well to design a path to help her reach that
level, just as we design a path for our students to grow into the
characteristics of the *Grad at Grad*.

The second glaring need is for catechetical formation. We do a
good job of helping our teachers experience and appreciate Ignatian
spirituality. It is attractive and often speaks to the immediate, felt
needs of adults. But we generally leave it to someone else, hopefully
their college, high school or parish, to have developed their
understanding of Catholic teaching. While this may once have been a
reliable approach, it is no longer. The catechesis received by even our
Catholic teachers is uneven and often outdated. This is problematic
for schools that pride themselves on being permeated by religious

values. We can't simply rely on our religious studies departments to carry the load. I hear teachers say they need more help when students in their biology or history, or even math classes ask them difficult questions about Catholic teaching. When I was a student in a Jesuit high school, we used to be able to derail our Latin lesson by asking Fr. Menard about some difficult aspect of sacramental theology. He always took the bait, and we were relieved of the boredom of Latin drills. Though our motive was distraction, we learned a lot. We don't need language or music teachers with the theological training of Fr. Menard, and we certainly don't need teachers as easily sidetracked. But the more teachers who can reinforce the faith by responding confidently during the "teachable moment," the more effective we will be.

Somehow, we need to allocate time and resources to helping teachers with at least the rudiments of Catholic theology. As with Ignatian spirituality, we need to design a path that allows teachers to gain this understanding over time. As with professional development, this process will work best if it is collaborative. Our faith is community-centered. The journey toward a deeper relationship with God is not one we make on our own. We need others to encourage us and at times to challenge us. This is especially true in the area of formation, because it cannot simply be enforced on the participants. While apostolic formation is the most important element of our school's unique mission, how we hold people accountable is tricky. Too heavy-handed an approach will result in a begrudging compliance, when we need them to freely embrace our spirituality. The more collaborative the formation process is and the more the pressure comes from peers rather than authorities, the more genuine and heart-centered people's commitment will be. Nothing less will do.

Beyond the faculty

The foregoing sections have focused on teachers, but the reality is that professional development, collaborative learning and apostolic formation must extend throughout the school. Administrators must be fully engaged in the collaboration, not only as participants but as designers and leaders. The office staff, the development and business departments, the facilities staff, admissions, food services, technology, all must be committed to continuous learning and growth, both professionally and spiritually. The mission and its essential elements cannot be delegated to one department or category of employee. All must bring their expertise, experience and insights to the table. This means that all departments must be recognized as key players in formation and their contributions recognized as essential to the success of the whole enterprise. All must share accountability for the mission which the school achieves together.

G. Accountability/Evaluation

If the school has hired the right people and put in place programs for their continued formation and professional development, the next challenge to building an apostolic team is how to keep them working together as a team. Accountability can be defined as how we assure that individual members of the community do what is necessary for the community as a whole to succeed in its mission. The individual must not only function at a high level of competence, but must gear his performance to what makes the community succeed as a whole. Our schools are more like a ballet than a revue featuring individual dancers. We need everyone to not only execute his own role effectively and passionately, but understand the ballet as a whole and fit his performance into the greater work of art. He may be the most talented dancer in the world, but if he fails to execute his part in a way consistent with the whole, the ballet will fail and fail spectacularly. Accountability is how we align the work of talented, passionate individuals into a meaningful whole.

Education has an ambiguous relationship with accountability. On one hand, we have elaborate processes for holding students accountable. In any given course, hardly a week goes by when they aren't being tested about what they've learned or done. Generally, the results of these assessments will affect their final grade, which will affect their GPA, which will affect the college they get into, which will, or so it seems, shape the sort of life they will lead.

On the other hand, when it comes to having our own performance measured, we are mindful, even fearful, of how measuring performance can go wrong. Teachers who relentlessly assess their students mistrust processes for assessing their own performance. They worry that an observation on a bad day will give an unfair impression, or student evaluations will punish demanding teachers, or measuring teaching by student performance won't account for differences in student aptitude.

Administrators who hold teachers accountable dread their own evaluations, feeling that the administrator, or Board of Directors, above them are prone to undervaluing parts of their job that they themselves feel are important, or to not appreciating the difficulty of their work. I would say that most people I have supervised would not complain if I simply forgot to do their evaluations, until and unless the gulf between us became so wide that they demanded to know why. Even then, I suspect most of them would want to control what was evaluated and how. I would too.

The anxiety of being evaluated leads to an anxiety about doing evaluations. Supervisors fear that their assessment and their subordinate's self-assessment will be at odds and this will lead to conflict, the sort of conflict that few of us relish. I once heard of a study in which 90% of the people interviewed felt that they were better than average. Unfortunately, that can't be true, and honest evaluations are bound to run into that contradiction. Supervisors often face the delicate task of explaining to subordinates, who may be exceeding their own expectations, that they aren't even meeting their boss's. Or to point out that someone who is pouring his heart and soul into his job may be wasting energy on something that isn't that important to the school. I remember one of our facilities staff storming into my office one day to complain about the evaluation he had received from his supervisor.

"He evaluated me as just 'meeting expectations'. I can't believe it. I do everything that is asked of me."

I said, "Ned, that is the definition of 'meeting expectations.' Is it your goal to exceed your boss's expectations?"

"I felt I was," he replied.

"What are his expectations?"

"I don't know."

"I suggest you ask him," I said. "Set a time to meet with him and ask for greater clarity on his expectations. Ask him what you could do that would exceed his expectations." It took a few years, but Ned finally got it sorted out and is now delighting his supervisor by going above and beyond his expectations in ways that are valuable to the school.

Both the supervisor and the supervisee must take responsibility for clarity in expectations. This is hard to do because it involves potential disappointment and conflict. The person who is being evaluated has to hear about ways her performance has not measured up. And the supervisor has to articulate clearly to a defensive listener what his expectations are and in what ways they haven't been met. The person being evaluated may argue and bring up counter evidence. She has the advantage of knowing more about her work than he does, so if this were a debate, it's not a comfortable place for the supervisor to be. But we are operating in a consultative management model, which we defined earlier as one where "authority and responsibility for making decisions on behalf of the organization are vested in certain individuals or groups, with the requirement that they listen to and take into account the experience, insight and needs of those being affected by their decisions." The supervisor has the responsibility to listen to the input of the person he is evaluating, but he doesn't have to win a debate. At the end of the day, he must determine whether his expectations have been met or not. He must then do the best he can to communicate what they are and how the person he is responsible for supervising can meet or exceed them.

Because this is difficult, persons responsible for evaluating others can fall into several avoidance patterns. First they can simply not do evaluations. I have been in a number of positions where I have had to bird-dog my supervisor to give me a formal evaluation. Second, they can avoid confrontation by not being honest in evaluations. I have found that supervisors more often than not want to use the evaluation as a way of giving encouragement. They are afraid of hurting morale by giving negative feedback. I once reviewed a supervisor's annual evaluations of his staff and was surprised that the people he had been complaining about all year were all exceeding his expectations. When I asked him to explain, his answer was that they were all trying hard and they would feel he had pulled the rug out from under them if he gave them negative evaluations. My question was, "With positive evaluations like these, how will you ever convince them that they need to do better?" Too often, supervisors think their frowns and grumpiness will sufficiently communicate that their expectations aren't being met. The more dishonest the evaluation, the grumpier they get, hoping to get their point across. My friends who do personnel law tell me that in wrongful termination cases, the employee often has a fat folder of positive evaluations from their supervisor and then a sudden termination. The supervisor is shocked that the employee didn't see this coming.

Annual evaluations are a minimum. Supervisors should be giving their subordinates constant feedback. Since we tend to be more aware of when our expectations aren't being met, we need to discipline ourselves to look for and acknowledge the positive. We can sometimes be like the man who was asked by his wife of 50 years why he never says he loves her. "My dear," he said, "I told you I loved you when we got married. If anything had changed, I would have let you know." As laughable as this sounds, we tend to assume our employees know when they are doing acceptable, or even exceptional, work. But they need to hear it from us. In addition to the accolades, we need to be honest about where subordinates aren't meeting our expectations and willing to work with them to correct the situation. Even with constant feedback, an annual, formal evaluation is critical for clarifying where the employee's work is or is not supporting the overall mission of the school. Annual evaluations are also important documents in those cases where an employee's dissatisfaction leads them to pursue legal remedies.

Evaluating different categories of employees

If annual formal evaluations are the minimum, how they are carried out will vary for different categories of employees. In general, all evaluations should be based as much as possible on the performance of employees against expected outcomes. These can be hard to define, but as much as possible goals should be measurable and formulated with, rather than simply for, the employee. The following is a brief outline of how this is done with the three main classes of employee in the school: teachers, support staff and administration.

1. Teachers

In many ways the teachers in a school are the hardest category of employees to evaluate. First of all, they are the largest group of employees with the flattest supervision structure. Second they perform their work for the most part in isolated classrooms. Third, their outcomes are difficult to measure. And fourth, they actually have several roles, with different outcomes and different supervisors. For these reasons, teachers are best evaluated on a multi-year cycle.

The first year of the cycle might include observation and follow-up by the principal (or when necessary by the vice principal). This requires an enormous amount of time for the principal, but few things she does will have as salutary an impact on the school. In these observations, the principal gets an on-the-ground feel for how learning is taking place in the school. She builds relationships with the teachers. And she is able to communicate one-on-one what the mission of the school is and how it should permeate the culture. The talented teacher who is captivating the students but only marginally contributing to the school's unique mission can be coached to coordinate his methods or content with what the rest of the team is trying to accomplish. The teacher who supports the mission but lacks proficiencies in certain methodologies can be coached to strengthen his skill-set. Just knowing the principal cares enough to observe the teachers in their work is a great source of encouragement and motivation to excellence. Observation by the principal is important, because she is the one generally making hiring and assignment decisions, but this doesn't preclude observation by the AVP, department heads or even peers. These will have great formative value, though they will not generally be used for summative purposes. For new teachers, observations by the principal or her delegate may take place more than once a year, as she grounds them firmly in the mission, culture and professional standards of the school during their early, formative years.

The second year, the teacher might be evaluated by students using an anonymous survey. This can be a source of anxiety for the teacher, who may fear students inflicting retribution for a low grade or disciplinary action they may have received. But a skilled principal treats the student evaluations as a data point, not as the ultimate assessment of the teacher. She will not be swayed by out-lier comments, and she will administer the evaluation in such a way that a student with a grudge can't organize a coordinated negative response. Teachers should value the formative feedback such a survey can provide. If they rely solely on anecdotal feedback from students who may be trying to curry favor or parents reacting to what their child says happened in class, they may get a distorted view of what the students in general are experiencing.

Year three might involve evaluation of the teacher's role beyond the classroom—as a coach or club moderator, as a department head, or as someone providing substantive leadership on school committees.

In one of these years, the principal or her delegate can set three-year goals for the teacher. These would include goals for professional development, apostolic formation and collaboration. The principal can make sure that these goals are consistent with the department's and school's goals. Shaping the individual goals of teachers is a key opportunity to coordinate them into the ballet being performed by the whole school. The principal can employ the same principles of "backward design" used in curriculum development, starting with what outcomes both she and the teacher are aiming for, discussing what would give measurable evidence of that outcome and then how the teacher can go about achieving that outcome in his work. This is a difficult process, especially at first, so they must resist the temptation to make it too complex. The goals should be limited to 3-5. The teacher can give himself as many goals as he likes outside of this process, but for this three year evaluation cycle, simplicity will greatly increase the chances of success. During the three years of the cycle, the principal and the teacher can discuss progress and make adjustments as necessary. At the end of the three years, the outcomes are recorded in a summative assessment and the teacher, with the principal, sets goals for the next three years. Of course, if serious issues arise before the three-year cycle is complete, the principal may notify the teacher that performance must be improved in a shorter period or the teacher's job may be in jeopardy.

2. Support staff

Supervision and evaluation of support staff comes closest to what one would find in a typical employment environment in the business sector. Support staff include those who work in the front office, facilities, technology, development, admissions, business, food service, security and student health. Generally they have job descriptions that outline specific responsibilities and expectations and they are supervised by someone who can regularly observe their work and its results. As support staff the school administration might tend to give a lower priority to their performance, but they play a key role in the effectiveness of those who work directly with students. It is critical that their supervisor give them ongoing feedback on their work and a formal evaluation at least once a year.

Unlike the faculty, different support staff members can be doing very different sorts of jobs, requiring different work schedules and radically different skill sets. In order to assure quality and equitable treatment of employees, a core process should be spelled out for how staff are evaluated throughout the school. Supervisors will need to adapt and augment the core process, but whatever they do must include it. Another challenge is that the person supervising staff may have limited experience with evaluation and need assistance. Much of the process is counter-intuitive and, as mentioned earlier, there are human proclivities that can pull us in directions that undermine honest, effective evaluation.

The first step is to make sure all support staff employees have job descriptions. The second is to make sure these job descriptions are written so that they can be used to evaluate job performance. This means they need to focus on a few key performance areas rather than a long list of tasks. Job descriptions should list 8-15 items. Task lists are less helpful because they change too often, and they devolve into check lists of whether the employee did this or that, rather than helping the supervisor assess the employee's performance.

Job description elements should be expressed in terms of outcomes, but in a general way. This raises questions for the employee. If one of the items in the job description is "Maintains the safety of the building for which the employee is responsible," what does "maintain safety mean?" The supervisor and the employee might have very different understandings of what this outcome should look like. The supervisor needs to tell the employee more precisely what his expectations are, what he will be looking for to confirm that this outcome is being met. The more measurable he can make the outcomes, the clearer his expectations for the employee will be. For instance, he might say that the goal is "zero accidents due to maintenance lapses," or "fewer than 10 observed violations of safety procedures in a year." These metrics would not be included in the job description itself, because they change over time while the job description should remain stable. The metrics should be updated and given to the employee annually as supporting documentation to the evaluation.

At the time of the evaluation, the employee should also be setting goals with the supervisor for the coming year. The number should be small enough that the employee and the supervisor can keep them in focus over the year, probably between three and five. They should address only the most pressing areas for personal professional growth, job performance and support of the school's strategic goals. By having the employee take ownership of these goals, the supervisor encourages continuous growth as well as alignment of the employee's efforts with what the school really needs from them. The setting of these goals and reviewing them on a periodic basis is the most important part of the evaluation process.

To put this all together, here's what the staff evaluation process might look like. Each supervisor receives from the President's Office (or whoever is handling HR) the most recent job description/ evaluation form on file for each of her employees. She then forwards to her supervisees a copy of last year's evaluation, a blank job description/ evaluation form for each to do a self-evaluation, and a copy of each employee's annual goals. She schedules a time to meet with each employee.

Anyone who has done staff evaluations knows how difficult they can be. It is difficult setting metrics and getting them right; it is time consuming to lead an employee through the process of setting goals; and it is stressful to tell employees that they are not meeting your expectations, especially when they think they are. For these reasons, doing evaluations is for supervisors more like eating their vegetables than either dessert or even the meat and potatoes at the core of their job. We need to remind new supervisors that nothing they will do is more important than empowering people under their authority to grow and increase their contribution to the mission of this important apostolic work. The good news is that it gets easier and more effective the more they do it. We just need to help them through the early, awkward stages as their skills develop.

3. Administration

Much of what has been said about evaluating other categories of employees applies to the evaluation of administrators as well. It is important to have job descriptions which are written in outcome language; they should also have focused goals which address personal professional growth, job performance and support of the school's strategic goals; expectations should be put in as measurable terms as possible. But because of their leadership roles in the school, three additional elements must be part of the process.

First, in setting annual goals, greater emphasis must be placed on alignment with the school's strategic goals. As a general rule, the higher an employee is in the chain of responsibility, the more his goals must explicitly align with the goals of the school's annual and long-range strategic plans (discussed in Chapter VI Strategic Planning). The president's goals, by definition, should include all of the annual strategic goals approved by the board. The principal's goals should include any strategic goals over which she has responsibility, and likewise for the development director, the CFO, the dean and so on. So the goal-setting process must begin with a review of the strategic plan and any areas for which the administrator has major responsibility

Second, the evaluation must include some discussion of the administrator's spiritual growth. This is tricky, because spiritual growth is by its nature personal, subjective and not programmable. Accountability for spiritual growth exerted by an outside authority disrupts the subtle conversation happening between a human being and God. On the other hand, spiritual growth of an administrator is critical to the school's effectiveness as a Jesuit apostolate. The benefits of having all administrators doing a daily *Examen*—discerning where God is working in their lives, revisiting difficult encounters to see for the first time how the Holy Spirit is working through a student on the edge, or a troublesome faculty member—cannot be overestimated. Yet accessing the power of the *Examen* is not simply a matter of requiring everyone to do it and reviewing how faithful they have been. Here, the supervising administrator must be more like a retreat director, gently reflecting God back into the conversation, asking the administrator he is supervising to consider the importance of her personal relationship with God to the school's mission, suggesting some possible tools for strengthening that relationship and asking that the administrator set goals for spiritual growth. My experience has been that they will often not choose what I think they most need. I sometimes sense some avoidance in the choices they make. But I have chosen to trust that God is at work in them and recognize that even avoidance is a natural part of the journey to a deeper relationship with God. So I try not to be prescriptive, and I have found that, in the long run, God does the work and my patience and trust are rewarded. Taking on the role of the retreat director is somewhat awkward and even confusing, especially in the context of evaluation. Sometimes it has to be scheduled at a different time so as not to be caught up with those areas where accountability is stressed. But over time it can become a natural part of the relationship between supervising administrator and his supervisee.

The third element which must be added in the case of administrators is the 360° survey. Because they are leaders in the school, they and their supervising administrator need to get feedback from the people who work for them and with them, as well as those for whom they work. This is best done by a survey which is confidential but not anonymous. Since these surveys are part of the administrator's evaluation, the respondents are required to give their names, but are assured that only the supervisor will know which respondents gave which ratings or comments. This strikes a balance that produces both candor and responsibility.

At first, the person being evaluated can feel vulnerable in this process, knowing that people about whom they have had to make tough decisions may be using this as an opportunity to strike back. I use several approaches to allay these anxieties. First I develop the survey with the person being evaluated so that they trust the questions being asked. Second, I involve them in selecting the respondents. They may add a name or ask me to remove the name of someone they don't think will be fair. Often we decide to include the name, but my knowing more about the context will help me interpret that person's response. Third, I make clear that the 360° survey does not constitute their evaluation. While I listen to what other people say, I take it only as input. For instance, one administrator was rated low in some areas because supervisees felt he was not a good listener. It was clear to me that the reason they felt this was that he made decisions that didn't accord with their input. They assumed that their input had been ignored. I knew the process he had followed and knew he hadn't ignored their input. I praised that administrator for both listening to their input and for making the right decision despite the push-back he received. Finally I help address the anxiety of the 360° survey by pointing out that people will express their frustrations one way or another and that it is better to have it come though a channel where it can be balanced and interpreted. Over time, administrators come to trust the process and appreciate getting feedback through a healthier channel.

Merit pay

I have experimented with tying evaluations to compensation and have come to learn that paying for performance is a powerful tool for supervisors to improve that performance, but that it also puts tremendous stress on supervisors, employees and the evaluation system.

Leadership trainer John E. Jones has said: "What gets measured gets done. What gets measured and fed back gets done well. What gets rewarded gets repeated." It is difficult to change behaviors when we are rewarding people just as much for what they are currently doing. Without performance-based pay, the only way supervisors can retain top performers who can command a higher wage elsewhere is to promote them to a higher paying job, and Jesuit school just aren't big enough to do much of that. Conversely, the only way a supervisor can send a pocket-book message to an underperforming employee is to fire them. Merit pay gives the supervisor something short of the "nuclear option," the ability to reward someone who is contributing more value to the school, and to avoid terminating underperforming employees who could be saved if the message can break through their pattern of denial. I've seen the performance of departments improve dramatically with the introduction of merit pay.

But be ready for unintended consequences. With merit pay, evaluations that were once harmless feel-good or nagging sessions, suddenly become events that affect people's financial wherewithal. This not only creates greater accountability for the employees, but for their supervisors as well. A supervisor may have been able to procrastinate and do a rushed evaluation at the last minute. But when wages depend on that evaluation, it becomes a significant component of a supervisor's job. One way to deal with the anxiety of higher stakes evaluation is to simply give everyone good grades. Believe me, some supervisors have great difficulty resisting that temptation. But it will come back to haunt them. When everyone in the department is being paid as if they were exceptional employees and the department itself is getting only mediocre results, the supervisor is painting a target on his back as the problem. And he has no leverage to tell his employees that they need to improve their performance. Their response will be, "I'm already working at my maximum, and besides, you told me that I'm an exceptional employee and I'm being paid at that level. What more can you expect of me?" In addition, when this path-of-least-resistance supervisor leaves, his "exceptional" employees will be shocked when a new supervisor comes in and evaluates them as only "meeting expectations," and adjusts their pay to match. Finally, the evaluation system will itself be evaluated by employees who start comparing their pay. When someone finds out a colleague is getting more pay than she is, you won't lose any money betting that her first explanation will be that the system is unfair.

I support the use of performance to help determine wages, but it has to be done right or you will regret ever calling down the firestorm upon your head. Without going into too much detail for this treatment, here are three suggestions for minimizing the negative consequences. 1) Involve all the employees who will participate in the merit-based compensation in formulating the program. Let them tell you where the problems will be and how they would solve them. Let them take ownership, which will help with acceptance during the early, critical phase. Keep in mind that by some mystery of human nature, the ones who oppose the idea will tend to be underperformers and the ones who are excited about it will be the high performers (imaging that!). 2) Train your supervisors. Make sure they understand the power, for good or ill, that you are giving them. Address all the corners they can paint themselves into. Until they are fully competent in giving evaluations, require that the supervisors go over their evaluations with you before they show them to the employees. Use this as an opportunity to foster equitable appraisals across departments. 3) When an employee's performance rating declines and she is at risk of having her pay lowered, use a probation system to cushion the impact. Give the supervisor the authority to maintain the current pay level for a specified period of time to let the employee get her performance back up to match her pay level. In some cases, for instance where an employee has been inherited by a new supervisor with different expectations, the probationary period may be as long as a year. This takes pressure off the system by cushioning the financial impact without undermining the honesty of the evaluations. What we want most from the evaluation/merit pay system is to give honest feedback to our employees and to reinforce productive effort. 4) Set the performance component of pay at a level that provides incentive but doesn't have a drastic impact on the employee or the school as a whole. Incentives are like fuel additives, a little bit goes a long way, and too much will blow your engine.

In thirteen years of using performance based pay for more that 70 support staff employees, we have only had to actually lower pay twice. About 25% have maintained their pay level and 75% have improved their performance and moved up the scale.

H. Open-book Management

Pioneered by Jack Stack, CEO of Springfield Remanufacturing Co., in the 1980's, Open-book Management is a philosophy that an organization will do better the more its employees know about how the organization works. Stack and other business leaders used the approach to maximize company profits, but if you read his description of how it works, it's easy to see how it can help an apostolic organization better accomplish its mission:

> The more people know about a company, the better that company will perform. This is an iron-clad rule. You will *always* be more successful in business by sharing information with the people you work with than by keeping them in the dark. Let your people know whatever you know about the company...Don't use information to intimidate, control or manipulate people. Use it to teach people how to work together to achieve common goals and thereby gain control over their lives. When you share the numbers and bring them alive, you turn them into tools people can use to go about their business every day. That's the key to open-book management.[3]

Stack's point is that people will be more effective if they understand what makes their organization successful. This is no less important when the organization's mission isn't to maximize profits, but to graduate students animated by faith and committed to justice. The reason is that any organization relies on meaningful collaboration to be effective. Perhaps at one time, collaboration wasn't necessary or even possible. During feudal times, perhaps human beings needed a highly authoritarian structure in which kings, landed gentry and the Church made all the decisions and the rest of us just did what we were told. Then came democracy. Democracy grew not just out of a need for fairness but out of a recognition that much human wisdom is wasted when only a few people are charged with thinking, being creative or making meaningful decisions.

Well after our political structures had put more faith in the individual participants, our industrial model was content to have the vast majority of workers perform mindless functions on assembly lines designed by the few. But in the 1960's that changed. Edwards Deming and others had found ways to tap into the insights of factory workers through "quality circles," in which people working on the same or different steps of the process began sharing their ideas about how the process could be improved. It took us a long time after we realized the incredible intelligence of ordinary human beings to begin developing processes to harness it. And though the leader in developing this process was an American, it was the Japanese who first transformed their industrial process around this principle. Americans got on the bandwagon only after being badly bested by the Japanese in sectors like electronics and automobiles. Grudgingly at first, American industry began adopting more collaborative approaches to process.

While I think most of us understand collaboration in principle, it's not always clear how practical it is. Administrators often experience faculty as resistant to change and unwilling to take responsibility for the bigger picture. Why would we entrust them with decision-making power if we have experienced times when they have used any power they have to scuttle change? I've seen faculty members move into administrative positions and be surprised at how former colleagues, who used to dream with them during a free period about how to improve the school, suddenly become truculent and grumpy. What's going on here?

I had an insight into this when my wife Mary described a trip she took with her sisters to a canyon in Eastern Oregon. Mary and another sister were in the back seat of a mini-van as they drove up the winding road along the canyon wall. From the back seat it felt to Mary that her sister Eileen, who was driving, was careening near the precipice on each curve. At one point, Eileen saw a view turnout off to the left and decided to pull into it. To Mary in the back it looked like she was about to drive off the cliff. She screamed and demanded that Eileen stop the car immediately so she could get out. It took a while for her to trust Eileen's driving again and realize she were suffering from an optical illusion that comes with being in the back seat.

Being in a classroom all day with administrators making decisions that affect your life can be like riding in the back seat of a van. You can see some of the road from the back, but not what the driver sees and not enough to know that she is making the right decisions. Even if you know better, it's just hard to trust your life to something you can't control.

The solution is to put people as close to the front seat as possible. Share information with them and involve them in the decisions. If they are worthy to teach in our schools, they are worthy of this responsibility. But it requires planning and creativity to involve busy people in meaningful ways in steering the school. It is only human nature to come to conclusions based on the knowledge we have at hand. If that knowledge is limited, it will be hard for us to see the big picture and to participate in decisions as if we had responsibility for the school as a whole. We fall prey to what economist Paul Samuelson referred to as the "fallacy of composition,"[4] assuming that what is good for an individual is good for the group. Their individual experience in the classroom or on the playing field is indispensable for sound decision-making. But to take advantage of that, administrators need to move their colleagues beyond the fallacy of composition. They must both provide them the information that drives institutional decisions and respect the considerable time demands placed on classroom teachers. If they can find ways to give teachers the big picture and create opportunities to work collaboratively with the administration, they can make pedagogical decisions that harness the full wisdom of a team of talented, committed educators.

Open-book Management is based on the belief that people not only can be trusted with information, but they need it to make their optimal contribution to the team. The opposite would be closed book management. I don't know of any school that says it practices closed book management, but I know a lot of them that would be nervous to have faculty participating in board meetings, or having access to all the financial information, or knowing the administration's real assessment of performance in some areas. Mistrust leads to de facto closed-book management, which in turn precludes meaningful, school-wide collaboration for the mission. The genius of the individual experts who work in our classrooms, offices, computer rooms and boiler buildings cannot thus be harnessed to meet the school's ambitious goals.

One of the reasons for closed-book management is the legitimate fear that employees will misunderstand the information they are given. This is actually more likely to happen than not, especially in the beginning. A librarian reading the consolidated financial statements may see investments of millions of dollars in the restricted fund for endowment and wonder what the school didn't have more money for raises last year. Or a German teacher may see a cash flow statement that shows a high cash balance early in the year when the bulk of tuition has been paid, and assume that the school is running a surplus. Stack stresses the importance of education. It takes time to learn how to read financial statements, to understand the difference between positive cash flow and positive fund balances or the consequences of a large pledge in accrual-based accounting. The reality is that most school employees don't have much time, and even less interest, in mastering this knowledge. But if they are getting woozy riding in the back of the van, this is the only way to cure their car-sickness. And it's the only way we can align their considerable potential with that of their colleagues to accomplish the mission. So we have to think through carefully how, over time, we will teach the players the rules of the game and what they have to do to help the team score.

We need to set aside time, at in-services, faculty meetings, employee meetings, brownbag lunch meetings or optional study sessions, to gradually raise people's awareness of how to keep score in the game we are playing. And it's not just about the financial piece. We need to share with our colleagues the progress we are or aren't making apostolically, educationally and relationally. How many students are going to mass, here at school or with their family? How many are enrolled in AP courses? How are they doing on the tests? How are they doing in college? How are they demonstrating sportsmanship at our games? How satisfied are our employees with their work environment?

We also need to learn how to present information in ways that are understandable and time-efficient. Many organizations develop "balanced scorecards" or "dashboards" that present metrics on key performance areas. My experience is that not only is it difficult to identify and begin tracking these metrics, but it takes a while for the school's adult community to understand how to use them in evaluating the school's progress and directing their own efforts.

My rule of thumb for what to share with employees is this: whatever we share with the board of trustees, other than certain legal and personnel issues, should be shared with employees. It may need to be reformatted to meet their needs, but if the information is helpful to the board in its work, it probably will be helpful to the employees. Some of it may only be available if they want it, but some will be "pushed out" to them. Employees will also need detailed information that the board doesn't require and this information will vary depending on the employee's department and role. But the goal is to give employees all the information that will help them engage the school's mission and engage their full gifts in executing their part of it.

All the information in the world, however, cannot replace the trust that teachers and support staff have to place in their leaders. Information can contribute to the level of trust, but not everyone can sit in the front of the van. Various people at various times will be seated further back from where decisions are being made, and they have to place trust in whoever is driving the vehicle if they hope to arrive at the destination along with everyone else.

I. Team Building

A friend of mine was giving spiritual direction to a woman who kept insisting that her life was her prayer. He finally said to her, in a gentle way, "Yes, but it helps if you actually pray a little, too." In a similar way, all the sections of this chapter describe ways of building an apostolic team, but it helps to engage in activities that directly build a sense of team as well. As reasonable as this may sound, I find that people often resist team-building exercises even though they are enjoyable and help us enjoy working with each other. The resistance comes because they take time from our urgencies and they require a certain level of vulnerability. Somewhat like actual praying.

Team-building activities focus not on producing a direct result in the operation of the school, but on how people work together, on helping them know and empathize with each other. They help reduce the friction in human relationships that can waste the precious energy we need for our mission. Here are a few elements of team building which I and my colleagues have used.

Check-in

At the beginning of meetings set aside some time for people to talk about what's going on in their lives beyond the work they share together. I find it helpful to know that a colleague's mother is suffering from serious illness. I want to know the struggles of people I care about so that I can hold them in prayer, be patient with them when they are having trouble completing their commitments and be consoled by their courage and wisdom as they deal with adversity. They also find it freeing that the people they work with care about their burdens and can be called upon to share them. Sometimes this level of intimacy occurs naturally in work relationships, but more often than not the feelings and experiences we might share get boxed up and put to the side. We each have unique jobs, and the challenges we face can isolate us from colleagues. The expectations we have of others and they have of us can increase this sense of isolation. Check-ins are an explicit way of dealing with this.

But simply adding 15 minutes at the beginning of a department or administrative meeting will not automatically produce a flow of sharing about our personal lives. It cannot be legislated. People are under no obligation to share information about what is happening outside of work. They may choose not to for many reasons. The most common is a lack of confidence that others will care about their struggles and treat them gently. For check-in to be fruitful, it has to allow freedom to share or not to share. For people to have that freedom there must be an atmosphere of trust. I talked about the importance of trust earlier in this chapter. I mentioned the importance of honesty and transparency if one is to trust. I also spoke about how love leads to trust. But the converse is also true: honesty and transparency depend on trust, as does our ability to love others. The check-in creates a space where trust and the free exchange about what we're thinking and who we are can happen. Everyone, but especially the team leader, must work to create safety in that space for people to share themselves.

Having fun

As serious as our work is, if we aren't also having fun at it, we're doing something wrong. We know this about our students. On one hand we challenge them in ways that make them work very hard. But we also put on dances and spirit assemblies and have them play games. When people are playing together, they are able to see each other, not in terms of what they need or expect from them, but as who they are in themselves. Other dimensions of their humanity emerge. Laughing together builds trust within a team. But, like check-ins, it doesn't happen automatically. People can become competitive, which makes it harder to trust. I like to choose games and activities that make it hard to compete, either because no one knows how to play them (like acting out the names of Christmas songs) or because the skilled players have to cooperate with the unskilled (like a team challenge on a ropes course). Team-building games can allow people to take risks they wouldn't normally and laugh at their failures because no one really expects them to be good at, say, juggling. They can also reveal to people how teams can accomplish things they never thought were possible, like getting to the top of a mountain with people of various strength and skill levels. Hopefully some of that realization will transfer to their work together and they will be less afraid of failure and more trusting of their team's ability to climb the mountain together.

Explore differences

Strong teams have a diversity of gifts. If all the people on the team have the same interests and skills and tend to see things the same way, the team may seem strong because it can communicate easily and come to decisions quickly. Conversely, a team of people with different backgrounds, different skill-sets and different thinking styles can seem dysfunctional. Divergent teams can be dysfunctional, but they also have the greatest potential for producing remarkable results, the sort envisioned by our ambitious mission. It is harder to build trust and communications in divergent teams than in convergent teams, but it can be done. One way is to explicitly explore those differences. Identify who has what strengths and how they can be better put to the service of the team. For instance, the "visionary" can help the group see where the path might lead, while the "realist" will help it see what pitfalls must be avoided to get there. In this example, the visionary may tend to trust the vision as the one necessary ingredient for the team to accomplish its potential, and dismiss the realist as a curmudgeon incapable of stepping into the unknown. The realist may see the visionary as a dreamer who doesn't seem to care whether there is any practical probability of reaching the vision. If these two people are on a team, they may mistrust each other. And so the more "out there" the visionary is, the more the realist counters with warnings about what will go wrong. And the more pessimistic the realist is, the more the visionary will counter with inspiring dreams. If one gets the upper hand, the other will either become a disaffected opponent or a sullen non-participant. In either event, the important contribution of the loser is no longer available to the group.

To avoid this scenario, the team has to find ways to identify, value and harness the diversity within it. One way to do this is to use instruments like the Myers-Briggs personality profile, the Firo-B, the Enneagram, StrengthsFinder, or any one of a number of tools which help people identify their strengths and their characteristic ways of viewing the world. People can be threatened by the prospect that these profiles will put them in a box. If their experience in the team is that their way of approaching issues is not valued, they may look at the questionnaire as a way to justify dismissing their perspective. Sometimes it may be helpful to have an outside person come in to administer the questionnaires and explain what they mean. This person can talk about the strengths of each type of profile and help the team see that all of them can contribute to better leadership of the school. The team can explore ways of working together that not only respect differences but take advantage of them.

Praying

As Jesuit schools we have available to us the most effective team building tool of all. Jesus said, "Wherever two or three are gathered together in my name, I will be there in your midst" (Mt 18:20). God in our midst is where our power comes from. Prayer engages Jesus and calls forth his grace in our work in a special way. Like check-ins, games and personality profiles, prayer reminds us who we are. It lays open our humanity, moving us beyond being vice-principals and facilities directors and basketball coaches to fully human people working together for something they know is important. In prayer— as in check-ins, games and personality profiles—manipulation, or making a point or making people change has no place. We are acknowledging that Jesus has called us together, as he did the apostles, and what we most want to know is how we can help him in the marvelous work he is doing in our school and in the world. A version of the serenity prayer captures what the team is seeking in prayer:

> Lord, grant us the serenity of trusting that everything is in your hands;
> Grant us the wisdom to discern our role in your work;
> And grant us the courage to cooperate fully.

J. President-Principal Relationship

In Jesuit schools, the core of the apostolic team is the relationship between the president and the principal. This structure once unique to Jesuit schools is becoming more common in other private schools as they face the challenges ahead.

The president-principal model has its roots in the structure of the early Jesuit schools. A local superior, also called a rector (though canonically, not all local superiors are rectors), was assigned as the head of the local Jesuit community, and a principal, also a Jesuit, was tasked with running the school. As superior of the Jesuit community, the primary responsibility of the rector was *cura personalis* (care for the person) for the Jesuits who staffed the school. But he also had some responsibility for *cura apostolica* (care for the apostolate). The rector had the primary responsibility to the provincial superior for the fidelity of the school to the Jesuit mission and assisted the principal in finding the resources the school needed, which generally went beyond what tuition could provide. Eventually, as schools incorporated, the rector was named the president of the corporation. Over time, it became clear that the rector's responsibilities as president were becoming a full-time job in itself. It was also clear that the gifts needed to be a president were often different from those needed to be a local superior. In the 1970's, provinces were appointing separate presidents along with rectors and principals. As the schools became autonomous, their boards appointed presidents, who in turn hired principals, and the province appointed the local superior, or rector.

Despite its firm roots in the history of Jesuit education, the president-principal model can be confusing to people not familiar with it. It sheds some light to compare it to other better-known administrative models. The president performs many of the functions of a superintendent in a public school system, freeing the principal to focus on the educational process within the building. Comparing it to a common business management model, the president would be analogous to a chief executive officer (CEO) and the principal a chief operating officer (COO).

The president has three primary responsibilities: mission, resources and presence. The president is hired by the board of trustees to lead a team that will accomplish the mission of the school. As such, the president must lead the community in articulating what that mission is, help the community understand why it is important, identify the means to accomplish it and hold people accountable for their roles in its accomplishment. In this role the president must represent the school and its mission to the broader community and represent the community and its needs to the school. The president will delegate nearly every aspect of running the school to someone else, but she can never give up responsibility for whether and how it pursues its mission.

The president is also responsible for assuring that the school has the resources it needs to accomplish its mission. While the president will be assisted in this role by a development director, a business officer and others, she must be prepared to devote a substantial portion of her time to fundraising, marketing and assuring an adequate and stable resource base for the school. The president's role in cultivating the trust and participation of major donors and community and church organizations cannot be emphasized enough. No one can replace what she can bring to these relationships as the head of the school, and both the president and her staff must carefully optimize this finite resource.

Finally, the president is often the human face and presence of an institution. If the president attends a funeral, the school is attending and saying how important the deceased was to it. If the president attends a music concert or spends a weekend with the juniors on retreat, she is sending a message about the importance of these activities. As important as presence is for a president, however, this aspect can be over-emphasized. Despite our tendency to identify a whole institution with one person, the reality is that it is many people. The more the broader community sees the depth of a school's leadership and how the mission is embodied by all the administrators, faculty and staff, the healthier the school will be. And the president will be healthier if she can avoid the trap of feeling she is the sole spokesperson and personification of the school.

To the principal is delegated the leadership of the school's core mission activity as a school: the curriculum, students' spiritual formation, the extra-curriculars and all the programs that support these. The principal supervises the majority of the school's employees and sees to their spiritual, personal and professional development. Like the president and in conjunction with her, the principal is responsible for mission. His work is hugely important in shaping what the mission is, how it is understood and how it is pursued. The principal has some responsibility for resources, but generally his focus is internal. Nevertheless, the principal must manage a large budget and plays a key role in assuring the financial stability of the school. And the principal, like the president, has a responsibility to be the presence of the school, especially internally, but to the external community to some extent as well.

Because the roles of the president and the principal are not always familiar to the school's publics and because there is so much overlap, there can be confusion. Even for the president and principal themselves, the expectations of others and the overlap of leadership responsibilities can lead to confusion. Studies by the JSEA in both 1991 and 2005 have indicated that tensions between the president and principal are not uncommon. These may arise because each is trying to exercise important leadership responsibilities and that is difficult to do without impinging on the authority of the other. For instance the principal may have determined that a teacher who is popular, but nevertheless not living up to her responsibilities, must be terminated. The school policy may be that only the president has the authority to terminate employment, and the president may be reluctant to lose a popular teacher. The president may feel that the principal shouldn't be making that call, but the principal may feel powerless if he works patiently and follows evaluation procedures but can't expect that his decision will be upheld by the president.

Both positions require the exercise of authority, but what happens when one interferes with the other? Both require vision, but what happens when visions contradict? The easy answer would be that the president is the boss so her authority prevails. But, considering the importance of the principal's position, and the immense responsibility he has, the president would do well to exercise this option cautiously. The school is not served by one of them being a strong leader and the other not. They both need to be strong leaders, and they need to work together.

The president and the principal are in a position to model collaborative leadership, trust, and good communication to the rest of the school. Like parents in a family, if they can't get on the same page, the result will be some level of dysfunction. They owe it to themselves and the apostolic community they lead to attend to their relationship and make sure it is healthy. A good way to do that is to pay attention to the ways things can go wrong.

Conflict can enter the president-principal relationship when both have the same skill-sets. We have a tendency in stressful circumstances to use the tools that have worked for us in the past. If I had been a successful principal and am now president, and I were worried about whether I was doing a good enough job, it would be natural for me to want to step into areas like curriculum or faculty development and exert influence where I know I have skill. It takes a great deal of trust to let go of those areas. It means trusting someone else (who may have far less experience than I) to manage them. It means trusting myself to develop new skills that a president needs which I haven't needed before. And it means trusting that the community will be patient with me and give me time to work through the awkwardness and develop those new skills.

Conflict can also arise from the opposite situation, where that president and principal have completely different skill-sets. A president well-versed in finance and management may have trouble finding common language with a principal whose strength is curriculum development. Each may be aware of blind spots in the other's view of how the school works and even doubt each other's competence in areas they consider key. If they can resolve the communication issues and develop a respect for what each brings to the relationship, the complementary skill sets can be a valuable asset for the school.

Research by the JSEA suggests that conflict between the president and the principal occurs most commonly when there is a lack of trust. The most common reasons for this lack of trust according to surveys of presidents and principals are a lack of communication; unclear delineation of roles resulting in overstepping (by principals) or micro-management (by presidents); a lack of understanding or respect for each other's roles and responsibilities; and divergent understandings of the school's mission.

The presidents and principals surveyed by the JSEA offered several suggestions for strengthening the relationship. Leading the list was the need for open and honest communication with both formal and informal meetings on a regular basis. Others suggestions included clarification of roles, improved evaluation processes, collaborative decision-making, mutual public support, shared prayer and the assumption of good will.

K. Hardwiring the Culture

Hardwiring culture is a bit of an oxymoron. Hardwiring implies that a process can be put in its final form so that it can be repeated over and over with sustained effectiveness. Culture, however, is ever-changing, developing different processes and shifting boundaries. This is true for human culture in general, the culture of a nation and the culture of a school community. How does one hardwire the culture of a Jesuit school?

The first part of St. Ignatius' life was spent breaking boundaries. Reaching adulthood with a reputation as a fighter, he first broke through the barrier of his own assumptions about what happiness and glory would mean. He developed a new approach to fostering spirituality, and ran into trouble with religious authorities in the process. He founded not only a new religious order, but a new kind of religious order, one that would trade extensive communal prayer for apostolic presence at the very frontiers of human need. This was a time of explosive change and new insights for him and for the people around him.

The second part of Ignatius' ministry, after he was elected superior general of the new Society of Jesus, he spent writing letters and writing the order's *Constitutions*. Through both his letters and the *Constitutions*, Ignatius was hardwiring the culture he had been instrumental in creating. How would he assure that the charism received by him and his early companions would perdure through successive generations of Jesuits to follow them? One might have questioned the very possibility that this could be done, and yet he did it. Through the *Spiritual Exercises*, the instructions he wrote in letters, the *Constitutions*, and through the subsequent General

Congregations, *Complementary Norms* and decrees, he and his followers shaped a culture which has a rich repertoire of approaches to common challenges. The Jesuits refer to this as "our way of proceeding." I suspect there are few if any organizations in the last 500 years which have maintained such continuity and quality of process in pursuit of a mission. Ignatius and the founders of the Society succeeded in hardwiring the culture.

One of the reasons they succeeded is that they built in flexibility. In the *Constitutions*, which is the compendium of regulations governing the Society, Ignatius would give detailed instruction governing some aspect of Jesuit life and then end by saying something to the effect of, "but use your judgment, depending on the circumstances." Ignatius trusted his followers the way Jesus trusted the Apostles. Jesus also gave many instructions, some quite specific. But he knew that they and the many generations to follow them would have to adapt and adjust in order to carry the core message forward. Along with instructions, Ignatius communicated trust and left room for the genius of the people who would follow those instructions.

Similarly, when we as administrators hardwire the culture of our school communities in the ways described in this chapter, our intention should not be to take decision-making away from people, but to give them tools and guidelines to build upon. Understanding *cura personalis* and the chain of care, the profile of a Jesuit educator, how our communities work together in a consultative model and how to use Ignatian discernment are indispensable for our way of proceeding as Jesuit schools. We need effective tools for hiring and evaluating employees and educating them about how to create and use metrics to determine where we need to adjust to accomplish our mission. We need tools for building collaboration within the team and fostering the healthiest and most fruitful ways of working, playing and praying together.

What the Jesuits have accomplished has not happened by accident. And it wasn't just because of the original inspiration of Ignatius of Loyola, as powerful as that was. It was because Ignatius and those who followed him identified and inculcated those ways of proceeding that would preserve and strengthen the inspiration of the

Society as it progressed through the ages. And in our own school communities, we can do the same.

Chapter V: Business Model

To this point we have discussed three models that must function effectively for a Jesuit school to achieve its mission: apostolic, pedagogical and community. As we have looked at each, it has become clear that each model does not operate independently but should support the others. The final model to be examined is the business model, and already in our discussion of the other three we have been looking at this model. The apostolic model becomes the core competency around which the business model is built, the pedagogical model produces the product, and the community model describes both the labor force and the customers. The business model might not be the primary lens through which we view these other aspects of our schools, but it is constitutive to their success, as they are to its.

A business model is the assumptions, components and interactions of an enterprise's system of producing and exchanging products for sufficient financial support to accomplish the enterprise's mission. Some like to use a simpler definition: A business model is how a business makes money. So why would Jesuit schools need a business model if their mission is not about making money? The answer is that since schools need to make money to accomplish their mission they need a business model.

Even for profit-oriented business enterprises, it isn't always obvious how the business model functions. At the end of the last century a "Dot.com Bubble" was created by on-line businesses with ingenious ideas about how the internet could be used. Their ideas attracted a lot of investment dollars. But many of them could not figure out how to "monetize," or make money, from their product. When this became obvious, the value of many of them collapsed and the bubble burst. Even today, on-line businesses are trying to figure out how to make their businesses work as businesses. In a 2011 interview on National Public Radio, the co-founder of Twitter, Biz Stone, explained that he had three goals for his company: To have a positive global impact, to have fun and to develop a very successful business. With over 200 million users within five years of the first "tweet," —including other businesses, heads of state, astronauts, NGO's and protesters battling despotism—he said that they have accomplished the first two goals, in many ways beyond what he had imagined. For Twitter, which didn't charge for its service and didn't sell advertising, the remaining challenge was to find ways for the business to make money without undermining the first two goals.[5] This is similar to the challenge for Jesuit schools. We wouldn't be concerned about making money at all except that unless we do, we won't be given the opportunity to continue our work.

All organizations have a business model, whether they know it or not. Even monasteries which depend entirely on the grace of God for donations to support their work have a business model. Their product is their prayer and modeling the possibility of a deeper, more direct relationship with God. Their customers are those who feel it is important for that prayer to continue and take solace in seeing humans like themselves living lives centered on God. And so they are willing to take money from some other use and make it available to the monks. If the product deteriorates, the donations will cease. If the product is unknown, the customers will be meeting their needs by other means. Surely God's grace is operative, but it works through decisions made by people to whom God has entrusted resources. There is a logic to how those decisions are made and we deceive ourselves if we think that as apostolic institutions we are somehow exempt from that logic.

A. The Components of the Business Model

The way to assure one's business model is healthy is analogous to making sure a car engine is sound. You identify the essential components of the engine and verify that they are doing their part in the overall operation of the engine. For a business model, the major components are five P's: Product, Purchasers, Price, Promotion and Production Method.

Product

We tend to think of products as material goods rolling off an assembly line, destined for Wal-Mart or Safeway. We can also see commercial services, like lawn care or consulting as a product. We can even see the formation, education and community our schools offer as a product. But referring to them with the same word we use for TV's, Barbie dolls and pizza seems to diminish them. Formation, education and community are not commodities. They are not produced on an assembly line. Even with skilled workers and the best facilities, something more is needed to produce the experience we are striving for. Nevertheless it is still being produced. And as much as we would like to think that our product is not competing with TV's, toys, cars, second homes and orthodontia, it is. So it is important for the health of our business model that we be able to state clearly, for ourselves and others, just what our product is. Is it spiritual formation, college preparation, character development, emotional growth, self-discipline, safety? Some combination of these? Whatever our customers conclude is our product is what they will weigh against the other uses of their limited resources to see if it is worth it.

Purchasers

The purchasers are the people who make the decision to commit money to obtain our product. They are our customers. And who are our customers? This is actually a tricky, but important question. Are the true customers our students or their parents? One way to approach that question is to ask who benefits from the product, whose needs must our product satisfy. Since the students receive the education we offer, surely they are the customers. But they may not be very interested in the product described in the previous paragraph. A 14 year old boy may only be interested in playing baseball or being with his friends. His parents on the other hand are probably much more interested in the full capability of our product and more demanding that all the components be present. So who is the customer? From a business model perspective, the answer lies in who makes the decision to commit money to obtain the product. Obviously that is the parents. They write the checks, and they won't write them if they are not satisfied with the product. This would suggest that the parents are our customers and our business model should be geared to meeting their needs. This was probably clearer 50 years ago than it is today. Today, students have a greater say in whether their parents purchase our education. Not many parents will pay for private school if their children are unhappy with it, constantly nag them to send them to the public school or refuse to cooperate with the learning process. In such a case, the student becomes the customer, or more precisely, to borrow a term now being used in computer games, the student is an avatar. Students don't make the decision, but it is their experience on which the true customers, the parents, base their decisions (more on this in the section on marketing, below). To have sufficient enrollment to support our costs, our business model needs to treat both as customers. We have to have a product that motivates parents to write the checks, but also motivates students to support that decision.

As if that weren't complex enough, we also have another important set of customers. Jesuit schools rely on donors for a substantial portion of their operating revenues. Donors are also customers. We may not think of them as purchasing a product, but they are also making decisions to take money from some other use, whether it is eating out, investing in a business, or saving for retirement, and spending it with our school. Contrary to popular belief, nobody, not even Bill Gates, has *extra* money. Everyone's money is being used for some purpose and the only reason anyone would give it to us is that what we're doing is more important to them than what they are currently doing with that money. I ran into a friend in a restaurant who is president of a Jesuit school in the Midwest. I joined him at his table, not realizing that the fellow he was talking to was a prospective donor. The man was a successful businessman who hadn't given much to the school in recent years and had suddenly taken an interest. Matthew was listening carefully to learn why. It turns out the man's granddaughter had applied and he realized that it might help her cause if her grandpa were a benefactor. I was able to listen as Matthew deftly used the opportunity to help the man learn more about the school in the hope that his interest could be based on broader understanding of the product.

This example emphasizes the obvious self-interest of many donors. But even those who don't plan to directly benefit from their donations are still basing their philanthropic decisions on some level of self-interest. Maybe they don't have grandchildren who will attend the school, but they want to invest in something that will help the world be a better place for their grandchildren. Maybe they were the beneficiary of a scholarship that allowed them to attend and they derive joy from thinking that some younger version of themselves will have that opportunity. People's reasons for donating to our schools are complex and varied. Like my friend Matthew, we must listen deeply to what those reasons are. It can help us to stop and look at the potential donor as a customer and ask what it is about our product that might meet his needs.

Price

Most of the board members and schools I have worked with have at least some anxiety about having to charge tuition. When the idea of the Jesuits getting into the school business was first proposed, Ignatius agreed on the condition that they observe what he called the "radical gratuity of ministries," in other words, that they be free. The idea was that we should freely give what we have freely received. Yet it wasn't long before the Jesuits who operated these schools came to believe that the apostolate simply wouldn't survive without charging tuition, and that there were many middle class and wealthy families who could well afford to pay for the value their sons were receiving. Today, administrations and boards experience anxiety every year as they set tuition. If they set it too low, will they not have sufficient resources to maintain the quality of the program? If they set it too high, will enrollment drop, or even if it doesn't, will the school become less economically diverse? These are difficult questions at the core of our business model. It is also why they are better answered by looking at the business model as a whole.

Unfortunately, stakeholders in the institution look at the tuition question in a fragmented way. Teachers might say they feel it is unjust for them to be paid below what public school colleagues are paid when affluent families are getting a bargain. A parent may say that providing Catholic education for their children shouldn't require putting their family's financial well-being at risk. They may think the school needs to cut costs, although they are reluctant to see any programs that involve their own children rolled back. The CFO says the school needs to balance the budget and it can do that only by raising tuition or cutting costs.

Here's the reality about pricing in schools. First, parents will not pay one penny more in tuition than the school is worth to them. If you doubt this, understand that the statement is simply tautological. What something is worth to a person is what they will pay for it. It can be worth more than they will pay for it, but it cannot be worth less or, by definition, they will not pay. That doesn't mean they are paying the money for the reasons we think it's worth it. They may think our education is over-priced, but they don't want to disappoint their child, or they like the prestige or the safety it provides. But whatever *their* reasons are, the cumulative worth of those reasons has to at least equal the value of the tuition they will spend. This axiom brings some clarity to the tuition-setting process: from a business model perspective, tuition must be set at a level at which enough people find that the benefits of the school's product meets or exceeds its cost to them. This assumes that people have enough money to pay what the product is worth to them. This leads to the second reality.

The second reality is that affordability, while it seems like a hard and fast limit, is quite mercurial. It drives me crazy when people say a school's tuition is not affordable. Not affordable for whom? It's as if there is some mythic number beyond which tuition is now out of the reach of the paradigmatic family. The reality is that any tuition level will be unaffordable for some and easily affordable for others. Affordability isn't just tied to how much money someone has. It floats with the perceived value of the product. For instance, I can't "afford" a boat. With the income available to me, I couldn't come close to justifying the purchase of a boat. I have enough money (and credit) to buy a boat, but it would involve taking resources from other things that are crucial to me (like housing, transportation, and food). So I simply say I can't afford it. But if I lived in a place where boating is a key part of transportation, or if my family's recreational life revolved around boating instead of other things, all of a sudden, I could afford a boat. Just so, one family sends its children to a Jesuit school, while another family, with the same number of children and income, says in all sincerity that it can't afford it. What they are really saying is that they don't see it as worth the sacrifices they would have to make. And they have every right to make that decision. The importance of this for the school is that how much money people have is something it has no control over. But it has a lot of influence over how the value of its product is perceived relative to other uses of family resources. One of the ways is by improving the product through strategic planning and attention to the other three models, apostolic, pedagogical and community. And the other is by promotion, which will be discussed next and later in the section on marketing.

The price, itself, is an important dimension of the business model, but equally important and often overlooked is how the product is purchased. Again, look at the model of internet companies like Twitter. Most services on the internet are free to users. Most make their money by advertising. In a way, we as users pay for the service by putting up with advertising. If it becomes too annoying, we are unwilling to pay that price and we stop using the service. If we stop using the service, advertisers stop buying ad space. Website users like us are avatars for the true purchasers, advertisers, the way students are avatars for the true purchasers of our product, parents.

Another model used by internet firms is to offer free basic services, but charge if people want the feature-rich premium version. Schools can also base their price on what features customers want.

On-line schools find it easy to charge students by the course. Community colleges charge by the course. Jesuit schools tend to view their program as a totality and so are reluctant to use unit-pricing. But some will keep tuition lower by charging fees for various courses, sports or activities, especially if it considers those optional. In cases where all students are expected to access those services and pay those fees, this is just a way to make the tuition look more attractive.

The pricing model for most Jesuit schools is to set a standard tuition which they feel is attractive to enough customers that it will generate enough revenue to support the product. Discounts are offered to families of lesser income using financial aid and a means test. In the education industry it is acceptable to ask people who want a discount how much money they make and thereby target the discounts to the people who could not otherwise afford our product. Few other industries have that option.

Extra revenues are sought through fundraising. For parents, fundraising is like being offered optional premium services (relief from the guilt of being subsidized, recognition in the annual report, special dinner with the president, etc). For non-parents, fundraising packages aspects of the school's product to meet the various needs of benefactors (recognition, being part of a community, expressing gratitude, making the world better, etc).

A variation on this is a model called *Fair-share*. In this model, the school sets tuition at a level which would cover all its costs per student, but lets people pay whatever they can afford toward that full cost. The advantage of this pricing model is that it strengthens community and defeats any claims that some families cannot afford the school. Schools with this model vary in how much they trust the families to set their own price and how much accountability they incorporate through means testing.

One Jesuit school, Regis High School in New York City, charges no tuition at all. Beginning in 1912 one donor and her family underwrote the operating costs of the school until the 1960's , and provided a substantial endowment with the stipulation that the school be available to students tuition-free. In this model, the ultimate customer is the deceased donor, and the students who accept the support from the endowment are her avatars. It may seem that Regis is thus removed from the demand for a business model, but they still need to identify who their (avatar) customers are and produce a product that will attract them to make whatever sacrifices (including accepting the rigor of their academic program) they need to make. In addition, the endowment could not provide enough to keep pace with rising costs, so the school must still raise a substantial amount of money from parents, alumni and other benefactors. Their product must be such that it justifies the philanthropic decisions it is asking people to make.

There are other pricing models in use in Jesuit schools and other possibilities yet to be developed. The point is that how people are asked to pay for our product is a key part of making a business model work. In the years ahead, if financial challenges continue to become more daunting, pricing models will be a key to adapting and flourishing.

Promotion

A business can have a great product, perfectly matched to the needs of its customer and available at an attractive price, but it will still fail if no one knows it. There was a great ad early in the development of the dot.com sector. A group of 20-somethings was clustered around a computer screen, watching a new website they had just launched to sell some product. Their first "hit" was registered to smiles all around. In a few seconds the numbers started doubling and a great shout of joy went up. But the numbers kept doubling and these new business people realized to their horror that they were already beyond what they could handle. Their product was apparently so attractive to the public that orders poured in faster than they could hope to fill them. Pure fantasy. The ad was sponsored by a company that said it could help these youngsters out of their predicament. Such phenomena have happened, but a product going "viral" without extensive promotional efforts is extremely rare. We'd be much better off worrying about how we get people to know about our product in the first place.

Without a way of getting the word out, of creating awareness of and interest in our product, the other components of the business model form a bridge to nowhere. This is especially true for our business. We compete with less expensive schools, even free ones, that promise the same things we do. How is a potential customer to know why their investment in tuition will be worth it to them, unless we engage in a vigorous effort to explain who we are, what we do and why it will benefit them and their children? Promotion is part of a bigger marketing process that will be explored further in the next section of this chapter. Suffice it to say here that it is important enough to be included as one of the five P's that make up the business model.

Production Method

To discuss the method of production, we need to return to what the school's product is. I suggested earlier several possibilities, and these generally fell into two categories. We can see our product as the programs we provide to the students or we can look at the students themselves as our product. An argument can be made for each. By looking at websites and brochures, it appears that schools generally think of their programs as their product. It appears that our customers, the parents, are shopping for schools this way— looking for who has the most AP classes, the lowest student-teacher ratios, the best college counselors or the best computer technology. But these are really just *inputs*. What happens with our students, who they become, those are our true *outcomes*.

In a manufacturing firm, it is pretty clear what the product is. It's the item that rolls off the end of the assembly line after all the parts have been glued together or bolted on. It's not so obvious what the product of a school is. It looks like what's rolling off the end of our assembly line is the students themselves. And yet, it seems distorted to say that the students are our products. For one thing, a manufacturer has substantial control of its product. Every car that comes off the line will look and function exactly the same. If not, the manufacturer knows it has a problem. Our students, on the other hand will not look and act the same. If they do, we know we have a problem. This is one of the reasons we tend not to look at the students as our product. Because they are autonomous people, who are only influenced but not controlled by us, we don't want to be held accountable for outcomes we can't fully dictate. We would rather sell as our product the programs we offer, over which we do have control. Yet, however good our programs may be, if they don't produce better students, who cares?

What an organization sees as its product has big implications for its production method. If our product is programs and classes then we want a process that will create programs and classes that measure up to accepted standards for programs and classes. Our goal will be to emulate the current paradigm and conventional methods, but just do them better than our competition. Given the variability of students, we tend to take them out of the equation and instead evaluate the programs by criteria like how many students are in a class, how far they get in a textbook, what technology is used, how good a presenter the teacher is. If a parent complains that a student isn't learning very much, it must be the student's fault because we have put everything in place the student would need to succeed. If students in general aren't learning much, this will cause us to question the model, but short of irrefutable evidence, we will stick with what we're sure works best.

The danger of this approach is that if it's all about us and what we do rather than the students and what they do, we can do so much for them that they rely less on themselves. If we're in the business of helping people become better, smarter and stronger, that's not a good thing. An example might be a high-powered college counseling program. College acceptances are critical to a school's reputation. So a school that wants a premier reputation will view college acceptance as an important product. It will hire more counselors who will know that they are being evaluated, explicitly or implicitly, by how many students are accepted to selective colleges. Of course the weakest link in the college application process is the students themselves. They often procrastinate, write superficial essays, and ask the wrong teachers, too late, to write their letters of recommendation. The college counselors can improve their quality control by reducing the role students have to play in the college application process. They can set appointments, build in checkpoints to make sure students are on track and chase down teachers for recommendations. They can coach students on their essays and might even coach them so much that it isn't clear whose essay it really is. This may increase the college acceptance numbers, but what impact does this have on the students long-term? Have they learned to take responsibility for themselves, or that it is up to someone else to make them successful? I realize that I am describing an extreme that I haven't observed in our schools, but this is the direction things head when we focus on a product other than the students themselves.

Once we see our product in terms of what happens to students and who they become, we are freed up to use a variety of methods to achieve results. For instance, the program-as-product model tends to confine us in a class structure in which a group of 20-25 students sits in front of a teacher for six periods a day. This provides high accountability for quality of *input*. But shift to quality of *outcome*, and a student might be able to take eight classes, learn more from each and not work any harder, and the school might be able to lower its costs. If we can measure learning, that is outcomes rather than input, we can free students to take courses in the best way for them. So they might take three classes in a traditional classroom setting (English, Religion and Art); two on-line, at the student's pace and time-frame (Statistics and Swahili); one could be a hybrid with occasional in-class sessions (Social Studies); one could be an independent study (Women in Media); and one could be an extra-curricular (Debate or Soccer) that has adopted rubrics to demonstrate students are mastering essential learnings.

The biggest challenge is how to measure student learning and growth. This is not easy, but it is not impossible. As we develop assessments that measure student transformation, and as we grow to trust those assessments, we will free ourselves to find "production methods" that best achieve those outcomes. We will also be able to offer our customers, the parents, a way to evaluate our school in terms of what they really want, the transformation of their children into successful, virtuous and happy adults. But more on that when we discuss marketing, and specifically the *value proposition*.

Finance

The last major element of the business model is finance. For many, the word finance is intimidating. It brings to mind a lot of other words they only vaguely understand, like return on investment, cash flow, market timing and general ledger. I remember a campus minister I worked with who would use the word "fiduciary" in every meeting about budget as a way of teasing me about the incomprehensibility of financial management. I've slowly learned these concepts over the years, but for me finance is best understood as analogous to electricity. A friend of mine built a vacation home on a small island he owned in the inland waters of British Columbia. Because he was on his own little island he decided to use solar energy to run all his lights and appliances. Unfortunately, solar energy, especially in the Pacific Northwest, is not constantly available. It disappears entirely each night and many days it is available at reduced levels. So he had to add big batteries to the system to store up solar energy when it was available and feed it out when it wasn't.

In a school, tuition and fundraising revenues are like solar power. They provide the electricity we need to run our programs and to produce our product. But they are not constant. Tuition revenues cluster at the beginning of the year and fundraising dollars come in during the various drives and events used to attract them. Sometimes we go through periods where the availability of one or both is greatly reduced. My friend had to budget his electricity, anticipate times of greatest draw and least availability and consider how these cycles occur in relation to each other. He needed to calculate how big his solar panels needed to be (revenues), how efficient his appliances needed to be and how many he could support with the system (costs), and how big his batteries needed to be to balance out electricity needed with electricity available (cash flow). No one would trust living on an island like this unless they had thought through all these factors. Similarly, everyone in a Jesuit school has a stake in making sure resources are being managed similarly at their institution. Just as the sunlight in general may be enough to sustain the island home, but not consistently, so all the other elements of the school's business model—product, purchasers, price, promotion and production method—will usually provide enough financial electricity to run the school. But black-outs and brown-outs can cause a disaster. If you haven't had trouble meeting a payroll because of cash flow problems, ask someone who has.

What I have said so far about the role of finance in the business model will not be revelatory to anyone reading this book. More will be said in the section on financial management later in this chapter. But this brief look at its role is important because many we work with get impatient with the influence that finance can have on decisions. They can treat it as something that operates independently of the apostolic work they are doing. When it interferes, it seems to have overstepped its bounds and become an end in itself. "Money drives everything in this school," they may say. But the whole point of paying attention to finance is to keep money, or the lack of it, from interfering with our mission. Certainly this is of greatest concern to the president and the CFO, but it is something we all at least need to appreciate. Which is why the open-book management approach discussed earlier is so important. If anyone on the island lives as if the management of electricity is not important, they will soon learn what it is to live without it.

B. Marketing

Even if all the components of the business model are in place and functioning in a sustainable way, the business model may still be operating below its potential. We may have a great product and it may match the needs of the people we hope will purchase it. But for some reason we can't command a price that allows us to improve that product. And so we struggle along, dreaming of what we could do if only we had more resources. This is where marketing comes in. Even if the product meets the needs of its intended customers, they may not know it. As a result, many customers who would benefit from purchasing the product don't, and many who do are not willing to pay what it is truly worth to them.

Marketing is the process of connecting products and customers. I envision in the Middle Ages, just as the mercantile system is beginning to emerge, a serf raising enough turnips that he can feed his family, pay off his obligations to the local baron and the Church, and still have some extra. So he loads them onto his cart and brings them to town where a market has been formed. At this market, the farmer can find buyers for his turnips. He can learn what these buyers are looking for in turnips and see how much other farmers are charging for them. He can make a case for why his turnips should command the price they do. And he can sell his turnips and use the proceeds to expand his domestic economy, including making some changes to his farming methods to get more turnips that conform to what people are looking for. I don't know if this is where the term marketing comes from, but it captures the essence of the process for me.

Marketing is the process of identifying what people need (research); producing it (product); presenting it to them in a compelling way (promotion); and asking them for their commitment to purchase it (sales). We market our schools for a lot of reasons, but the three most important are to align all the school's constituencies with the school's true mission, to increase the quantity or quality of enrollment and to increase the level of philanthropic support. A fourth reason, less pronounced than these, is to attract and retain the best employees. Although all four of these are distinct goals, the marketing efforts to support one will tend to support the others as well.

Components of Marketing

1. Research

People never do anything for our reasons, only for theirs. They don't send their children to our schools because we think it is a good idea or because we think they should. They don't make donations because we care so much about young people getting opportunities through financial aid. This sounds obvious and yet, when we actually wade into the world of marketing, it is striking how hard it is not to focus on our reasons. Ignatius said well that we must bring them in their door if we are to bring them out ours. People never come in our door, no matter how important it is to us. They always come in their door. Their door may be the same as our door at times, but it is only because it is their door that they come in. As educators we may continue to improve our product, adding this program and that resource, without ever asking whether our customers see it as adding value. This is the role of market research. It tells us before we go and make big changes whether those changes are likely to make a difference to our potential customers. We may make the changes even if they don't, but we shouldn't expect that to strengthen our business model.

Market research can be quite elaborate and expensive. Firms can conduct on-line, mail, phone or canvassing surveys. They can conduct focus groups and access databases of existing research. Companies like Microsoft and Proctor and Gamble, with billions of dollars at stake with each product line, do extensive research, more than would be justified for organizations on our scale. Market research can be as simple as stopping to ask ourselves, is this something our parents, or their avatars, our students, would value? Just doing the mental exercise of standing in our customers' shoes can break through the blinders of our own motivations to consider the motivations of the people who are actually deciding whether to invest in tuition or make a donation. We can conduct simple surveys which can uncover the motivations of our constituencies. And we can test market ideas as well. For instance, before we roll out a full bus service, we could provide it to an underserved suburb, and see what kind of response we get. We can also learn from patterns of students coming to and leaving our schools. People voting with their feet is compelling data. Administering exit surveys or interviews will help us better understand why our school did or did not meet people's needs.

Surveys are not easy to design. I have learned by trial and error how disappointing the data can be when I didn't word the question right. Maybe I rolled two questions into one and then didn't know which part they were responding to. Or maybe they gave a response I didn't expect and I wish I had added another question that would help me understand. To overcome these difficulties, we use an approach that parallels the backward design process for curriculum development. We begin with identifying the marketing decisions we need to make and then work backwards to the data we need, and to the questions that will elicit that data. This seems obvious, but there is a human tendency to want to start writing questions as a first step, and this generally leads to much wasted effort. Despite the pitfalls, it is possible to design surveys in-house. In fact if we relied only on outside professionals to design surveys, the cost would prevent us from getting the regular feedback we need from our customers. It is worth training people in-house to be able to design and administer effective surveys and save the expense of outside firms for more critical data collection.

My experience with surveys at my school has identified three consistent motivations parents have for sending their children to our school. First, they want their children to be successful. I'm disappointed that some deeper, more spiritual motivation doesn't top the list, but that's my door not theirs. Even religious parents and faithful Catholics tend to hold the promise of success as a *sine qua non* for spending money on a Catholic school. I think this is because as parents see their children enter adolescence they become anxious that in four short years these very children who can't take out the trash consistently will have to support themselves in the world. Getting their children into a "good college" is of great importance to them.

The second motivation is that parents want their children to be good people. Again I wish this were first, but I believe the main reason it is important to them at all is that as their children reach adolescence, they become selfish and petulant. Although this is a by-product of gaining autonomy and a necessary part of growing up, their present rate of development looks to parents like they are turning into monsters. Catholic parents desire that their children somehow appropriate the values of the Catholic Church. Non-Catholic parents, even non-religious parents, are hoping that some value system will take root in their children, and Catholic values can look as good as any. But anxiety about their children's character is still less than their anxiety about their ability to succeed on their own. If you doubt this, consider how parents weight college decisions. The allure of a pathway to success eclipses whatever a college may promise in the development of virtue.

The third motivation is that parents want their children to be happy. It is only third because they believe the first two will lead to their children's happiness in the long-run, which is more important to them than their current happiness. The long-run is more important because that's when parents won't be around to provide a safety net for their children. But short-run happiness is important too. They want their kids to have friends, to make the team or be cast in the play, and even to have some fun. They hate seeing their kids miserable, hearing them say that no one at school accepts them, or observing how getting cut from the volleyball team has seemingly destroyed their sense of self-worth.

If these are the big three parent motivators for your school, those doors must be there for them to enter. How consciously is your school making sure they are present in the product?

2. Shaping the product

Research, even very simple research, will help the school understand better what its customers want. With this knowledge, the school can then look at its product, the impact it has on students, and the program that produces it. If it sees that its product has just what customers are looking for, it simply needs to help these customers understand that as they make their decisions. How this is done will be addressed in the next section, on promotion. If the school finds that its product is deficient in what customers desire, it must use this information to review the product and consider changes.

At this point we need to remind ourselves that this approach is not suggesting that our mission is to provide a product that the customer likes so that we can sell more of that product and make more money. While this may be the mission of for-profit businesses, it is clearly not our mission. But neither can we pretend we don't need a functioning business model in order to accomplish our mission. And this means we need to make sure that our "apostolic product," or outcome, is seen as sufficiently valuable to those making decisions about where their money goes. If we find that our product is lacking in features that the decision-makers are seeking, we have to ask whether those features can be added and thereby strengthen the apostolic outcome, or at least not weaken it.

It can be disconcerting for us in education to consider becoming more customer-centric. This calls up images of pushy educational consumers telling us they're paying good money to see that Johnny gets into an Ivy League school. We think of non-educators dictating how schools should be run based on values that have nothing to do with our mission. This could happen. But the solution is not in refusing to listen to those desires, but in making sure we hear them and use a clear process for determining whether we can or can't accommodate them within our mission.

For example, let's say we learn that there is a market for students from East Asia desiring to enroll in American schools, including ours. It would require adding ESL (or now, ELL) classes, special counseling and supervision services, and recruiting home-stay families. We then ask ourselves both how this would impact the business model and how it would impact our mission. We might find that it helps our business model by providing a new revenue stream that exceeds the added costs, but it hurts our mission by bringing non-Christian students whose only desire is to prepare for an American university. In this case, we probably would choose not to alter our product to accommodate these potential customers. On the other hand, we might determine that the school's apostolic mission would benefit from students who bring experience from another culture, and that the idea of exposing future leaders in other countries to Christian values is a wonderful apostolic opportunity. In this case, we might well be willing to alter or add to our program to accommodate this desire identified in a group of potential customers.

A third conclusion in this scenario might be that the move would not help the business model, that it would cost more than the revenues it brings in, but we feel it will greatly strengthen our apostolic mission. In this case we might decide to make the change, but if we do so, we know we have to adjust the business model in some other area to cover the costs.

Other product changes we might hear our customers asking for include adding more advanced placement classes, adding more remedial classes, adding or expanding summer school programs, adding more electives, adding more sports or other extra-curricular opportunities, making sports teams more competitive, or less competitive, having greater ethnic diversity or having less ethnic diversity, or even eliminating features from the product to lower tuition. As the examples demonstrate, some would contradict what we stand for and many contradict each other. We must not be afraid to listen to all of them, and then pursue the ideas that will help us accomplish our mission.

Successful for-profit businesses do this well. That might in itself convince us that this approach is not consistent with our mission. But is it inconsistent with our mission to listen to the people we say we are serving? To want to hear their desires, what they think their needs are? Would it be more consistent to assume we know what is best for people and they can take it or leave it? Jesus said that he came not to be served, but to serve, going so far as to wash the feet of his disciples. How much more should we be willing to ask the people we serve what they feel they need, and at least consider using that information, as well as our own experience and expertise as educators, to shape our product.

So how do we use customer feedback to shape our product? This is done on three levels. On the first level, it can be as simple as teachers paying attention to what their students are asking for, or what they hear during parent-teacher conferences. Some teachers have a knack for listening to people's needs and adjusting their approach in mission-appropriate ways to accommodate them. This might include adding periodic reviews, cutting down the amount of lecture time, or posting information on their website. This is not only great educational practice, it's great marketing, and it behooves us to find ways to help all employees develop this knack.

The second level is those changes that require persons or groups in authority to make decisions about the appropriateness of customer desires. An example would be a desire that non-cut sports be available to students. This might involve the athletic director and the principal working with coaches to determine whether and how this might be done. When customer research surfaces a list of possible improvements, the administrators and departments in charge of the affected areas should receive the information. They should evaluate whether the suggestions can be incorporated into their programs without causing negative collateral consequences. An example might be a request that the deadline for financial aid applications be extended. The business office might want to accommodate this request, but can't do so without delaying the process for enrolling new students. It might, however, find another way to address this concern, like getting information and forms out earlier.

The third level, big changes, ones that require a shift in approach by the school, should be considered as part of the strategic planning process, discussed in a later chapter. The way to identify these decisions is that they significantly impact several departments in the school. For instance, adding a new language doesn't just affect the language department. It could affect student enrollment in other electives. It might require additional resources, which either must be generated by the school or taken from some other use. Adding a support program for students with learning disabilities will require additional funding, facilities and additional training for classroom teachers. If the school's customer base indicates a strong desire for changes on this level, they should be considered, and the appropriate place to do so is in the context of the school's strategic planning process where their impacts on other areas of the school, both positive and negative, can be identified and addressed.

3. Promotion

Customer research provides valuable information about possible improvements to the school's program that could enhance the value of its product for its customers. More often, however, it reveals that potential customers don't realize that many of their needs actually are or can be met by our product as it is. Software companies often have this problem. People who purchase their products often understand only a fraction of the product's capabilities. For instance, customers may be dissatisfied with a word processing program because they want the ability to convert documents to web pages. If the product already has that capability, its maker doesn't need to add it, it needs to promote it. Two days before writing this paragraph, I was approached by a man at a Rotary meeting who asked me if our school had a religious instruction program. He said that a parent of students in one of our

Catholic feeder schools had told him that we didn't. This is anecdotal, but it clearly indicated a breakdown in our promotion of the product that we have. How many other customers might have the same misperception? I could ignore the comment or I could pursue it through customer research to see if it is an anomaly. If it isn't, we need to use that information to improve our promotion of the product we already have.

Promotion is fostering an environment of understanding and favorable perception of a product by an organization's publics. Promotion is often considered synonymous with marketing. If we are promoting our product, especially through advertising, then people feel we are marketing it. I hope it has become clear that promotion is only one piece of an overall marketing process, and it does not stand alone. Promotion cannot function without the other elements of marketing: customer research, shaping a product that customers will want, and selling it to them (which will be discussed in the next section). We have to know what customers are looking for to know what to tell them about our product, we have to have a product that truly meets their needs. Once they are informed about our product we have to have a way to convince them to make a decision to invest. That having been said, let's take a look at how promotion works as part of the marketing process. I want to draw out three major elements: the value proposition, branding and communications.

At the center of promotion is something called the **value proposition**. A value proposition is the justification for buying a product, which demonstrates that benefits to the customer exceed costs. Businesses have been using this concept for years, and it can help schools get clarity about the economic decisions that parents and benefactors are making and how we can influence those decisions. Consider this equation: Value = Benefits – Cost. In English, the value of a product for a customer is its perceived benefits (which the customer will subjectively and unconsciously translate into dollar terms) minus any costs the customer incurs to get those benefits. If the value is greater than 0, the customer has a reason to buy. The higher the positive value, the more compelling the reason to purchase. If the value is 0 or less, the customer has no reason to buy.

The higher the negative number, the more compelling the reason not to purchase.

Let's look at a purely economic example of a value proposition, where we are the customer. The lights in our gymnasium are 20 years old. Since they were installed, more energy efficient lighting has been developed. An electrical contractor proposes to install new light fixtures for $10,000. She says that installing the new fixtures will save me $500 per year in electricity costs, but also earn me a $5,000 energy rebate from the utility. If I look at a ten year window, Benefits ($500x10 + $5000) – Costs ($10,000) = Value ($0). The contractor's proposal has 0 economic benefit to me in ten years, so I could wait 10 years and take advantage of even more efficient technology and not lose any value in the meantime. This value proposition is not compelling to me. But then the contractor points out some non-dollar benefits, like better environmental stewardship and improved illumination. She has improved the value proposition, and I might well be convinced to make the investment.

Two other important factors will influence my decision. The first is how much risk I'm taking. What's the likelihood that we will actually lower our utility bill by that much? Will the fixtures even last ten years? The second is opportunity costs. I'm not likely to invest in this program if we can get the same benefits by buying the fixtures from another contractor for $8,000. Or if I can invest that $10,000 in something else that gives the school a higher return.

Our customers, though probably not consciously, are constructing this same equation when they look at our school. Potential parents are looking at tuition and asking if they will get enough benefit to justify the cost. The benefit may be economic (increased chances for college scholarships or for lucrative careers) or they may be non-economic (children becoming virtuous adults, status, belonging to a community). But whatever they are, the value they put on these benefits must exceed the costs, which include not only tuition, but costs like fundraising expectations, parental support required by a more challenging program and time driving kids to a more distant school. In addition, the parent must factor in the risks that they will not receive the benefits we promise. Will their child really get into a good college? Will this really be an accepting, supportive community? And the parent will be seeing if there is a less costly way to access the same benefits. Is there another Catholic school of comparable quality charging less tuition? Can they send them to a good public school and use the tuition money saved for college?

Our donors are also customers who are considering a value proposition. The benefits of making a donation of $1,000 might include a tax deduction, some recognition, access to people they care about, and the good feeling of having contributed to a cause that makes the world better. What is the likelihood that the donor will actually accrue these benefits? Are there alternative ways to invest that money to get those benefits more efficiently? Just because donors aren't preparing spreadsheets with a cost-benefit analysis, does not mean they are not consciously or unconsciously considering the validity of our value proposition.

The second element of marketing which is key to establishing the credibility of the value proposition is **branding**. Branding is a bit of a buzzword now, but it simply means building the identity of our school in the mind of its publics so that they have a clear and accurate, if not detailed, impression of who we are and what we do. We'd like to think our mission statement is our brand, and the closer these two are the better. But we don't have the same control over our brand that we do over our mission statement. Brand is how the mission interacts with public perception to produce a public image. It's like writing a 300 page book and having someone turn it into an hour and a half movie. Hopefully some of the original story will survive, but we know it's going to be changed. Branding is the process of paying attention to how our story will come across to the public as it is picked up and broadcast by the media, individuals and other transmitters. When the all-state football player is quoted in the newspaper saying the most valuable thing he learned this year was teamwork and gratitude for the opportunities God has given him, that builds brand. When he says "Football is my life!" that erodes it.

The key to successful branding is consistency and discipline. After researching what messages its customers are listening for and reviewing its mission and program, the school needs to decide on a few key messages and martial all its resources to get those messages out to the public. This sounds simple enough, but there is an inherent disconnect that makes this counter-intuitive for people. Those of us inside the school think that because we have heard the message, everyone has. We've heard the message so much that we're bored with it, so we assume our publics are too. The fact is that if we aren't sick of hearing the core messages, we haven't even come close to saying them enough to seat them in the minds of our publics. If you doubt this, listen to the speeches of successful and unsuccessful politicians. The successful ones manage to stay on message and do it so consistently that to their campaign staffs, it must be mind-numbing.

The school's logo and graphic identity are a good example. We underestimate how difficult it is to plant that image in the mind of the public. Our school has had the same logo for over 25 years and we think it's pretty effective. Every once in a while, I'll ask an alum to describe it from memory. Usually, they can't. I ask them if it has a cross in it. Some will say yes. I'm pretty sure I would get a higher response if I showed them the logo and asked them to identify it. And yet, people at our school talked about changing it within five years of its creation. Every department wants to develop its own logo, some using and changing the school's logo to do so. They do this, presumably, because they think their department can create with a few brochures or a T-shirt an identity it has taken the school as a whole 25 years to begin to shape. This desire to be creative with the logo, and messages in general, is a constant undertow which every organization must contend with if it is to build a brand in the mind of the public.

Note that promotion is, ultimately, about creating a favorable perception of the "product" and not, as we often assume, the school. Most promotional work of schools is aimed at promoting the school. It is natural for us to want people to know what a great school we have. The assumption is that if people know what a great school it is, they will want to send their kids there. As intuitive as this sounds, it isn't actually true. People send their children to a school because of the results they anticipate. Those results are our product, which is ultimately what we should be promoting. Knowing and trusting our brand is a necessary condition for people to believe in our product. But it is not a sufficient condition.

The third major element of promotion is **communications**. Like promotion, communications is also seen as synonymous with marketing. Communications is the way we transmit information about ourselves and our products to our potential and actual customers. It includes both advertising, in which the school pays for access to public attention, and media relations, in which it convinces third party news organizations that conveying some message or story about the school is in its own journalistic interests. Advertising has the advantage of being under our control. As long as we are willing to pay the price we can have advertising say pretty much whatever we want it to. Unfortunately, our publics know this too, and so they discount the credibility of advertising. Imagine a continuum which has paid self-promotion (advertising) at the left end and third-party endorsement to the far right. As you move leftward on this continuum, you gain more control over your message, but lose credibility. As you move rightward, you gain credibility, but lose control. The strategy of public communications is to achieve an optimal balance.

One component of the public communications program will be to send out press releases and cultivate media contacts so that the school can get the media to pick up stories that carry its messages out to the public. It takes skill to identify and frame a story so that the media will pick it up, and further skill to keep adverse messages from getting in. It's great to have a story about underprivileged kids getting scholarships to your school, but not so good if the reporter thinks the story is that a private school recruits minorities for its basketball team.

As you move to the left on the continuum described above toward advertising, you also spend more money. There are an amazing number of places to spend advertising dollars. Newspapers, TV, radio, internet, symphony programs, welcome packets, event sponsorships, parish bulletins. The list is infinite and the biggest problem is that it is difficult to evaluate what impact any of these have. Our school asks people on their applications how they heard about the school and advertisements hardly show up. Most of the applicants say word-of-mouth referrals or personal experience of the school. That doesn't mean that advertising hasn't reinforced the impact, but it's difficult to say whether the cost is justified by the return on investment.

One of the advantages of internet advertising is that there are ways of measuring how many people see your ad, and if there is a link, how many follow it to your website. This is one reason your website should be the hub of your public communications program. But there are others, even more compelling. If you can get people to your website, you have the opportunity to tell them your story, as thoroughly as they want, and as accurately as you want. You can also quantify how much traffic you're producing. There are even ways to track where that traffic is coming from so that you can adjust your strategies accordingly. You can also save money on advertising dollars. You can spend advertising money on brand building and use the internet for information transmission. An example is putting a job notice in a classified. Spend money on your logo and a message that will catch a potential applicant's interest, then send them to your website for the details. The same can be done for potential student applicants and rummage sale customers.

All this suggests that the school's website must be well-designed. It must be attractive, easy to navigate, and up to date. The design must anticipate what people are interested in, balanced with what you want them to be interested in. The principal of bringing them in their door so that you can bring them out yours is key. And it must be designed so that you can learn about your publics. What are they interested in? What are they clicking on and why? Quick survey questions can help gather information and feedback from your customers.

4. Sales

Promotion is the process of fostering understanding and favorable impressions of our product with the customer, but it does not complete the marketing process. People could have a favorable perception of a product and never get around to buying it. I've always wanted to learn more about painting with watercolors. Several community colleges offer what look like good classes at a reasonable price. But I just never get around to signing up. They have already created in me a favorable perception, but they haven't made a sale with me. To assure that an organization is making sales it needs a sales force.

Schools don't think of themselves as having a sales force, but they do. The admissions director is, or should be, a salesperson. Development officers are salespeople. The principal is a salesperson when he is wooing a teacher to join the faculty. The campus minister is a salesperson when she is trying to get that reluctant senior to go on the Kairos Retreat. The problem is that because we don't see ourselves as salespeople, we don't attend to what makes the sales process successful. This has two major impacts: The first is that we don't dedicate enough people to selling when we need to. In fact when schools are struggling with enrollment and fundraising, when it needs to shift resources to ramp up sales, there is pressure to use diminishing resources to protect teaching positions. This is in part because the faculty is the largest and most influential block of employees, and partly because the school wants to protect the quality of its product at all costs. We believe that the students we have came because they saw a quality product. This is true, but it misses an important step. It's the same step Emerson missed when he is reputed to have said that if you build a better mousetrap the world will beat a path to your door. That does happen, about as often as a solar eclipse. Most of the time someone needs to be tirelessly contacting potential customers and helping them review the value proposition and leading them to make the decision it suggests.

The second problem with a school not appreciating the role of sales is that it prevents it from seeing who its sales force is. It can lead an admissions director to believe it is enough to send out materials, conduct an open house and wait for the applications to come in. It can lead the development officer to miss the connection between the number of in-person calls they make and the dollars raised. And it can lead a teacher to believe he doesn't need to share the good things he knows about the school with potential parents.

As counter-intuitive as it feels, we will strengthen our schools if we understand and strengthen the sales function. This means understanding that we have customers, that they are looking at our product, that they are using a value proposition, consciously or unconsciously, and that while some customers will sell themselves, the rest will need some help. They are the people who will make the difference between our being able to pursue our mission with vigor, or limp along from year to year.

If this makes sense, and you are willing to look at the sales function in your school, then it will make sense to look at some principles of the sales process. A full development of sales theory and how it functions in a school environment is beyond the scope of this book, but let me highlight a few key concepts in the hopes that it will spark interest in learning more.

Features and Benefits

One of the main ways we falter in making our value proposition is confusing features with benefits. I do this a lot. I explain all the features of our school and expect people to be convinced that it's a great school and that alone will compel them to send their kids or donate. Would you buy a car because it had torsion-bar suspension and an overhead cam engine? I wouldn't, because I have no idea what these are or why I would want them. Even if I know what a feature is, I don't always understand the benefit of it. I may know that a school offers an extensive retreat program, but I may not see how that will mean I have a happier, healthier teenager living with me or that she will more likely have a faith that feeds her for the rest of her life. I'm always pleased when a parent tells me they came to our school for the academics and only after a few years realized that the real benefit is the spiritual experience. I'm pleased that they finally got it, but I wonder how we can do a better job of cluing them in from the beginning, especially during that time when they are in danger of choosing another path because they undervalue the benefits our school would provide.

An important marketing discipline, whenever we mention a feature, whether it is in a recruiting brochure or during a talk to donors, is not to stop there. Take the next step and state what the benefits are, even if we think they're obvious. Paint a picture, help them see it, hear, taste, smell and touch it. That's what people mean by the saying, "Sell the sizzle, not the steak." In the table below are examples of features I have heard my colleagues presenting to prospective customers, followed by what they should also say about the benefits:

Customer	Feature	Benefit
Prospective Parent	Small class size	Personal attention helps children develop their own individual gifts.
Prospective Parent	Rigorous graduation requirments	Your children will be more attractive to colleges who evaluate transcripts, and they are more likely to finish college once they get there.
Prospective Donor	25% of the students attend on financial aid	Your investment is working with that of others to help kids who need opportunities to accomplish what you have.
Student	The school has a strict dress code	We are helping you develop an awareness that how you dress affects the way people will see you in the adult world

In converting features to benefits, we need to keep in mind that what one person would see as a benefit, another might see as just a feature. For instance, if we point out that the rigorous academic program (feature) will lead to increased chances for success in college, we assume that all prospective parents would see that result as a benefit to themselves. But if the student would be the first in his family to attend college, they may not be sure succeeding in college is worth the sacrifices. In that case, it's the salesperson's job to help them visualize what it could mean. For instance, it might be important for them to know that on average, over the course of a lifetime, a graduate with a college degree is expected to earn over $500,000 more than one without.[6] That means their child would have a better chance of not only becoming independent, but having the resources to provide even more opportunities for their grandchildren. We would hope that they would be coming to our schools for reasons beyond anticipated personal income. But if financial issues are a concern and they don't understand this benefit of a college preparatory program, they might make a faulty decision that prevents them from experiencing all the other benefits.

Handling Objections

Sales requires good listening to learn what customers desire. Based on what we learn we can point out the benefits of our product that address those desires. Ignatius talked about a similar sort of listening in the *Exercises*. In prayer, we should be working to understand what our own deepest desires are, and what God desires of and for us. Unfortunately, we are often afraid of what these desires might ask of us, so we avoid listening to them. Something similar can happen in the sales encounter. We can be afraid to hear what the customer desires or perceives because it might be at odds with our product. So we fill the time with talking about our product, hoping that something motivating for the customer will emerge. In so doing, we don't hear what sales people call the "hot buttons," the key drivers in the buyer's decision. Often these come out as objections to buying the product. We're afraid to hear their objections because they come across as negatives. But objections are key opportunities to learn about people's true desires. Perhaps you've heard the saying, "The sale begins with the first objection." There is a method for handling objections, called "feel-felt-found," that can help us hear the objections and, when appropriate, be used to uncover for the customer why our product might be just what they are looking for. In summary it follows this path, "I know how you feel; I felt that way myself; here's what I found."

Feel: The first step is to empathize with the customer. Clarify what they are feeling. See if you understand it correctly, then acknowledge their feelings and let them know that you understand. Often the objection may come across as a question of fact and the first tendency might be to respond with another fact. Resist this temptation and use the opportunity to listen to the deeper feelings behind the objection. For instance, a prospective parent might say, "I don't want to send my daughter there because I've heard that your teachers are mostly non-Catholic and don't know anything about Catholic doctrine." Your first inclination might be to say, "Actually, 86% of our teachers are Catholic, and all of them participate in an ongoing formation process." But they don't want to get into an argument with you, and most people will be reluctant to even voice their objections for this reason. Instead, recognize that the parent has just said something important about his desires for his daughter's education and try to address it at a deeper level. Reflect back what you think you've heard: "You're concerned that our school won't be able provide your daughter a good Catholic education because you've heard that most of our teachers aren't even Catholic." This may spark a further discussion about why this information is so important to the parent, where he heard it and how much credence he gives the information.

Felt: The next step is to express empathy and let the parent know that you share his concern. Rather than putting him on the defensive for having wrong information, you validate the concern. "If this is what you've heard, I don't blame you for being concerned. I felt that way about the school myself before I came here, because I heard many of the same rumors." Or you might say, "I understand because I've felt that about institutions that call themselves Catholic, and it raises deep concerns for me as well."

Found: Then you let the parent know how you worked through your own doubts. "So I did a pretty thorough investigation before I came here. I decided I have one life to give and I wouldn't spend it working for a school that didn't reflect my own values as a life-long Catholic. What I found is that this school recognizes how important the teachers in the classrooms are and they are careful about whom they hire. I found when I came here that 83% of the teachers were Catholic, and since then the percentage has grown to 86%. And what really surprised me is how committed our non-Catholic faculty is to understanding and supporting who we are as a Catholic school. I also found that they have helped us prepare our students for the religious pluralism they will find in college and the work world."

Following this process, you will end up with three things you didn't have before: a deeper understand of what the customer's real desires are (his door); a beginning relationship of trust based on your affirming his desires; and an opportunity to give him information about your product that centers on his desires, rather than what you think he should care about.

This approach works for any sales situation, whether it is recruiting students, asking for campaign contributions, or recruiting a new band director. But it can also be helpful in other contexts, for instance, resolving complaints from parents. When a parent tells me a coach has been unfair in cutting her son from the team, I find it helpful to first acknowledge how painful that is, not only for the student but for the parent. And we talk about that. I share with them my own pain when my daughter was cut from the basketball team and never played again. And we talk about that. Then I share with them what I learned about parenting in the process, that my most important role was to assure my daughter that we loved her and had confidence that she would not let this defeat her. If I have listened well and demonstrated that I understand how parents feel when this happens, I find they are able let me share my own experience as an educator and parent.

Incentives

Most sales organizations have found that getting people to sell—that is, meet with potential customers to help them make a decision to buy a product—requires incentives. On the other hand, organizations have found unintended consequences to paying commissions. The economic recession of 2008, as an example, was caused in part by securities traders who were over-incentivized to sell financial products in situations that had long-term negative results for everyone. Still, it is appropriate for schools to ask whether they are giving proper incentives to their sales force. To under-incentivize runs the risk that admissions and development officers will generate only promotional activities and hope that enough commitments will emerge to meet the school's goals. In some cases, say for a school in a large city with a great reputation and a waiting list as big as its freshman class, this could well be true. But when the school falters because enrollment or fundraising targets aren't being met, it's time to ask whether people are being rewarded for results that matter.

I wouldn't advocate that admissions and development people be paid on commissions. This raises serious ethical issues because it fosters too much short-term thinking and not enough care for parents and donors as more than customers but potential members of our apostolic community. It may be enough to simply keep accurate track of results so at least the salespeople can keep score on how they are doing and know when to ramp up and down. It may mean giving special rewards or recognition when sales targets are met. And it may mean setting up compensation packages with a component based on meeting certain performance objectives. I have done this with some key personnel and they like the ability to track their own performance and to influence the compensation they receive by working harder and smarter.

In the foregoing discussion, I have focused on the development and admissions officers as the school's sales force. The reality is that full effectiveness requires that everyone be part of that sales force. Delegating sales to only certain people is expensive. If a custodian doesn't make sure the school has a welcoming environment, if a teacher who meets a prospective parent doesn't extol not only the features of the school but also the benefits, if an administrator doesn't handle objections of current parents with an approach like feel-felt-found, then we will have to spend a lot of money hiring people who will. And they will have to make up for the impression given by an apostolic team that doesn't seem convicted enough to sell their product. That's an expensive proposition.

To some extent, the responsibility for promoting and selling the school must be shared by all. They must be willing to abide by the school's branding discipline, which means accepting the parameters for use of the logo, and being familiar with and transmitting the school's key messages when opportunities present themselves. They must also assist those who have primary responsibilities for sales by giving them information about good things happening at the schools which can become features and benefits. They must let them know of prospective parents, donors, employees and volunteers who might be drawn to the school's mission if properly asked. This means extra work for people who already have a lot of responsibilities. What's the incentive? If the school is already as good as it can be, if the enrollment and financial outlook could not be improved, if there are enough resources to provide program quality, adequate salaries and a healthy working environment, there may not be an incentive to assist with selling the school. Most schools, however, and the people who work in them, have aspirations to be better off than they are currently. In this case, open book management, discussed in Chapter IV, will help them keep score and see where the school can be doing better and how they can help. That and a little sales training may be enough to engage them in marketing the school. Generally they will just need to do the things they're doing now, but differently. What this can do for the mission will be strategic and powerful.

Goals of Marketing

With the foregoing understanding of what marketing is and how it is done, let's turn to what the results of marketing should be. We generally think of marketing as living in the business model. When people think of marketing for schools, the first thing they think about is selling the school to get more students. The next thought might be that marketing is also needed to achieve fundraising targets. But marketing should support all four models of the school—apostolic, pedagogical, community and business. If marketing is the process of connecting products with customers, for a school to achieve its mission that connection must be made on many levels, and marketing should support them all. The marketing process should reinforce for parents why volunteering and attending conferences are important. It should encourage students to make maximum use of the opportunities they are being given. It should foster greater engagement of employees in the school's mission. This should be expected of the marketing process because the messages for people from whom we are seeking monetary commitments shouldn't differ from the messages we give to anyone else, including ourselves. Effective marketing is not a superficial process. It should emanate from the very core of our mission and identity, and in turn reinforce that core. Otherwise it will be like that seed that falls on rocky soil, which quickly flowers and fades in the heat of the sun (Lk 8:6).

How we do marketing will impact and be impacted by every aspect of the school, but there are four major areas that require a deeper understanding to assure its effectiveness: mission alignment, admissions, development and employee engagement.

C. Mission Alignment

A Jesuit school can be like that proverbial elephant being described by the blind men. The one touching its trunk announces that an elephant is like hose. The one with his arms wrapped around a leg says, no it is like a tree. Next to him is one whose hands are flat on the Elephant's side and says it is like a wall. The one behind grasps the elephant's tail and says it is like a snake. Same elephant but vastly different perceptions. Our missions can be like that. We may have a mission statement that we feel clearly states what we are about, but how it gets interpreted can be bewilderingly diverse. The mission may talk about "graduating students of competence, conscience and compassion." To the social studies teacher, this might mean that students must understand history well enough to be responsible agents within it. To the campus minister, it might mean they are committed to fostering those qualities within the Church. To a soccer coach it might mean that they can balance both individual skills and teamwork, as evidenced by the ability to win games. To the development director it might mean that students graduate with a sense of stewardship that will lead them to support the school for future generations. All of these are elements of the school's mission, but each fails to describe its totality. If we stay in touch only with the part of the elephant nearest to us, we again fall into the fallacy of composition, assuming that what is true of a part (our part) is necessarily true of the whole. As a result, our schools fall short of having a coherent identity for us and for others who might join us. Our marketing efforts must raise the vision of all participants to an understanding of mission that unites all their individual efforts.

How do we market for mission alignment? We're trying to lead people from different stakeholder groups to commit to and support a common understanding of mission. The keys to doing this are:

- selecting focal messages
- communicating them to all the key audiences
- and adapting or contextualizing them for different audiences.

We tend to formulate messages to get particular people to take particular actions. For instance, we used a phrase in our advertising for new students, "Worth the investment." We felt this answered a major question parents might have when they face the prospect, some for the first time, of paying tuition dollars to send their children to a school. We worked with the assumption that what parents desire is to use their limited resources in ways that will most benefit their children. We wanted them to see that tuition is not an expense, but an investment. We hoped the parents would hear the claim that our school is "worth the investment" and think that they can justify the economic sacrifice because it will be an investment they can make in their children. Our hope was that this would get them beyond any sticker-shock they might have, to come and learn more about the school's value proposition, and ultimately be drawn whole-heartedly into the mission. But if they don't take those additional steps, if they only hear the message, "worth the investment," we risk having them conclude that we see our education as having only economic value.

If parents, the target audience for this message, could hear it in a way that skews their perception of our mission, what about other audiences? It has been my experience that, while parents are most concerned with benefiting their own children, alumni are concerned that the school not become available only for the wealthy. They could see the message, "Worth the investment" and think, "Wow, the school must be getting expensive." Our own employees are another audience who will see the message through a different lens. They don't want the school to become financially elitist, but they are sensitive about subsidizing parents who can easily afford higher tuition by keeping their pay low. A teacher might see "Worth the investment" and think, "The school is telling us we need to sacrifice, yet pandering to parent consumerism."

To prevent the perception of our mission by our constituencies from fragmenting, the messages we send to any one audience have to connect to our bigger mission and also connect to other audiences who will hear it. One of the ways we did this was to make sure that the phrase always followed another, more general message which we have used for 25 years, "Educating for Life," This phrase, in turn, follows the school logo, which includes a cross, making clear its faith-based mission. In this way, anyone who reads the message— parent, alum, employee—will be alerted that we are faith-based, that we provide a holistic education, and that such an education is worth making an investment.

Marketing for mission alignment requires more than using a logo and a few catch-phrases. The school will develop a marketing plan based on research into constituency desires and perceptions of the school. Using this information, the school identifies the key messages that will convey who it is and what it is about to the constituencies that matter. One challenge is to craft messages that both project the mission and capture the felt needs of the school's internal and external audiences. Another is to narrow the list down to a handful that the school can transmit consistently enough that they seat themselves in the memories of the audiences. Once these messages have been identified and agreed to, using a participative process similar to that for building the strategic plan (see Chapter VI), the school should martial all its communications resources to transmit these messages. These include:

- advertisements,
- press releases (both internal and external) with stories that illustrate the messages,
- articles in the school's newsletters,
- items on the website,
- talks at parents meetings, faculty meetings and alumni reunions,
- messages on the readerboard,
- prayers,
- T-shirts,
- Facebook posts,
- tweets

The list is endless. The point is that once we know the critical messages that advance our mission, we focus communications on those messages until we are sure they have penetrated into the collective consciousness of our stakeholders and prospective stakeholders. This doesn't mean that every piece of communication the school sends out will be about one of those select themes. But a heck of a lot of them had better be. When we are convinced that everyone has the message, we will be just beginning. As stated earlier, if we ourselves aren't already tired of banging these same drums, we probably haven't yet had any impact on our audiences' perceptions.

If all this seems familiar, it is because the process is basically the branding we discussed earlier in the chapter. Branding must be around mission. If the school's branding doesn't strengthen the mission by creating a climate of understanding and favorable perception for it among its constituencies, even if it brings burgeoning applicant pools and millions more donated dollars, the school will not last as a Jesuit school. What we are is defined by who we are. If our marketing doesn't attract people who understand and support our mission, if it doesn't discourage people who don't (or won't), we will eventually wonder how we got to be a school where parent groups, employees and key donors have re-centered the mission, or given it no center at all.

D. Admissions Recruiting

Admissions recruiting is the process of attracting, selecting and bringing in new students to the school. Admissions and recruiting are actually two very different aspects of bringing students to the school that nevertheless have to function together. Recruiting is the attracting part, how we get parents and students to make the effort to become part of our school. Once we've done that, the process switches gears as the school decides whether it wants to accept a student into the school. Then, when the student is accepted, the process shifts gears again and the school works to make sure the student actually matriculates. The director of admissions role has unique challenges because one person generally has to straddle both sides of the process. She builds relationships with students, as well as parents, counselors, principals and others as she sells what the school has to offer and encourages them to support the student in applying to the school. Then she works with an admissions committee to select only those students who will bring the most promising attributes to support the school's mission. She must maintain relationships with applicants' teachers and counselors who in some cases are advocating for students who may not meet the school's admissions standards. As a recruiter she has more in common with entrepreneurs and business people who have to market their products. As an admissions officer she has to work with school personnel who often have little experience, or patience, with the marketing process. In her work she has a huge impact on shaping what the school is by shaping who comprise it, yet her work is seen as ancillary to the main task of education. As a result, admissions recruiting is sometimes under-resourced and understaffed and when it isn't, underappreciated.

Building an Applicant Pool

Some Jesuit schools, especially those in small markets, struggle to maintain a stable enrollment adequate to support the business model. Others have huge waiting lists and struggle with annual controversies over children of alumni or benefactors or prominent community members who aren't admitted. It may be tempting to believe that a robust recruitment effort is needed only for the school with no waiting lists. When applications fall short, a school can switch into emergency recruitment mode, invest in advertising and send out an all-call to the school community to go out to the highways and by-ways and bring in students. Then when the pool of qualified applicants exceeds spots available, the effort subsides, especially if people are not comfortable with the prospect of having to turn away qualified applicants. But there are three arguments for maintaining a robust recruitment effort even when the applicant pool seems healthy. First, it's good insurance. Economies can collapse and drain away applicants. Public schools can get better or competing Catholic schools can be founded. Feeder schools can close. The bigger the applicant pool, the better it can withstand these changes in the school's environment. Second, admissions recruiting is about not just the quantity of enrollment, but its quality as well. The more students you have to choose from, the more sure you can be that the ones you select will support the mission of the school. This doesn't mean necessarily narrowing the school's selection criteria. It can actually mean that the school can admit a more diverse student body, ethnically, economically and academically, because it can select students from otherwise underrepresented groups who have the greatest chance of success. Third, by building a large waiting list, a school builds a case and a market for more Catholic schools. It helps strengthen the Catholic feeder schools because they provide better access to a desired and selective secondary school. And it provides the justification for the founding of additional secondary schools. This latter outcome may sound like more competition, but it actually strengthens the school in the long run by raising the awareness and cachet of Catholic schools in general. We once helped start another Catholic high school in a neighboring county and actually got more students from our overlapping catchment area because they did such a good job of getting people excited about Catholic education.

Building the applicant pool requires a marketing effort, as described earlier. It requires knowing who your customers are and what they're looking for; it requires knowing your product and maybe even changing it in response to what people need; it requires promoting that product and making a value proposition that speaks to the motivations of potential customers; and it requires a sales effort to get people to take the necessary steps to apply and matriculate. I want to emphasize this last step, because as schools, we're just not used to selling. It is true that some of us have a natural proclivity for building relationships with prospective families; for helping them understand not only the features of our school, like program and plant, but how those will benefit them; for listening for objections people are feeling and sharing what we've found out so that they can evaluate how valid the objections really are; and for setting goals and being persistent until they are achieved. These are the characteristics of successful salespeople that we discussed earlier. Some admissions directors have them, and others' strengths are more on the selection side. They have a good feel for who would make successful students but are not comfortable with helping them see, if they don't already, what the school could do for them. If these sales skills aren't naturally present, we need to help the admissions/recruiting staff understand why they are important, have them acquire them through training and reinforce them through the school's planning and evaluation processes.

It helps to set up clear goals and monitor progress toward those goals over the course of the year. It is not enough to say the goal is to have as many students as possible apply. A specific target should be set, for two reasons. First, it sets common expectations for everyone involved. Without specific admissions targets, the admissions director might be pleased with 500 applicants, only to find that the principal was hoping for 600. Finding this out after the fact can be demotivating to an admissions director who otherwise feels that his efforts produced the results they were supposed to. Second, once a specific goal is stated, there can be a discussion about the resources needed to achieve those goals. Do we need to spend $50,000 on advertising, or $10,000? This is a difficult question to answer under any circumstances, but impossible if we don't know the results we are hoping to produce.

To set this goal we first need to know the outcome we want. The ultimate outcome, of course, is accomplishing the mission of the school. This means having a student body size necessary to support the apostolic, pedagogical, community and business models of the school. What this level is should be clear from the long-range strategic and financial plans. To maintain the desired student body size we need to have a freshman class of a certain size. Based on the school's experience with yield (the percentage of applicants who accept their acceptance to the school), we can set a goal for the number of students we want to admit. Some schools use point systems to identify students who show *prima facie* evidence of meeting admissions requirements. This point system can be used to set a goal for the number of applicants who have a minimum profile score. Based on experience, we can project the percentage of applicants that will have that score or higher, and using this factor, we can set a goal for the size of the total applicant pool. This then becomes the target for the recruitment phase of the admissions/ recruitment process.

With a goal for the total applicant pool established, we can set up intermediate goals so that the admissions director can track his progress toward the applicant pool goal and make corrections if necessary. Past experience will tell us how numbers at various points of the process relate to the numbers for total applicants at the end of the recruiting phase. For instance, the first indication of interest may be the number of people registering on a web portal to receive more information. If the number of registrants by a certain point in the year is higher than the previous year, this may presage a higher number of applicants. This correlation can be honed by collecting data over the years. The next indicator may be attendance at open house, and the next, school visits by prospective students, and after that, the numbers taking the entrance exam. Intermediate goals can be set for all these steps. If no data has been collected in prior years these will have to be guesses initially, but as data gets captured more accurate correlations can be made between early indicators and ultimate outcomes. This information can then be used to increase or decrease efforts to achieve the target. For instance, if fewer people than expected have registered on the web portal, additional mailings might be sent from the school, more targeted advertising purchased, or additional presentations made to feeder schools.

Intermediate metrics are especially important if the school's applicant pool has been or is projected to be lower than needed to sustain the school. Enrollment is critical to a school's viability as an apostolate and a community, in some ways pedagogically, and of course in a fundamental way, as a business. Even extraordinary success in fundraising cannot make up for an eroding student population. If enrollment is declining, it is harder to convince donors that they are investing in a quality product. Eventually, teacher and staff morale declines, fueled by reductions in positions and constraints on salaries and budgets. All this makes it harder to market the school, which leads to further declines in applicants. It's just not a healthy cycle for a school to get into. When the 9.0 earthquake and tsunami struck Japan in 2011, it had the most advanced system of early detection of any country in the word. As a result they were able to give people 30 seconds warning before the earthquake struck. 30 seconds isn't very much, but it's a lot more than nothing and probably saved a number of lives. What if they had had 5 minutes or a half hour warning, how many lives could have been saved? It is not clear whether that could ever be achieved technologically for earthquakes. But it is possible to develop an early warning system for a seismic shift in our enrollment. If a school has enjoyed a healthy surplus of applicants for some time, the need may be less critical. But any school that faces concerns about loss of quantity or quality in its applicant pool needs an early warning system to make adjustments during a recruitment cycle before it is too late.

1. Who makes buying decisions?

Earlier we asked the question, "When the school markets itself, who is it marketing to, who is the customer?" It is critical to the admissions/ recruiting strategy to answer this question. Is it the parent, or is it actually the student? Fifty years ago, the answer clearly would have been the parent. But in the last half of the twentieth century, there was a shift toward giving the student more say in the decision. Now in many families, the students at least have veto power over where they go to school. This veto power grows stronger as tuitions rise and parents are reluctant to make such a big investment unless their children will commit themselves to optimizing it.

Earlier, we used the term "avatar" to capture the student's role in buying decisions for our schools. Avatar is originally a Hindu concept, meaning an incarnation of a deity, often Vishnu. The computer industry has adopted the concept for personae or identities that computer users can adopt to be present in a chat room or a role-playing game. The avatar in this case interacts with other characters and may even make some decisions on its own, but is ultimately controlled by the computer user who makes the final decisions. In a similar way, parents give their children much more autonomy today than they did a generation or two ago, but parents still retain the ultimate decision. They follow their avatars, seeing how they respond in situations, letting them make decisions when appropriate. When the stakes are high, however, children have influence but the decision is the parents'.

This concept is important to marketing for enrollment because it suggests that we have to market to both the student and the parent, but in different ways. For most families it will be critical that students tell their parents that they would like to come to our school, or at least would not object to coming. They will generally base this on different criteria than their parents. Most want to go someplace that will be fun, where they will be accepted, where they will have friends. They don't want their next school to be too stressful or put them at risk of becoming failures. But they also would like the school to help them become successful, to satisfy expectations that others, especially parents and peers, have of them. These all connect with attributes that our schools also desire for their experience. We want them to enjoy learning and growing, to become part of a community, to be able to balance stress and achievement with self-acceptance. It shouldn't be hard for us to show them "their door" into our program.

Parents, on the other hand, want most of all to give their children tools for success in life. The amount of maturation needed between middle school and college is enough to induce anxiety in any parent and cause them to wonder whether their children will survive as independent adults. Parents want their children to become better people, to develop the virtues and sense of responsibility that will not only contribute to their success but contribute to a better world. And parents want their children to be happy. They realize that there are trade-offs between what will make them happy now and what will make them successful later. In most cases, they are more concerned about their ultimate success, but they have a limit to how much current unhappiness they can put up with from their children. As with their children, what parents desire is not at odds with what we offer. College preparatory programs give students tremendous tools for success in life. Our faith-based education offers the best possible grounding for growth in virtues and responsibility. And our strong communities, our sports, activities, retreats and charismatic faculties go right to the heart of an adolescent's sense of well-being. These are the parents' door into our program.

I hope it is clear that the aspirations of students and their parents are at once overlapping, yet distinct. They are distinct enough that we must craft common messages that speak to both at once and also separate messages that speak directly to the needs of each. As an example of the first, I remember giving a talk to a mixed audience of parents and eighth graders at an open house. I wanted to talk about the rigor of the program, but I didn't want to scare the middle-schoolers. So I talked about something I have observed at our school, that students figure out that the best way to have fun is to work hard. Our football team was in the state semi-finals at the time. I said, "Those guys have worked hard to be where they are, but not one of them would complain, because they are experiencing the fruits of their efforts." I explained that our teachers know how to help students take ownership of their learning, to answer their own questions, achieve their own goals, and become the persons they want to be. That's fun. Finally I pointed out that it doesn't take our students long to realize that nothing is more boring than following the path of least resistance. By the responses I got, I felt that both the students and the parents liked the message. I was hoping I wasn't inflating what we actually accomplish, when a sophomore named Ryan, who had been in the audience waiting to perform with the drama department, came up to me, beaming, and said, "Mr. Peterson, I love this school!"

An example of the latter, delivering separate messages, is a strategy our admissions director used for an open house. Part of the agenda had the parents go to the auditorium for a presentation on curriculum requirements for the various departments, which we find is mortally boring for middle-schoolers. The students went to a series of presentations by our student government officers on what life at the school is really like. As you can imagine, the high school students were enthusiastic, honest and charming. They had instant credibility with their future underclassmen.

The important point is that there are two audiences we have to sell to. What they are looking for is distinct yet overlapping. Their perceptions will eventually flow together at the dinner table at home and result in a decision about where the avatar will be placed in school. Our communication strategy must give both currents in the decision making process reasons to flow our direction.

2. When do decisions get made?

The answer to this question will drive the timing and nature of the admissions marketing process. The first answer might be that the decision is made after the acceptance letter is received and the deposit check is written. But really, this is just a final decision in a series that may lead prospective students toward our school or away from it. If a decision was made not to take the entrance exam, then that's when the decision was made. If it was made not to attend open house to find out more about the school, then that's when the decision was made. If it was to pull students out of a Catholic feeder school in 7th grade and send them to a public middle school so they will start making friends with their future public high school classmates, then that's when the decision was made. Some parents decide where their child will go to high school when they enroll them in elementary school.

Part of our marketing challenge is to determine when parents need information from us to make an intelligent decision about their child's future. If we are assuming it can all be done when the child is in eighth grade, we will be too late to influence the decisions of a large number of parents. As tuition rises faster than incomes, parents are deciding earlier and earlier whether they will be able to afford our schools. Or, to put it more precisely, whether our value proposition is compelling enough to keep moving closer. One of my board chairs used to tell me that some people don't want to find out how good our school is, because if they do it will cost them a lot of money.

Most of the people who came to our open houses were already intending to attend the school anyway. Many have been to the school a number of times. Many have already had children at the school. That's okay, because it's important to confirm their intentions and to "close the sale." But open houses are intended to give people an opportunity to come and see what they don't already know, to explore possibilities they have considered or at least haven't decided against. This means they need to be targeted at parents with younger kids. Even though they are already forming opinions about high school, they are often reluctant to come to open houses for three reasons. First, they think they are not welcome, that the open houses are intended for imminent applicants, and that they would appear over-anxious. Second, they don't know about them, when and where they are, because we don't have them on our mailing lists or presentation schedule. And third, they feel that even going to an open house will expose them to the pain of either denying their children a great education or having to make financial adjustments.

If we want to reach these parents we have to address these objections. It may involve having special open houses just for younger parents (challenge: reaching a critical mass of attendees so it doesn't look like a ghost town); finding ways to get them on our mailing lists; recruiting peers who will be ambassadors to this group, or perhaps hosting coffee hours with school personnel. It may mean hosting presentations on preparing parents for adolescence, with expert presentations by school counselors, teachers, coaches, thus exposing parents to the school and building its credibility.

Where in the parenting cycle the school commits its marketing resources is a strategic question. It requires knowing where the center of gravity is for the population the school is trying to draw, and this may require market research. One school may find an outreach to primary grade parents productive (though they will have to wait 6-8 years to know for sure), and another may find it taxes scarce marketing resources with only marginal results. But it is important to at least think about when decisions about your school are getting made, and adapt your marketing to that reality.

3. Advertising vs. word of mouth

I have seen ads for electric toothbrushes for several years now. They claim they are far more effective than regular brushing and will help me avoid decay and gum disease. I care a great deal about my teeth. Maybe not as much as my children's education. But I realize as I get older that I want them to last a while longer (my teeth I mean). I can afford an electric toothbrush. So with all the advertising, why hadn't I bought an electric toothbrush? Then a couple months ago, a friend of mine, a sociologist who knows probably about as much as I do about teeth and dental care, said he bought one and he thinks I should consider it. Then my wife said her sister, also not a dental expert, has one and recommended it to her. So now, thanks to the referral of two people who are not experts, we have electric toothbrushes. This shows me the power of word of mouth (oh, please, no pun intended). We discussed earlier a continuum, with self-promotion on the left and third-party endorsement on the right. As we moved left we increased control, but decreased credibility. As we moved right we increased credibility but lost control. If my toothbrush example is any indication, apparently credibility is a huge influencer. But that doesn't mean that the advertising played no role in my decision. If the value proposition needed more than $180 of perceived benefit to tip the scales in favor of purchasing, advertising might have added $10 or $15 of motivation, with word of mouth supplying the rest. As schools, we need to continue to invest in advertising, but we want it to be as cost-effective as possible. And we know that the real influencer is either direct experience or word of mouth. Is there anything we can do to increase word of mouth endorsements?

If I had an easy answer to that question, I would be a wealthy man. The answers are as varied as the communities that surround our schools and the concerns that the culture pushes to the top of their agenda at any given point. But we can begin answering the question by looking at what motivates people to make a referral, or not make a referral.

First, people need to be pretty excited about the product. They need to have a good experience. Even paid salespeople are less effective if they don't have a positive personal experience with the product. For a parent to suggest that friends send their children to our school, their own child's experience has to be, not just positive, but so much so that it's likely a different child would have a similar experience. Why would a parent run the risk of a friend coming to her later and saying, "Boy, were we disappointed with what we found when we sent our son there." How do we influence the satisfaction level that leads to a referral? 1) Make sure the product is as good as it can be; listen to what delights our customers and see if that can be achieved by the product without detracting from other more important features. 2) Reinforce people's positive perceptions of the product. Continue to market to them even after their children are enrolled. Make sure they hear good news about what their children and all the students are accomplishing. I wonder if that sophomore, Ryan, who came up to me after my presentation and said, "Mr. Peterson, I love this school," heard me say something that increased his appreciation of his own experience.

Second, people need to feel competent to express the message. We need to give them language, stories, statistics and a conceptual framework they can use to convey what they and their children have experienced. This is where advertising can help. The cost of and short attention span given to advertising forces us to make our message as concise and accessible as possible. The same messages can be used by third-party endorsers (as long as it captures their actual experience) to convey their enthusiasm to a peer. Communications to current parents must be strategized to include information that will support them as endorsers.

Third, there needs to be an element of self-interest. As much as it may seem so, people do not behave randomly. They expend energy and make themselves vulnerable only if they expect to see benefits in their lives. This doesn't mean they always act selfishly. Since they are transcendent beings, the benefit can be a transcendent one, accruing to the ones they love or the world they live in. But, frankly, while we sometimes go the extra mile for transcendent reasons, we generally do it for more proximate reasons. Endorsing the school isn't always easy, so people need some motivation. The motivation may be the desire to be helpful to friends, to appear knowledgeable or to confirm their own wisdom by getting others to make a similar decision. They might feel that by endorsing the school, they are making it stronger and therefore better for their own children. They might even do it for a direct, financial benefit, such as a tuition credit offered to anyone who gets another family to enroll. While such incentives are worth considering, beware of unintended consequences. These might include creating credibility issues because parents are being compensated to bring in more bodies, or creating a pressure group to accept unqualified applicants, or losing money by rewarding parents for students who were going to enroll anyway. There are more nuanced ways of rewarding parents who make the effort to attract other parents to the school.

One area of admissions recruitment where word of mouth is critical is attracting under-represented minorities. Part of the reason some ethnic groups are under-represented is that they are mistrustful of institutions that were designed by and for the power elite. An African American parent may see the school as way to give his daughter a leg up in a world where success is hard to come by, but at what cost? Will she be the only African American student in some of her classes? Will she be subjected to, if not overt racism, subtler, unintended forms that are every bit as vitiating? To overcome this built-in resistance to our efforts to diversify, current students of color must be having a good experience. If not, they will want to warn others not to make themselves vulnerable, or at least be reluctant to endorse the school. If there have been negatives, they have to be addressed and the positives celebrated enough and brought to their attention so that they see that part of the picture as well. They must be given the information to pass on, like the graduation rate of African American students, where they go to college, how they do, their stories of success. They have to see that the school will be a better experience for minorities as the numbers grow, and the numbers won't grow without their help. Every time I meet with our Parents of African American Students Association, I ask them to help us make our school a better place for minorities by making the opportunity better known to their friends and neighbors who value education. Their feedback suggests that they appreciate the assurance that the school welcomes them and isn't trying to limit the number of minorities but expand it. They understand their role in making that happen.

4. Different audiences

The foregoing discussion of parents as third-party endorsers, points out the reality that there are different groups of potential parents and students, different subcommunities within the greater community. Admission recruitment strategy requires that we disaggregate these groups, at least to some extent, to address their differing needs and perceptions. These subgroups might include families of:

- students from Catholic feeder schools
- public school students
- students from other religious or secular private schools
- minority students, like Latino, African American, Southeast Asian
- the affluent, middle class and poor

These are just a few, and each school will have its own subgroups that deserve special attention. In marketing, one size does not fit all. Each subgroup has different needs and perceptions. A message that is positively perceived by one may be negative to another. For instance, saying that we are open to all faiths may be welcoming to non-Catholics but dilute the Catholic parents' perception of the school's religious identity. It is advantageous to consider each of the major groups and how the messages are likely to be received by each. On the other hand, there is a point of diminishing returns, where the disaggregation process adds greater complexity without producing commensurate results. The point is that the differing needs of different groups should not be ignored. How much effort should be expended on differentiated approaches is an important strategic question.

Selection of students

An in-depth treatment of the selection process is not appropriate here because different schools design their process around their needs and the pool of applicants they receive. But a few general principles might be helpful to keep in mind. Who is admitted to a school is a subtle but powerful shaping force for the school's identity and mission. Each student admitted changes the school. The impact of each admission may be imperceptible, but the cumulative impact is profound. While this should remind us of the seriousness of the admissions process, it shouldn't tempt us to believe we can completely control the results. One of the ways God shapes our apostolate is in the students He sends us. We want to be intentional in selecting our student body, but at some point we have to trust that God is in charge.

1. Selecting a class

While it seems to some that we are selecting individual students who fit our mission, what we are actually doing is selecting a class which collectively fits our mission. The ideal candidate might be a Catholic, 4.0 GPA, athlete with varsity potential, but the ideal class is not 100% Catholic, nor 100% geniuses, nor superlative athletes. We need to select a group of students who will complement each other, teach each other, challenge each other and populate all the teams and activities. This is often hard for people outside the selection process to understand. They want to know why one student was selected when another who seemed to have comparable credentials was not. Even a board member or the president may not be able to understand a particular decision, because only the admissions committee can see the choice in the context of the entire class.

2. Diversity

One characteristic of a healthy class is diversity. Balance of gender (for co-ed schools), diverse ethnicities, religious diversity, even different academic aptitudes help create an environment that approximates the real world. As such, it grounds the education and fosters the ability of students to work with and understand different kinds of people. Perhaps the only kind of diversity that isn't desirable is level of receptiveness to the mission. We may take some chances on 14 year olds who haven't fully demonstrated that receptiveness yet, but the one thing that will make our schools different than the real world is the general level of motivation and commitment to becoming the *Grad at Grad*.

3. Legacy

Although it is primarily the students' attributes that we are concerned with, we are also selecting the families who shape our community. We need families who will support the mission, who will pay tuition, come to parent-teacher conferences, uphold the discipline policies, volunteer, donate and be a positive influence in the school and broader community. We want to keep families together when possible, by giving some preference to qualified siblings. We want children of alumni because such families connect us in living ways to our traditions. We want children of benefactors (and not just the wealthier ones) because they have shown a desire to support our mission beyond the minimum. Legacy is an important part of the selection process. It should augment and not displace the more important attributes that the student brings. It would be a mistake to ignore a family's past support or involvement with the school, but it would also be harmful if students drew the conclusion that their presence at the school was more a matter of what their parents do than what they do. So while legacy can be a contributing attribute, it should not be the preponderant one.

4. Who selects

The task of selecting should be entrusted to a committee of people who comprise as a group the expertise to evaluate the qualities of the applicants needed by the school. Collectively, they should bring knowledge of how to assess academic ability and special gifts like art, athletics, music, drama and demonstrated leaderhsip; how to evaluate receptiveness to the school's formational opportunities; how to gauge the context of diverse cultures; and even how to identify any special physical, emotional or psychological needs the applicant may have and whether the school can meet those needs. Once the committee is impaneled, it needs to be trusted with the authority to make the final decisions. Others, like the athletic department, development, etc., should be given the opportunity to offer input, which should be used by the committee to make the final decision. I have heard presidents say they reserve the right to make a certain number of decisions, which they feel they must do for financial, political, institutional or community reasons. I understand this, but I have always been reluctant to take any decisions entirely out of the hands of the committee, which alone has the expertise and the context needed. I prefer to give them the input I have and let them decide how my concerns stack up with the other criteria.

5. Admissions policy

It can be helpful to have a written admissions policy, approved by the board and understood and agreed to by the administrative team. This policy can be used to guide the activities of the various people involved in the process, including any administrators who have supervisory responsibility for the admissions recruiting process, the admissions director, the admissions committee, those assisting the recruitment or marketing effort, the board and any board committee that has oversight over the process. It should also be disseminated to anyone not listed above who interfaces with the school's publics to help them answer questions or concerns that may arise from the process or a particular admissions decision. The policy should incorporate the school's mission statement and explain how the admissions policy supports that mission. It should talk about the general goals for admissions (enrolling students who can succeed in the school's college preparatory program, supporting diversity, fostering intergenerational commitment, building a community of diverse gifts, etc.) and perhaps some key elements of the process (how test scores are used, teacher recommendations, student and parent statements, etc.) The policy should not be too detailed. It should not commit the school to using a specific process or a specific weighting of admissions criteria (see below), even if the committee uses a stable, well-defined process. The policy will be perceived as a promise and will be used by those with a high stake in the process to hold the school accountable (which is appropriate) and to second-guess decisions (which is not). If with a particular class or over time elements of the process need to be adjusted to accomplish the stated goals, it will be difficult to do without arousing the indignation of those who think the change affected the candidacy of their favorite applicant.

6. Admissions criteria

Internally, the school should have a set of specific admissions criteria. Though they are specific, they also need to be flexible in the sense that weakness in one criterion can be balanced by strengths in others. And criteria can be weighted differently depending on what qualities the committee is or is not seeing in the class as a whole. Finally, the criteria will evolve over time as the school observes the actual performance of students who were admitted and correlates these, formally or informally, with what the committee expected of them based on the admissions process.

7. Admissions scoring and review

In order to deal with the sheer numbers and the various perceptions of the reviewers, committees often develop scoring systems which assign weighted numbers to various applications. Generally this quantitative process is used only for narrowing the pool to the likely candidates, so that these can be given a more in-depth, qualitative review. Quantitative scores would not be used to make final admissions decisions. And there is often a process for giving one last look to those with low scores to see if there is a reason to take a deeper look. The scoring systems should be known only to the committee and administrators with responsibility for the process for two reasons. First, because those who have a high stake in the candidacy of a particular applicant may use the information to suggest that the committee didn't apply its criteria fairly, when the scoring system is not intended to be an ultimate decider. Second, some parents will try to game the system by engineering their child's application to hit the right buttons. The less known about the details of process by the general public, the better.

Welcoming/Matriculation

Once a student has been accepted, and even after they have accepted the admission, the selling must continue. For some students this can still be a fragile time. Parents may have pushed a reluctant child through the application process, hoping they would come around. Or parents may still be unsure whether they can handle the tuition and ancillary costs. Or the child may have been admitted to a competing school. The wording of the admission letter, the materials in the registration packet and the registration process itself, must reinforce the positive perception of the school and how it will benefit the student. Even during the freshman year, a difficult transition can cause students who would eventually be successful to convince their parents to let them go to another school. There is still some need to sell the product. Check in with the "customer" on how it's going, make sure he knows its features and benefits ("This English class will give you the writing skills that lead to success in college"). Make sure students and parents know that others are having a good experience ("95% of our students this year were accepted to at least 5 four-year colleges"). At this point, selling transforms into the *cura personalis* that has made our schools special. The actual experience of a caring, supportive and, yes, challenging educational environment will be the most effective means of solidifying the commitment of students and their parents.

E. Development

What I will be calling development goes by several names: for example, fundraising, advancement, or, from the donor's perspective, philanthropy. Development is the process of securing resources for an organization from people for whom at least some portion of the benefit is realizing their aspirations for the organization and its work rather than for themselves directly. In other words, as with any transaction, there is still a customer who is making an investment, and the customer is still expecting a benefit in exchange for the investment. But the benefit is, at least partially, an altruistic one. The desire for an altruistic benefit is called donative intent, and unless there is at least some donative intent in a transaction, we are talking about something other than development. Not-for-profit organizations, precisely because they are not-for-profit, can offer not only products that can be purchased, like other businesses, but an altruistic benefit as well. This gives their business model an added marketing dimension that we call development. A whole book can be written on the role of development in the Jesuit school, and there are a number of books treating the subject for non-profits in general. Our purpose in this current treatment is to highlight some key principles and ways of proceeding that incorporate development into the mission of the Jesuit school.

We tend to think of fundraising as a necessary evil. Most people, including most people in Jesuit schools, just don't like to ask people for money. More about that later, but the root of this aversion is that we often don't like to be asked for money ourselves. This leads to questioning the legitimacy of the whole process. But fundraising has been a key element of the success of Jesuit ministries since the time of Ignatius. The January, 1993, issue of *Studies in the Spirituality of Jesuits* was dedicated to a paper by Thomas C. Clancy SJ, former provincial of the New Orleans Province, entitled, "St. Ignatius as Fund-Raiser." In the article, Fr. Clancy discusses Ignatius' impatience with people who thought that God's servants should not be engaged in the business of the world. "Do not ever," Ignatius says, alluding to Jesus' admonition in Luke 16:8-9, "permit the children of this world to show greater care and solicitude for the things of time than you show for those of eternity." Clancy says that Ignatius encouraged the early Jesuits to "emulate the energy and enterprise of merchants" who were generally despised by nobles and churchmen, "rather than indulging in long prayers and senseless mortifications." Fr. Clancy points out that Ignatius' regard for fundraising developed later in life, when he saw the evangelical effectiveness of the growing education apostolate, as well as its awesome resource requirements.

Fr. Clancy offers five principles of fundraising drawn from the example and writings of Ignatius:

- Believe in the value of the work, in this case the schools.
- Let your light shine.
- Know your clients and be patient with their moral failings.
- Manage your assets carefully.
- Honor your friends and show them your gratitude.

We will not delve into these principles, but I encourage anyone in a Jesuit school who has fundraising responsibilities to read Fr. Clancy's reflections, which can be obtained from *Studies in the Spirituality of Jesuits* in St. Louis.

Development is not a necessary evil. It is a fundamental part of who we are, just as it was for Ignatius and the early Jesuits. But there are right ways and wrong ways to do development, both in terms of fundraising results and in terms of how it supports the overall mission. We will take a look at some basic principles of successful development, but before we do, let's take a look at how development fits into the four models of the Jesuit school, starting with the business model, then looking at the community model, pedagogical model and finally the apostolic model.

Business Model: Development as Marketing

Some people believe development lives only in the business model. While this is a narrow view, it is true that development lives primarily there. It is one of the two main ways we market ourselves, with the other being admissions recruitment, discussed above. We have defined marketing as the process of connecting products and customers, which involves identifying what people need (research); producing it (product); presenting it to them in a compelling way (promotion); and asking them for their commitment to purchase it (sales). Development incorporates all these functions.

Development serves as a conduit of the perceptions and desires of customers back to those who shape the product. This often constitutes, either formally or informally, the school's primary research function. An overly "siloed" view of development can lead teachers and program administrators to cut themselves off from hearing what development officers are learning from their customers, and for development officers to take no responsibility for the product. Businesses have found that a gulf between manufacturing and sales threatens their survival. But such a gulf still tends to develop in for-profit businesses, and for much the same reason it happens in schools: hearing what customers actually want can be disruptive to our paradigms. A healthy product feedback loop requires both open-minded educators who desire helpful feedback and sensitive development officers who don't lose confidence in the product whenever they hear a negative perception from a prospective donor. Both should develop ways to gather and evaluate data from supporters of the school.

In one area, often without knowing it, the development office has a direct responsibility for the product (defined as the characteristics fostered in the graduate by the school's mission). I like to point out to newly hired development officers that our students will learn from their teachers what our mission is for only four years. The rest of their lives, they will hear it from the development office. How are our alumni magazine, our website or our alumni events continuing to foster the characteristics of the *Grad at Grad*?

Promotion is a large part of the development task. Ignatius urged his companions in far flung parts of the world to write letters that shed a positive light on their work so that he could share them with benefactors in Europe. The development office has a major responsibility for bringing the school's accomplishments and stories to light and sharing them with the school's publics. Cooperation from others in the school is important, because it is difficult to unearth these stories unless those who are witnessing them and making them assist in the process. Unfortunately some of the most remarkable educators are the poorest at capturing their results in ways that can be shared with others. They are immersed in their work and not thinking about how it could be conveyed to others. It gets expensive to pay people to track down the stories, so methods must be developed that create a flow of information to the development office so that it can broadcast the school's accomplishments, thereby fostering understanding and favorable perceptions of the school by its publics.

Along with promotion, sales (or in the development context, solicitation) is universally identified as a marketing function. The development office must do more than produce great publications and an attractive website. People generally do things, especially altruistic things, because they are asked. A lot of influences may go into producing an act of generosity, but asking for a gift is what finally kicks the pebble from under the wheel. More on this later.

It is possible for a school to have a successful business model without development. There are after all many for-profit schools that don't rely on any donative intent for their revenues. But I don't think it is possible for a Jesuit school. From the beginning, Jesuit schools have seen themselves as having a special responsibility to provide opportunities to the poor and middle class. This mission imperative doesn't exist outside the business model; it has become an integral part of it. Our basic value proposition doesn't work for the poor, because they don't have enough money to pay for the benefits they would receive. Someone else also needs to benefit from their having access to this education. Fortunately there are affluent people who feel a need to provide opportunities to the poor but can't do it directly themselves. They are happy to purchase from us the ability to provide those opportunities. This sounds a little theoretical, but it isn't something I came up with abstractly. I learned this early in my career from donors themselves. Some of the most generous donors, after making what I considered a "stretch gift," would thank me for giving them the opportunity to make a donation. I was surprised, but I eventually realized why they would say that. Our school was helping them meet what was an important need for them. At the risk of over-simplifying, development is the process of marketing to potential benefactors our ability to provide altruistic benefits, and it is a key part of the Jesuit school's business model.

Community Model: Development as Community-building

I recall a letter my predecessor and mentor Fr. Dan Weber SJ sent to parents at the beginning of an annual fund drive. In it he described going out on his early morning jog around campus and having his eye caught by the glint of sunlight off something in the middle of one of the fields. He jogged over to discover something metallic jutting out of the grass, and as he worked it loose, he realized that it was some sort of chest. He opened it and discovered it was full of gold coins and what were obviously precious jewels. Just looking at the load he knew it was worth a lot of money, probably enough to endow the school for all time. His heart rose as he realized he would never have to do any more fundraising. He sat on the ground as the sun rose and began to fantasize about the prospect. No more awkward lunches asking for pledges, no more wearying auction set-ups and procurement committees, no more student chocolate sales. He imagined what that would be like, and the picture that emerged surprised him. No need for volunteers, no need for fundraising events, parents just dropping their kids off at the school, alumni not feeling responsibility for their *alma mater*. Gradually his joy turned to sorrow as he realized that the treasure he had found would mean the end of the vibrant community that had grown up around the need to raise extra funds. He looked around to make sure no one was looking, then quickly re-buried the chest. As he closed his letter, he told the parents that he would never reveal where that treasure was because it would destroy the greater treasure found in the generosity, sacrifice and love of the people who care about the school.

Community is at the core of who we are as Jesuit schools. Community provides the safe, nurturing environment that leads to spiritual, emotional and intellectual growth. It is where students experience love and where they learn to express love. Our schools would be far less without community and our community would be far less without the need to reach out to people for resources. James S. Coleman, renowned sociologist at the University of Chicago, and later president of the American Sociological Association, published studies in the 1980's, demonstrating the superior performance of Catholic schools, especially for students of disadvantaged minorities. He argued that one reason for their superior results was the presence of what he called social capital. Social capital is the network of adults forming a community around the school like an extended family.

When we recruit parents to serve on the annual giving committee, when we bring donors on tours of the school, when parents from different parts of the city meet the parents of their children's friends at the auction, when we acknowledge donors by placing their names where students can see who is supporting their education, we are not only raising financial capital so vital to our mission, but social capital as well. Knowing this should help us think about how we do development in ways that don't pit the business model against the community model, but strengthen both.

Pedagogical Model: Development as Pedagogy

Development can reinforce the education process as well, and not just by providing the necessary resources. While we tend to think of student fundraisers as time taken away from academics, it doesn't need to be that way. To be done effectively, fundraising requires the development of skills, including oral and written communication, organization, graphic design and psychology. Conversely, ineffective fundraising requires none of those skills. Unfortunately, I think the tendency, when it comes to student fundraisers, is to opt for the latter on the theory that the less energy spent on student fundraisers the better. But it might make sense to move in just the opposite direction. It reminds me of the way my own children chose their books from the summer reading list. They would always choose the shortest books, even if they knew that a longer book would engage them more. The idea was to detract as little as possible from the major objective of summer, which is to have fun. I encouraged them instead to do an effort/ enjoyment analysis. If book A would take 15 hours to read and on a scale of 1-10 you got 0 enjoyment out of it, wouldn't you be better off reading book B which would take 20 hours but you got a 5 on enjoyment. 5 isn't as high as going to the beach, but at least by investing 5 more hours, you were having some enjoyment from the time it takes to the read the book. My analytic approach sounded as nerdy to them as it probably sounds to you. I could never convince them, though with maturity they eventually figured out for themselves that avoiding effort means forgoing the pay-offs as well.

Similarly, if a school takes a student fundraiser, does more design and preparation work and sets aside more classroom time, it may be able to produce an activity that has substantial educational benefit. We did this with a jogathon-format fundraiser in which students solicited sponsors for making so many laps around our track. The event was efficient to run but had very little educational value. Then an enterprising special events coordinator transformed it into the "Fitness Fun." Instead of walking around a track, the students participated in about 30 possible different fitness activities designed by the PE Department. One of them was fencing, which the local fencing association was only too happy to provide an instructor for. One of the kids who participated got so turned on to fencing she eventually became a nationally ranked competitor. When Fitness Fun had run its course, it was converted to Community Caring Day, where the students participated in one of about 30 different community organizations. One student did some computer programming for Habitat for Humanity and ended up founding a chapter at the school which became the largest in the state. These were fundraisers that actually enriched the school's pedagogy. Fundraising efforts could be used to teach persuasive writing or oral presentation, do psychology experiments (do two versions of a request letter and see which gets the better response) and so on. Not only does this produce direct educational benefit, but it excites donors and raises more money, which provides more resources to the education program. Yes, it's more work, and that's generally why we don't do it. But the point is that fundraising and learning aren't mutually exclusive. It depends on how we do it.

The Apostolic Model: Development as Ministry

One of the things that impressed Alexis de Tocqueville when he traveled through this country in the 1830's and wrote Democracy in America was the nation's reliance on voluntary associations and voluntary effort for the common good. In our culture it is unlikely that any of our graduates will exercise meaningful civic leadership without both engaging in philanthropy and encouraging the philanthropy of others. This is why I am always struck when parents say they don't want their children asking for money. It is comparable to saying they don't want their children voting, or serving on a jury or paying taxes. These are all indispensable to the social order and quality of life we enjoy as Americans. Parents sometimes don't see the connection between what their children enjoy and the substantial generosity that makes it possible. Nor the connection with a school mission that centers on fostering generosity in its students.

Development connects with the school's apostolic model on three levels. First our reliance on philanthropy gives students an opportunity to support their own education and the education of their classmates. They lack the personal wealth to be philanthropists in the traditional sense but they can help by selling coupon books or soliciting pledges for a read-a-thon. Second, it can help them appreciate just what it takes to produce the education they are receiving. This will hopefully encourage them to be more generous as graduates to a variety of causes, including their own school. I liked the theme one of my colleagues used for the alumni appeal. She told the story of a traveler who was lost and happened on a cabin that had a note inviting lost travelers to come in for shelter, welcoming them to build a fire and warm themselves. The note simply asked that in return the traveler, before moving on, take the ax and re-stock the woodpile for the next needy pilgrim. The minimum our alumni can do is to use some of their resources which the school helped them earn to re-stock the woodpile for the next generation. Third, our development efforts foster the spirit of generosity in the community around us. I remember a benefactor who funded a computer lab for our school. I asked him why he was so generous. He said that after someone talked him into making his first major gift he went to bed that night, woke up the next morning turned to his wife and said, "I don't feel any poorer, do you?" She said that in fact she felt a little richer. Thanks to whoever that first development person was, we had a new computer lab and there were two happier people in the world.

There is another dimension to development and the apostolic model. I alluded above to the fact that students receive the school's message for four years from the teachers and the rest of their life from the development office. I think we're missing a tremendous opportunity if we don't look at every one of our communications with our alumni in terms of how they do or don't reinforce the Gospel message. This can, and should, be done in subtle ways, not because we aren't proud of the message, but because people don't like to be preached at. I like the famous line of St. Francis of Assisi, "Preach the Gospel at all times. If necessary, use words." Support of the apostolic model in our development outreach can come from the use of quotes on thank you letters or cards, stories about students and alums, sending Christmas card which, though sensitive to our non-Christians friends, don't just say "Happy Holidays." This means that development officers have to know, not just how to raise money, but how to convey the school's faith-based mission in a compelling way. To do this, they may have to enlist the help of other school personnel more skilled in the nuances of the Catholic faith and Jesuit spirituality.

The Development Pyramid

I don't know who first developed the concept of the "giving pyramid." It might have been Hank Russo, founder of the Fundraising School, which used to offer seminars in development around the country and eventually found a home at the University of Indiana. I know it was a key part of Hank's course. The basic premise is that there are four tiers to a full development program. The bottom tier is broad because it involves many people. Each successive tier is smaller in the number of people involved, but not necessarily in dollars raised. Figure 2 shows what the pyramid looks like:

Figure 2: Development Pyramid

Special events comprises all those activities in which donative intent plays a relatively minor role in the participant's motivation to give money to the school. They include auctions, 10K runs, bake sales, sales of discount coupon books, craft fairs, spaghetti dinners, bingo, etc. Special events cast a broad net. They attract people who are strongly committed to the school, along with people who have a favorable view of the school but would not normally donate to it and even people who may not care at all that the school is sponsoring the event. Special events are basically transactional in nature and the participants are simply customers in a retail setting. While some may buy something, like a football signed by this year's team, merely to support the school, special events are aimed at the people who want something tangible for their money. Although Jesuit school development operations have generally decreased their reliance on special events, they are still attractive because they bring in "new money." Support comes from people outside the school community which often feels it is asked too much. They also are attractive to volunteers who generally feel less vulnerable selling something to someone than simply asking them to support the school. What they often don't acknowledge is that they will spend substantially more time, energy and money for each dollar raised than they would simply asking for donations. So when the school needs to raise more money and the development committee or the parent's club suggests putting on a marathon or a raffle, the answer should generally be no.

But special events do have a place in the development portfolio. It's just not, as one might expect, for raising money, which they don't do very well. What they do do well is build community, attract new donors and put people in touch with the school. When someone comes to an auction, they meet students and people who are enthusiastic about the school, they hear school leaders and they see a brief video about the school. They may look around and decide that this would be a nice community to be part of. The strategy is to design special events to play to these strengths. They need to accomplish four things: 1) be a good experience of the school community, which means meeting school personnel, students, parents and feeling welcomed by them into the community; 2) tell people about the mission and accomplishments of the school by pushing out what advertisers call interstitial messages, pictures, stories, facts about the school which are just part of the flow of the event, rather than something people feel subjected to; 3) capture information about those who came. By having them register or doing a door prize for those who sign in, use events to create a mailing list for follow-up to see if they have further interest. Auctions are great this way because you end up learning the attendees' contact information, who their friends are, the people who might invite them deeper into the community, and even a sense of their wealth by what they purchase; and 4) identify who in this broad net might be ready for the next level of the pyramid. These four outcomes are a crucial foundation for the development pyramid, and without them special events fundraising is generally not worth the effort it requires.

As we move up the pyramid to **annual giving** the breadth of participation narrows. While special events are able to attract people whether they care about the school or not, annual giving participants have to care enough to donate money without expectation of goods or services in return, other than helping the school get better. Certainly there may be less altruistic motives in the mix, like having their name appear in the annual report, or getting invited to a donor recognition event, but even these are attractive only because of the donor's regard for the school. If the special events participant is like the customer of a normal business, the annual giving participant is analogous to a shareholder. They are not looking for a product, in the normal sense, but for a stronger organization.

While most annual giving participants also participate in special events, and indeed need such events to stay bonded to the school, the converse is not true. Most special events participants are not annual givers. Annual giving prospects are a subset, and once you know who they are, cultivating their giving is a much more focused and cost-effective activity. The key strategy with annual giving prospects is to understand their motivation for giving and make sure the appeal speaks to that motivation. Like special events, the annual giving program should also be identifying, learning about and cultivating participants for the next level of the pyramid.

At the **major gifts** level, again the pyramid narrows. If special events participants are customers and annual givers are shareholders, major givers are investors who have taken a significant stake in the school. They have such high regard for the school and what it accomplishes that they see its mission as a significant part of their own and therefore a worthy recipient of a significant portion of their assets. Not all annual givers will become major givers. Some don't have the money, although they may give enough that in proportion to their own resources they have aligned their personal mission with the school's. Among those who have the money to be major investors, some will be satisfied to remain shareholders. Unlike the couple I mentioned earlier, they haven't seen the transcendent benefits of major giving, or perhaps they are more interested in other charities. But those who can and will deserve a lot of attention. It is reasonable to spend time, effort and money to learn about them—what their interests are, what their capacity is, who might be influential in asking them—to spend time building a relationship and to prepare carefully for making the ask. I once flew from Seattle to New York to go to lunch with a major donor. He was called out of town on an emergency and couldn't make the appointment. I felt bad about spending all that money on airfare and a hotel, but in this case it was worth it because my willingness to take that chance communicated in a way nothing else could how important he was to the school. It always strikes me as odd how reluctant I am to spend 5 times as much effort to prepare for a call that could result in 10 times as big a gift. I have a friend who sells airplanes for Boeing. He doesn't sell very many and he puts in a horrendous amount of work for sales that never happen. But when he does make a sale it feeds a lot of people. He has adjusted to that rhythm, but I think most of us would find that unbearably nerve-wracking. This is the adjustment we must make to have a productive major gifts component to our development program. In most schools major gifts are secured during capital campaigns, for dramatic, one-time projects. This works well, but has the disadvantage that the timing of such projects doesn't always match up with the donor's timing. For this reason, many colleges and some secondary schools have developed major gifts programs that continue to identify and secure gifts continuously, whether the school is in a campaign or not.

Planned giving, at the tip of the pyramid, is the donation of assets as part of the disposition of one's estate. When we reach the tip of the pyramid, it's not enough to use the business analogies we used for the other three levels, like customer, shareholder and major investor. At this level, the school becomes an heir of the donor, along with any children or grandchildren they may have. Again, the pyramid narrows. Not all major givers will come to see the school as an heir, although it can also be said that some who were not major givers will. In fact, I would say that over 50% of the planned gifts I have experienced are from people who were not prior major givers to the school. What that points out, however, is not that major givers are not likely prospects for planned gifts, but that the development operations I have supervised have not sustained an active planned giving program which deliberately cultivated donors from lower in the pyramid to consider gifts from their estate. This is generally because planned gifts, also called deferred gifts, may not be realized by the school for decades after they are secured. I found it difficult when the school hit bumps in the road not to redirect scarce resources toward the more immediate results realized at the other levels of the pyramid. This is unfortunate, because the rewards of a sustained planned giving program are as proportionately substantial as each of the other levels is to the one below it.

The development pyramid points out that the development strategy should always be pushing up the pyramid. More and more time for development staff and the president should be focused toward the top. Clear cultivation pathways should be in place to encourage constituents to move their giving involvement up the pyramid. And the school's strategic planning should identify projects and needs that create attractive giving opportunities at the upper end.

Getting results

Perhaps no other aspect of running a school gives as high an emphasis on getting results as development. It is painfully obvious when the annual giving appeal falls short, or a capital campaign is failing to achieve its goal. The whole school feels the impact and the broader community sees development success as a gauge of the school's vitality in general. In the classroom, it's not always clear what the results are, and even if we feel a teacher isn't the most effective in leading students to mastery of the subject, they may be contributing in other ways to the educational process. Our athletic programs are similar to development in terms of the public perceptions of wins and losses. Despite pressure from the competitiveness of fans, few Jesuit schools would terminate a coach for not winning championships if he is creating a good experience for the students. Even admissions recruitment, on whose results the school depends so heavily, can be judged by multiple yardsticks, including the quality of students and how well-oriented they are as they enter the school. Admissions recruitment results are also heavily influenced by other areas of the school, like those that impact retention and those which decide whether programs that reach a particular group, like diversity or learning resources, will be available for a particular segment of applicants.

But development must produce results and no other contribution to the mission will make up for a lack of success in terms of dollars raised. We need to be frank about this reality of the development function, but we also need to be careful not to let the concern for results disrupt the intimate relationship development has with mission. As we discussed earlier, development should support not only the school's business model, but its community model, educational model and apostolic model as well. The school's leadership must pay close attention to the fundraising results of the development function, and also to how it integrates with the rest of the school. When this balance is lost, the school will either acquiesce to substandard fundraising performance or, more likely, will judge the development staff only by how well they feed the school's insatiable appetite for resources. Symptoms that the latter is happening would be a feeling of separation between the development staff and the rest of the school. That can be deadly for both mission integration and financial results.

So how can the school leadership manage for both fundraising results and mission integration? This is a vast topic, and a complete treatment is beyond the scope of this present work. But I would like to highlight a few key principles that will help the school leadership get both financial and mission results from its development efforts.

The principles that follow apply the marketing model discussed earlier to development. Again, marketing is the process of connecting products and customers. It involves identifying what people need (Research); producing it (Product); presenting it to them in a compelling way (Promotion); and asking them for their commitment to purchase it (Sales). Adapting the model to development, research becomes prospect research, essentially finding out who your donors and potential donors are and what they desire; product becomes the project or reason you are raising the money, which in development parlance is called the *case*; promotion consists of materials and events that *cultivate* the interest of your donors; and sales is the *asking* process.

1. Case

Case is a term of art in development which means simply the compelling reasons the community should support a particular project, need or set of needs identified by a non-profit organization.

Once the case is defined, it can then be put into a case statement, a document that makes the case for the support the school is seeking. While the formal case statement is more of an internal document to maintain focus among staff and volunteers, it is translated into brochures, graphic presentations, slide shows, videos, presentations and other promotional materials that communicate the case for support to various potential donors.

Case statements tend to be articulated from the organization's point of view. Rather than addressing the needs of the donor, they usually give the reasons why an organization feels it needs something. For instance, the case may talk about the need for a new library so the school can take advantage of new information technologies. Internally, we may feel palpably how the lack of up-to-date facilities is holding back our ability to bring the capable students in our school to the frontiers of knowledge. Our experience of the missing ingredient motivates us to do something about it. We often assume that potential donors will be just as motivated as we are when the situation is described to them.

The term *case* is development's analog for the term value proposition, discussed earlier, and it should have the same functional properties. A *value proposition* is how an organization demonstrates to a potential customer that the benefits of its product to them will exceed the costs to them. It is not enough to make a case for why we want to do something. We need to take the next step and demonstrate why our *donors* would want to do it. We must not only describe the features of the project, we must describe its *benefits*. And we must challenge ourselves to describe the benefits, not just to the school, but to the donors. For example, the new library will accommodate remarkable new technologies. We might think that all we have to do is describe those technologies and assume people will be impressed and motivated to give. While some people have an innate faith in technology as the path to the future, many have seen or personally experienced technology installations which failed to do anything but temporarily dazzle and ultimately just confuse people. We need to demonstrate how the new technology will translate into better learning. If technology is a feature, better learning is a potential benefit. But we need to go an additional step and demonstrate why it is a benefit to the donor whose support is being sought. The new technology will prepare their children to succeed in a world where those who master technology tools get ahead and those who do not fall behind. For donors who have no children the technology will prepare the generation who will pay their Social Security and more importantly, carry forward the values they hold dear. This example points out the challenge of articulating benefits to the donor, because desired benefits will vary not only from group to group, but from donor to donor. We must make the effort to see and make a case for the project from the donor's perspective, both in documents that have general distribution and in our presentations to individual donors.

To be able to make the case from the donor's perspective requires an understanding of who our donors are and what they desire. We learn this in our prospect research, which will be discussed below in the section on the prospect pipeline. The knowledge we gain about our prospects should be used to shape the case, and to some extent the project itself. If we are asking individuals to give millions of dollars to bring a new library into being, it is only fair, and strategic, that they have the opportunity to give input on what it will be like. This is not only good marketing but good stewardship as well. The best way to do this is to involve potential donors in the process of building the case.

The *case statement* is a common element of a capital campaign, but we need to articulate a case for any fundraising appeal we do. What is the case for annual giving, for our auction, for student fundraisers? If we can articulate to ourselves how the success of the appeal will benefit not only the school but the participants, we have begun the process of providing compelling motivation for donor support.

2. Asking

At the core of development is asking. There was an ad for a stock brokerage a few years back in which British actor John Houseman would intone, "We make money the old fashioned way. We earn it!" A development version of this might be, "We make money the old fashioned way. We ask for it!" In the end there is really no other way to secure donations to the school. We can dress it up, sugar coat it and do it obliquely, but few donors will make meaningful gifts unless they are asked. Asking is the selling stage of the marketing model applied to development. It is where we help people make a decision to invest based on all the good information they received during the promotional (or cultivation) phase. The methods used in other sales settings—features and benefits, trial closes, handling objections (feel-felt-found), etc—can be used effectively in the solicitation of donor gifts.

But there is also a particularly Ignatian element to gift solicitation in a Jesuit school. We discussed earlier, in both our apostolic and educational model, how important it is to acknowledge the freedom that God has given each of us. As educators, we may be tempted to compel students to believe or to have an insight, but this wouldn't be consistent with how God created us. Anytime we try to bypass human freedom to compel behavior, the best we can hope for is short-term results. This is true in our work with donors. At times, especially after hearing a few no's from affluent people, we may want to somehow compel donors to give. We may want to use guilt, or extreme social pressure, or threaten to charge them more tuition, because we are convinced that they have the means and responsibility to support the school's needs. Whenever you start to experience this feeling, take a deep breath and don't go there, because it leads to several bad outcomes. First of all, people don't respond well to this. If they do, resentment will also be mixed in and at the first opportunity they will discontinue their giving. Second, it's at cross-purposes to our mission. God gave each of us free will, and seems adamant about not taking it back. Sometimes I wish God would just make me a good person, but he chooses instead to give me a lot of space to make my own decisions. If God treats me this way, who am I do treat others differently? Finally, riding roughshod over other people's freedom means that we are taking responsibility for their decisions. If you want to hate development work, that is a sure path. If we think it is up to us to manipulate people into making the "right" decision, we are bound to feel every no, or every lower-than-expected gift, as a failure. We will harbor bitterness toward the donors. Few of us can last long with such an accumulating sense of failure and bitterness.

When asking for a donation, it's important to ask for a specific gift amount. This may seem to contradict what I have just said. It may seem to put pressure on donors and prevent them from choosing their own gift level. This doesn't necessarily follow. In the asking stage of development, we are trying to help someone make a decision. If we simply say, "Give whatever you can," the donor not only has to decide whether to give, but fish out of an endless pool of possibilities the gift amount that would make a meaningful contribution to the success of the project. For most people this leads to acute indecision, which benefits neither them nor us. I remember working with a senior Weyerhaeuser Co. executive on a fundraising campaign for a building to be named for a revered colleague. Joe did a great job contacting other executives who had worked with Bernie over the years, but I couldn't convince him to ask for specific gifts. He said he didn't want to insult them by telling them what to do. I said he would be asking, not telling, but it just didn't feel right for him. I remember how mad he was at one of the donors who sent in a check far below what he was hoping for. I said, "Joe, that's not fair. He had no idea what you were looking for and now you're mad at him for not figuring it out."

Asking for a specific amount does put some pressure on a donor, but it doesn't take away her freedom, particularly if you ask in a respectful manner. I was once taught a way of phrasing an "ask" that was attributed to the great philanthropist, John D. Rockefeller. It goes like this:

> We would like you to consider a gift of $100,000, which would provide critical momentum leading to the success of the project. It may be that you were considering giving more to the project, in which case we will be doubly grateful. On the other hand, you may feel you are not able to give that much. Whatever you give, after having considered the importance of the project and your own circumstances, will be gratefully accepted.

In this approach we are asking the donor to consider an amount, and making it amply clear that the decision is theirs and whatever they ultimately decide will be appreciated. I believe asking for what you need respects people's freedom more than asking them to guess what you need. But we also have a responsibility to size our request to what they might reasonably be able to do, and this requires donor research. Donor research relies on past giving, information about their interaction with the school and publicly available information on their wealth to suggest a range of gift capacity. The gift projections that result are imprecise because there isn't much public information about people's wealth. Even if we knew their financial circumstances, we have no way of predicting their willingness to give, either in general or to our specific cause. But the research can get us close enough that we neither insult the donor and shortchange the project by asking too little, nor discourage the donor by asking too much.

Not all asks are alike. The Pareto Principle, or 80-20 rule, applies here as it does in so many areas: 80% of the dollars raised will come from 20% of the donors. In some contexts, 90-10 will be more the case. This means that large gifts will determine the success of the fundraising effort. It behooves us therefore to spend a proportionate amount of our time and energy identifying, cultivating and asking for those larger gifts. In this sense, fundraising is not a democratic process. It is true that in the eyes of God, the widow's mite is more pleasing than the donation made from one's excess. As Ignatian fundraisers, we hold any gifts, even those of the smallest amount, in gratitude. But we do a great injustice if we spend just as much time and effort soliciting gifts from people of limited means as we do from people of great means. We wouldn't think of taxing people with lower incomes the same as people with much higher incomes. We must ask people to take responsibility for the good works we do in proportion to their ability. Unlike taxation, fundraising is voluntary, so it follows that we must put greater effort into making a case and providing incentives to donors of greater capacity. In this light, development can seem elitist and contradictory to the democratic spirit of our schools. But given that the results of our development efforts provide critical resources to the poor, this concern about elitism is misplaced. The leadership of the school must assure that its development efforts are weighted toward the larger gifts that lead to success. We looked at the development pyramid earlier, which showed that as the school moves from special events, to annual giving, to major gifts and planned gifts, the donors become fewer and the dollars become greater. As we move up the pyramid, how we do our asking also has to change. The greater the ask, the higher its quality must be. This concept can also be expressed as a pyramid, as in Figure 3 below, showing different levels, and therefore kinds, of asking:

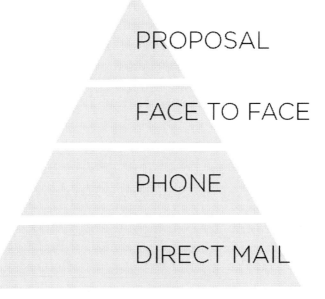

Figure 3: the Asking Pyramid

As the development program focuses on larger gifts, its energy should also be shifting up this asking pyramid, from less personal to more personal. If development is heavily reliant on direct mail, it will receive many smaller gifts. Even people who have great capacity and potentially high interest in the school will respond with small gifts. Direct mail simply can't provide the intellectual or emotional motivation to make a major commitment. The method of asking itself communicates to the donor that the cause doesn't merit much attention. If a development staff says it wants to increase results by reaching for higher gifts, but doesn't make many face-to-face asks, this is a case of cognitive dissonance. The school leadership needs to restructure the development effort to shift activities upward toward the top of the asking pyramid.

How will asking look different as we move up the pyramid? In general the asks will be more personal and targeted and will involve more preparation. In a word, the development program will become more donor-centric. Being donor-centric requires us to identify the *Four Rights* of asking: right person, right amount, right time and right purpose.

The **Right person** refers to who will make the ask. The adage is that people give to people, not organizations. If that's true, and it usually is, then an important ask should be done by someone whom the prospective donor is more likely to respond to. In some cases it may be a volunteer, a peer of the donor, whose good estimation the donor values. Her influence with the donor can be canceled out, however, by a lack of involvement or passion for the cause, or an unwillingness to do what it takes to make a good ask. Board members and volunteer leaders are critical to a campaign's success, especially if they have influence, and the willingness to ask, because they already have the involvement. More on this in the section on volunteers vs. staff, below. The right person in many cases will be the president of the school. Donors of truly significant gifts need to have confidence in the school's leadership before making a major investment. For them the president, as much as anyone, personifies the school. Reorienting the school's development program up the asking pyramid will require the president to be more involved in the asking process. The right person might also be the principal or a beloved Jesuit, teacher or coach. Many major asks will be made by development officers, who have cultivated strong relationships with donors and have the involvement and the training to make a quality ask. For a big gift, it is worth strategizing the best person or persons to make the ask.

The **Right Amount**. If you've experienced the difference between having and lacking confidence in the gift range you're seeking, you know the importance of the right ask amount. If you ask too much, you can inhibit the donor from finalizing a pledge and slow down the process. If you ask too little, you may forgo the higher amount she was willing to give and even insult her in the process. Having a reasonable but challenging ask amount is helpful to the donor, but it's even more helpful for the asker. A more relaxed and confident asker helps the donor to be less anxious and more open to the request.

There is no crystal ball that tells how much someone can give. Despite the internet and the vast amount of public information available, it is difficult to know someone's net worth. You may have information on the real estate they own, but not know their mortgage balances. You may be able to find information on stock ownership from a particular company's proxy statement, but you won't know what other types of stock a donor may own. The most valuable data is what they have already given to your school and to other charities. It's hard to get more than spotty data on previous giving to other organizations. Jesuit high schools can't afford the extensive research departments of universities and other large non-profits. Even if we could, it is impossible to know what is going on in the financial lives of our donors on any given day.

Still, some research is better than none. The more we raise the confidence level of the ask, the more likely we are to get a positive response. This research can come from several sources. First, from publicly available data. Second, from the observations of peers in prospect evaluation sessions. Third is the donor's giving record, media file and contact records in our own files, which I have been guilty of overlooking much to my chagrin. The fourth is my favorite and in many ways the most reliable: from the donors themselves. Donors are often willing to share information about themselves with people they trust, and it wouldn't be unusual, if they have a relationship that makes them a *bona fide* prospective major donor, for them to have that trust in us. If the relationship is sound, questions like, What are your philanthropic priorities? What's the biggest gift you've ever given? What do you see as the biggest gift you will give in your lifetime? Do you have appreciated stock that could be used for gifting? are not inappropriate. They may help the donor communicate her desires to you and provide invaluable information in crafting an attractive proposal. A big ask will generally take the form of a series of asks. I have often brought up gift amounts early in the cultivation process to gauge the reaction of the donor before presenting a specific proposal. Using methods like this, it is possible to determine a specific gift request and be comfortable making it.

The **Right Time**. Sometimes a donor's timing and the school's timing match up well. Just as we're beginning a capital campaign, the donor has sold his business and has cash and tax liabilities. But more often, our needs and the donor's readiness will be out of phase. Their market may be slumping, or they may be going through a divorce or have terrific investment opportunities that are tying up their cash. Part of the role of research is to strategize for each major donor the best timing for an ask. But a more successful strategy is to structure the major gifts program to take advantage of the timing issues of various donors. One of the disadvantages of capital campaigns is that they need to be compressed and urgent. At any given time there are many worthy institutions looking for donations, and a campaign asks the community to focus on our school's significant needs or opportunities. But we can only hold that focus for a brief time. If that time doesn't match up with a donor's readiness, the campaign will not benefit from their philanthropy. That's why schools should have ongoing major gifts programs, punctuated by campaigns. The campaigns will not only create a sense of urgency, but will identify the desires, capacity and timing of donors who can be followed up with later, when the time is best for them. A donor-centric—as opposed to a needs-centric—development program will track donors' timing and interests based on their feedback, and identify school needs that will match their timing and interests.

The **Right Purpose**. A donor-centric development program will also learn and track what donors are interested in. While the school will always have to push out its needs to its support community, the school should better understand the needs and desires of donors, at least at the top of the pyramid, and gear its requests to those needs.

A donor who loves the school but cares more about academics than sports might give us $100,000 toward a new gym, but $1 million for a new library. Maybe we don't need a library. But at least we can acknowledge her interests by asking her to fund the health classrooms and fitness center used by the PE department, and then retain the information about her interest in the library for when that project comes on stream. On the other hand, the school has to be careful that it isn't just generating programs to attract donors. Just because a donor loves horses doesn't mean the school should start an equestrian program. But the school should give serious thought to how its real needs match up with the interests of major donors and be strategic about presenting projects in ways that tap into the donors' desires.

As the development program shifts toward the top of the pyramid, it becomes more donor-centric. This is consistent with what must happen in any business model. We have to know who our customers are, what their desires are, how our product meets those desires, how it may need to be adjusted if it doesn't, and how we can show that the customer's own desires will be satisfied by investing in our product. This is another example of bringing them in by their door. It not only increases the effectiveness of our development efforts, but shows respect for the people who support us. The donor-centric development approach unites the school's business model with its apostolic, pedagogical and community models, because it invites benefactors to be part of the school in a way that makes a difference in the school's life as well as their own. For it to work, however, all school personnel have to see a picture bigger than the model they normally work in. The development office must develop a deeper understanding of school needs and programs. And non-development personnel must be able to view their needs from the donor's perspective. I remember completing a campaign feasibility study once and one of my administrative colleagues was upset with the results. The donors responding to the study had not prioritized the projects slated for his area. "That's not fair," he said. "We've planned for these facilities and it's our turn. Why should they be able to tell us what we can build?" I couldn't resist a little sarcasm and responded, "If you have the money to build those facilities, by all means go ahead. Otherwise, I think we'd better work with the donors on this." Five years later, we had finished all the projects we had planned in his area.

One last observation before we leave the topic of asking. Before sitting down to start writing this section, I decided I needed to brew myself some tea. Then I decided I needed to change my shirt and put on my slippers. I even decided to call my brother-in-law to talk about an upcoming hike. Finally, I realized I was doing all these things to put off getting to the work of writing. I love to write, but I really don't know how things will tumble out of my head. Maybe they will be brilliant, but maybe they will be stupid. If I never get started, I can avoid writing something stupid. Many will recognize these as the symptoms of writer's block. Once you start writing, you're fine. But if you aren't careful, you can put off writing forever.

Something similar happens in asking for money. It's known as *call reluctance*. When you pick up the phone to initiate an ask, one of two things can happen. The conversation can lead to a decision by the donor to support the school. More times than not the conversation will lead to indecision, a lesser gift than what you hoped for, or even an outright no. Most of us aren't good at dealing with those latter three outcomes, because they make us feel like a failure. So we procrastinate. We think of a hundred reasons why we shouldn't call now. We can even use the *four rights* discussed above, saying we're just not sure we're the right person, or that we know the right amount to ask for. Maybe we need more clarification on the project for which we'll be asking a donation. There are many reasons why this wouldn't be the right time to ask: it's tax season, it's Christmas, it's summer, it's a full moon. We want to wait till we know we will be successful. And we procrastinate. Imagine if a baseball player did that. He knows that to be successful will involve not making it safely to first base at least two out of three at-bats. But he keeps stepping up to the plate taking the pitches he's thrown and giving himself an opportunity to get a hit.

We need to be more like baseball players. We don't need perfect at-bats every time. We need to make enough calls to secure enough pledges to move our schools forward. Yes, we need to prepare for those calls, especially as they get toward the top of the pyramid. But we also need to recognize when call reluctance is preventing us from making the number of calls we need to be making. A key part of getting results in development is eliminating the barriers to making asks, from fear of failure, to over-doing the preparation. The way I do this is to consider what my goal is for the campaign or appeal, determine how many calls I need to make given that I may close only one in four, do as much preparation as I can without eating into the time I have to make the calls, then make the calls my top priority. I hold myself accountable for making these goals. If my calendar is getting full of other demands, I schedule time for making solicitation appointments, just as if I were scheduling a meeting. Sometimes I have other people sit in with me as I make the appointments, because this holds me accountable. The point is that for a development program to be successful, it must move its focus up the giving pyramid, and to do that people have to make more personal asks. And to do that, they must be honest about call reluctance and develop methods to eliminate it.

3. Staff vs. Volunteers

One of the vexing questions in development is whether to rely on staff or volunteers to make asks. Programs that rely on staff to make asks are paying for every ask. They must pay salaries to attract top producers and keep them motivated. Volunteers can be used to leverage a smaller team of paid professionals who support them in making the asks. Not only are volunteers free, but as peers of the potential donor, as people with no vested interest, they can make a more compelling ask. Or so the theory goes. In practice many institutions find that the effort to find, recruit, train, motivate and bring closure with volunteers is more than it would take for staff to do the asks themselves. Then at least they would know that the asks were done correctly. Volunteers often don't bother to present the case, don't like to ask for a specific amount and don't document call outcomes for future reference. But then again, using volunteers has the benefit of getting more people involved hands-on with the school, which is important for the long term. As volunteers, they develop a deeper understanding of the school, its needs and the case for support. When the campaign succeeds, volunteers can take pride in the result, which cements their support for the future. By participating they push themselves up the giving pyramid, hopefully becoming so close that they include the school in their estate plans. I once worked with a consultant whose strategy was to recruit a team of volunteers big enough that if they alone gave at the level they were supposed to be asking for, the campaign goal would be reached. If they actually asked others and got pledges, that was gravy. That takes a lot of effort, but it works.

So, what's the answer, staff or volunteers? The answer depends on two factors: The size of the organization and what you need done. In a smaller organization, fundraising tends to be volunteer-driven. First of all, there isn't much staff, so if funds are going to be raised the volunteer leadership simply has to put its shoulder to the wheel. Secondly, in smaller non-profits, the volunteers are more disposed to take this responsibility. They are generally close to the work, take more operational responsibility and have pride of authorship in shaping not only the organization's fundraising efforts but often its program as well. Third, the dollars needed are generally small enough that they fit within the volunteers' comfort level. They can provide a large portion of the money needed themselves and they don't have to press their friends too hard to get the rest. Finally, because the dollar amounts are small, the fundraising structure is simple and there isn't a great need for coordination of efforts. But as organizational size increases, it requires more professional management of every facet. Volunteers' roles and responsibilities in governance become more circumscribed. The dollars needed and therefore the ask amounts get beyond what they feel they can present without risk of being thrown out of someone's office. And more coordination is needed just to prevent duplication and to provide research for the *Four Rights*. As staff is added to support the fundraising, volunteers tend to rely on them more and more. They feel less that everything depends on their following through. After all, so-and-so is paid to do this, let her follow up. The staff obliges, as they are increasingly reluctant to have their results subject to undependable volunteers. So, as organization size increases, the scale tips toward greater utilization of staff.

The other way to approach this question is to take advantage of the strengths and weaknesses of both staff and volunteers. What does each bring to the party? Volunteers bring fresh energy, relationships with peers and the credibility of third party endorsement. Staff brings accountability, training and knowledge of the institution. These are generalizations because some volunteers are more accountable, trained and knowledgeable than paid staff, and some staff bring more freshness, relationships and credibility than volunteers. But as a general rule, these are the attributes of each type of asker. So in designing a fundraising effort, be it a campaign or an ongoing development program, the organization should play to the strengths of each. The diagram in Figure 4 below suggests a way of thinking about this. Imagine a radio dial. When you turn the dial to the left, toward using more staff, you increase the quality control of the ask itself (e.g. presentation of case and asking for a specific amount), and when you turn the dial to the right, toward volunteers, you increase peer influence. Both are important for the ask. But if the ask requires the elements to the left, you dial the process toward activities that volunteers just aren't as good at. They aren't as good as staff at doing prospect research, or at managing a relationship that requires coordination of steps, or stewarding a gift that requires a prompt and accurate acknowledgment from the school itself.

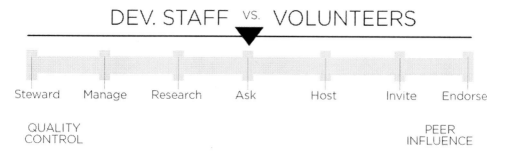

Figure 4: Staff vs. Volunteers

But if the ask requires the activities to the right, hosting a dinner, inviting people to an event or providing a more objective endorsement of the program, volunteers will be more effective than staff. In some cases you simply have to weigh the trade-offs and decide what on balance is most needed. In other cases, you can design the program to get the best of both worlds. For instance, a volunteer can call and make a solicitation appointment, but if he isn't an effective asker, a staff person can go along to present the case and make the ask. Or a volunteer can host a party and give an endorsement of the project and staff can make follow-up appointments to do the solicitation. At the high school level, it would generally be advisable to involve volunteers as much as possible so that broad and visible community support is maintained. The consultant I mentioned earlier used to ask me, "Are more and more people of stature being involved in the school?" If the answer is yes, the school will be healthy. On the other hand, volunteers need to be involved in ways that they feel good about and translate into progress for the school. This generally means that professional staff must be in place to make sure the job of asking gets done and done properly.

The Prospect Pipeline

The capacity of a school to raise money is to a great extent a function of the strength of its case. The clearer it is to prospective donors that investing in the school will bring results that match their philanthropic desires, the stronger the development program is likely to be. But there are two other important factors. One is who the prospective donors are, and the other is how well the school asks them. Identifying, cultivating and asking prospective donors is a process. It can take a long time, and all the steps generally have to be done in a pre-ordained order. Because of this, we describe that process as a pipeline. Imagine an oil pipeline from Houston to New York. Petroleum has to be loaded into the pipeline in Houston and it has to flow through all the states in between to reach New York, a process that will take about three weeks (depending on the viscosity of the oil). If the refinery in Houston delays loading the oil, or if there is a break anywhere in the process, New Yorkers will wait even longer for the anticipated results. The journey from potential donor to actual donor must follow a similar process. We can't just decide one day to start asking for money and expect immediate results. We have to have put our prospects in the pipeline at the beginning and taken them through the steps of the preparation process.

Suspects vs. prospects vs. donors. In sales theory, a distinction is made between suspects and prospects. Suspects are all those people who might have the interest and capacity to become donors. Prospects are those suspects for whom sufficient information on capacity and relationship have been gathered to justify an ask at a specific level. Donors are those who have actually made a gift. The pipeline that leads from suspects to donors might look like this:

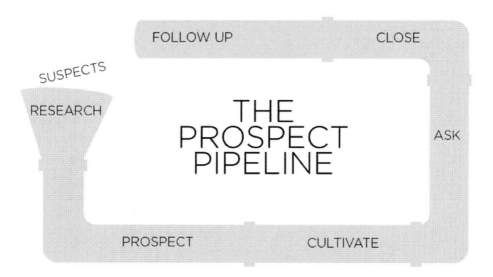

Figure 5: The Prospect Pipeline

Let's say the school is about to begin a capital campaign. It has various constituencies in its database (Houston), some of which will need to emerge as donors by the time the campaign ends (New York). It begins with various pools of suspects, for instance, all alumni who graduated 10 or more years ago for whom the school has valid contact information. The next stage is *research* to determine which of these might actually have the willingness and financial capacity to be considered prospects. The extent of the research is correlative to the level of the ask. Determining who are prospects for gifts of $1,000 may be as simple as running the constituent records through a filter that looks at prior giving. Determining which might be prospects for gifts of $100,000 or more may involve hiring a contract researcher to scour the internet, proxy statements, real estate filings and non-profit donor lists. It might also require interviewing peers and thoroughly reviewing the school's internal files. Here's a quick rule of thumb: A suspect can be considered a prospect when there has been sufficient research to support a specific ask for a specific amount at the upper end of the donor's capacity. Some of the $1,000 prospects identified by the giving filter will turn out to be suspects for gifts at higher levels. They are lifted out and input into a more rigorous research process necessary to validate the next higher ask level. This process is repeated until the upper capacity is identified for all the suspects. Only now can they be called prospects.

Once prospects are identified, the *cultivation* stage can begin. Actually, it is likely that there has already been a general cultivation of the prospects (sending newsletters, inviting to events, etc.), but now that we have a better idea of their giving capacity, we can target our cultivation efforts so that those with higher capacity are given more attention. I have seen school leaders do creative and powerful relationship-building with top donors, including special pilgrimages, thoughtful gifts for birthdays and anniversaries and special briefings on school progress. This may offend our democratic sensibilities until we recognize that we do our financial aid students no favors by failing to cultivate the philanthropy of the wealthy, or indiscriminately using scarce resources over-cultivating people who could never hope to give at a higher level. Cultivation based on prospect research is simply good stewardship, and done properly it respects the needs and circumstances of all members of the community we serve.

The next stage in the pipeline is the ask. As important as cultivation is, it's important not to delay the ask too long. If the cultivation phase takes too long, I find prospective donors begin to wonder why I haven't asked for their help, or they may even believe that I don't intend to ask for her help. When I do, they may think, "You mean that's all this was about, leading up to asking me for money?" I find it helpful to let prospective donors know early on that part of our relationship is based on the school's need for caring, generous donors. I need to make sure, for our own spiritual health and out of respect for the donors, that I don't reduce who they are to what they can do for the school. I take the perspective that one of the privileges of seeking support for the school is the unique and caring people it brings me in contact with. So I want to make sure I drink in the fullness of who they are. But I also have a job to do, and if they truly care about the school, it will be as important to them as it is to me that I do it and do it well. In this approach, their philanthropy becomes an important element of a bigger relationship. The ask then becomes more natural. But it still must be made and it must be made clearly and specifically, as discussed in an earlier section of this chapter.

Once the ask has been made, the work of *closing* the solicitation begins. Sometimes the prospective donor will respond immediately and fill out a pledge form on the spot. But more often, especially with larger gifts, they will need to consider the request, talk to a spouse or an accountant, or make some financial arrangements. Sometimes this can just be delaying a decision, and if this seems to be the case, you will do yourself and the prospective donor a favor by moving them expeditiously to a decision, positive or negative. Sometimes I have asked a couple in my office for a gift that I'm pretty sure they are capable of deciding about right then, but they say they want to talk about it and get back to me. Instead, I offer to leave the room so they can talk about it then. It works well. By doing this I save them the anxiety of a decision hanging over their heads, and myself several hours of trying to reconnect with them.

With larger gift requests, however, it is entirely reasonable that prospective donors will need to do some checking before they can finalize their gift. In this case the cardinal rule is not to give them the pledge form. It may seem natural that they simply take the form and send it in when they are ready, but you will play heck trying to bring closure to the gift. Rather, agree to a time when you will get back to them and hang on to the form until then so that you can record their intentions at that time. I remember once asking a university president for a gift to an organization we both belonged to. Violating my own principles, I gave him the pledge form and asked him to send it in. He said, "I know from my own development experience that you're not supposed to do that." I said, "I trust you." He nodded and smiled. Not only did he never send the form in, I never got him to return my calls after that. Unmade decisions fester and cause problems in relationships. Do everyone a favor and help bring fundraising requests to an expeditious close.

Once the ask has been made and the pledge form completed and signed, it's tempting to think that our work is done. That's my tendency—to look ahead to bringing the next prospective donor into the fold. But a pledge does no good unless it is paid. Despite the fact that the rules of the Financial Accounting Standards Board (FASB) require us to treat pledges themselves as assets, they are not contracts. No consideration has been given in return. So if the donor has a financial reversal, loses interest in the school or is wooed away by another cause, that pledge may never get paid. Good follow-up on pledges means having a reliable reminder system in place, the ability to generate account aging reports showing delinquency in payments, and a gentle but rigorous follow-up system for those who fall behind. For upper-end donors, it means continuing to pay as much attention to them as you do to the prospective donors you are cultivating.

The other reason for follow-up is that it is the best way of cultivating a donor for the next ask. If the donor's experience of giving is positive, he is more likely to repeat it. If it is less than satisfying, the climb toward a future gift has just been made steeper. Believe me, I have experienced both, and you probably have too. This is why the "Prospect Pipeline" picture in Figure 5, above, turns back on itself. Eventually donors emerge from the process, but if we are managing it well they go right back in. So the donor who successfully completes a $100,000 pledge becomes a suspect for the

$1 million level, or for a planned gift. The process begins anew, but hopefully at a higher level on the asking pyramid.

Feasibility Studies

Understanding the prospect pipeline will help assess the feasibility of a fundraising effort. Before embarking on a campaign, boards want to have some assurance that it will be successful. Perhaps they are mindful of Jesus' parable in the 14th chapter of Luke, "Which of you wishing to construct a tower, does not first sit down and calculate the cost to see if there is enough for its completion? Otherwise, after laying the foundation and finding himself unable to finish the work, the onlookers should laugh at him and say, 'This one began to build but did not have the resources to finish.'" Lk 14:28-30

The normal way to determine whether we can successfully complete a fundraising effort is by hiring a campaign consulting firm to conduct a feasibility study. Traditionally the study consists of interviewing 30-50 potential donors whose gifts would be key to the success of the campaign. The interviews determine what they think of the case, the school's credibility, and their own willingness and capacity to support the project in the current economy and fundraising environment. Other tools, like focus groups and an audit of the development office, may be added but the major donor interviews are the key to this study.

The traditional feasibility study is a good exercise and, properly done, provides indispensable data for making decisions about the contemplated campaign. It not only provides data to the school, but it also begins to educate key donors for the upcoming campaign and give them a sense of ownership through their input. Finally, if the counsel conducting the study is retained for the campaign, they will have begun building relationships with donors they may be working with later.

The interview-based study by itself can be inaccurate, and may not address the important issue of the readiness of the prospect pipeline to support the campaign. To be effective, the feasibility study must also include a thorough prospect pipeline evaluation, which is a kind of stress-test for campaign readiness. Here's how it works.

$5 million
$2.5 million
$1 million
$500,000
$250,000
$100,000
$50,000
$25,000
$10,000

Figure 6: The Giving Pyramid

In Figure 6, we see yet another pyramid. We have already seen the development pyramid (Figure 2), which showed the components of the development program and their relationships, and the asking pyramid (Figure 3), which showed the increasing quality of the ask as the potential gift size increased. Now we consider the giving pyramid, which is a tool for determining the gift sizes and numbers needed in a campaign. Like the other pyramids it is based on the Pareto Principle, which says that a small percentage of the donors will account for the majority of the dollars raised. The rule of thumb is that you start with the biggest gift you think you can get and move down the pyramid by doubling the number of gifts at each level. This produces a gift table, like the one shown in Figure 7 below:

Gift size	# needed	Cumulative total
$5 million	1	$5,000,000
2.5 million	2	10,000,000
1 million	4	14,000,000
500,000	8	18,000,000
250,000	16	22,000,000
100,000	32	25,200,000
50,000	64	28,400,000
25,000	128	31,600,000
10,000	256	34,160,000
Total Gifts	511	

Figure 7: Sample Gift Table

This exercise, as theoretical as it is, tells us that if we want to raise $34 million we will probably need a top gift of $5 million, and we will need 510 additional gifts of various amounts $10 thousand and up. This is the first reality check for the campaign. I did this exercise with an inner-city parish that wanted to raise a much smaller amount to pay off its debt. The range of gifts needed to reach their goal was from $500,000 down to $100. The number of gifts exceeded the number of parishioners, so in the space of about 15 minutes they had an answer to the feasibility question, in this case a disappointing one.

The next step is to see if there are enough prospects to support these gifts. I like to be conservative and challenge the school to identify five prospects for every one gift we hope to get. Not 5 suspects, but 5 potential donors that adequate research suggests have the capacity and interest to donate that gift amount. In the example in Figure 7, we would need 2,555 total prospects. If the school has done a great job of identifying, researching and cultivating its donor base, the ratio might drop to 4:1, but it's best to avoid wishful thinking. The next step is to put actual names by those numbers, especially at the top levels. If the development team can do this, then not only has the school substantiated the feasibility of the campaign goal, but prospects are researched and ready for cultivation and asking. The development director also can design the campaign structure, including staffing, resources and budgets, around the number of prospects that need to be asked. In this scenario, the role of the feasibility study interviews done by the consultants is to verify the probabilities for gifts at the top of the pyramid and begin cultivating those key donors.

The president's involvement in fundraising

Presidents of Jesuit schools come into their roles from a variety of backgrounds. Many, perhaps most, have served as principals and haven't been intimately involved with the school's business model. Some may come with backgrounds in development or finance, or leadership in other institutions in their provinces. Regardless of background, all presidents will need to be involved in fundraising.

First, the president is a key resource for development. No one else can replace the president when a donor or a constituency needs to hear from top leadership. The president must not only be available to share his vision for the school and what is happening on campus at fundraising or cultivation events, but must be willing to make asks himself. Some donors, especially those being asked to make large investments in the school, will need to look the president in the eye and hear in his voice just how important they, and what they are being asked to do, are to the school. They will want to know they can trust the school's leader and will want to be his friend in a concrete way, just as they are to the school in a more abstract way. This can be a little frightening to us introverts, or anyone who isn't used to having a relationship that involves a financial dimension. They might quote Moses, "O Lord, I have never been eloquent, neither in the past nor since you have spoken to your servant. I am slow of speech and tongue." Ex 4:10. But I have found normally shy people to be some of the most effective fundraisers. It is clear to the donor that what they are doing doesn't come easily, and it is powerful testimony to the importance of the ask when a president doesn't delegate this difficult task to someone else, but does his best to make the case himself. Nonetheless, it is reasonable for a president, especially one who is new to development, to expect his development staff to give him all the training and support he needs to be effective. Most development officers understand that this is a good investment, and are just waiting to be asked.

Second, the president must be involved and knowledgeable enough to provide leadership and direction to the development office. The president must be able to set reasonable goals and hold the staff accountable to those goals. And the president can't just focus on the dollar goals. If the development effort falls short of budgeted goals, the president has to understand why. Is it because of economic conditions? Is it because of school issues that have occasioned a loss of credibility? Is it because development staff isn't making calls, or involving volunteers appropriately or stewarding the gifts it receives? If the president doesn't understand what makes development work, she must either accept what she gets and suffer or else constantly replace staff until something works. This is why I have gone into some detail in the foregoing sections: to provide a framework for evaluating the development effort and to help the president see where steps in the process may be missing or weak.

But it isn't just the development staff that may need direction. Sometimes others in the school need be encouraged by the president to do more to support the development effort. It could be as simple as a club moderator sharing the story of a remarkable project or student that can be a compelling article for the alumni magazine, or teachers calling alums who looked up to them as students. The president needs to make sure the development staff has the resources they need. The need to invest in development is often misunderstood in schools. Hiring a development officer seems to divert money from our core mission, even though that hire brings more back into the school. We have to spend a buck to make three. And if the school needs a planned giving officer, he may not bring in more than he costs for several years, yet the potential long-term return could be a game-changer for the school. The president must be involved and knowledgeable enough to guide the school to the proper balance in supporting its development efforts.

Presidents will tend to gravitate to those areas where they have more prior experience and greatest comfort level. This is to be expected. But ideally, they should see themselves as members of the development team, just as they should see themselves as part of the apostolic team and the educational team. In each area, most of the authority and responsibility is delegated to others. But the school will be stronger if the president can be present to all areas of the school and the personnel in those areas can help the president to be a participant and a competent leader.

Measuring results

Unlike most other areas of the school, it is relatively easy to measure the results of development. In fact, it is almost impossible not to. The president, the board and the CFO will watch keenly to see how fundraising revenues are impacting the bottom line. Since development involves the public in accomplishing published goals, whether they be for a capital campaign, an auction or the alumni phonathon, everyone else in the community is also keeping an eye on fundraising. This puts a lot of pressure on the development team. In one sense, this transparency is good, holding the development effort accountable to the community it serves. But it can also cause so much pressure that it influences development staff to make decisions based on short-term rather than long-term results. For example, since the auction is such a public event, people will often use it to judge the effectiveness of the overall development program. This can lead development staff to allocate an inordinate amount of time to what is essentially a special event at the base of the development pyramid. Not only is more staff time taken from other areas like annual giving and planned giving, but donors can be diverted to asks that don't tap their full potential. The individual who could be giving $25,000 to a capital need is asked to be a table sponsor at $5,000 and thinks she is done. Auction sponsorship and capital giving aren't always mutually exclusive, but if not managed well, they can be. If the pressure is for immediate, visible results, the "four rights" discussed earlier may be abridged and long-term results compromised in favor of the short-term.

The key is to make sure we are measuring and incentivizing the right things. It doesn't do any good if the changes we make don't result in more dollars hitting the bottom line. But it also doesn't do any good if we stare at the bottom line instead of searching for the root causes of the results we're getting. Effectively measuring the results of the development effort will require setting metrics at various points of the process. We need to measure the outcomes we want; we also need to work upstream to measure the outputs, inputs and resources that produce them. Here's what that might look like, taking parent annual giving as an example.

Let's say our goal in the next five years is to increase parent annual giving from $500,000 per year to $1 million. Our outcome, or goal, is to raise $1 million, so we need to measure our progress from year to year toward that goal. We decide that this will require increasing both the percentage of parents giving from 50% to 91% and the average gift size from $1,000 to $1,100. These are outputs, and we would put in place metrics to measure our progress toward achieving those outputs. Our root cause analysis tells us that many parents don't give, or don't give as much as they might, because we're making a weak ask. It turns out that all we're doing is sending them a letter with a pledge form, and then phoning those who don't respond. We decide that if we schedule individual appointments with parents we can make a better case for supporting the parent annual giving program. So scheduling individual appointments becomes one of our inputs. We set up a goal of 100% participation in these appointments and measure how well we are doing against the goal for this input each year. Finally, we need resources to accomplish this change. We need people to meet with the parents, which may require adding development staff, or enlisting other school personnel like the president, other administrators or teachers. It can also be done with a group of volunteers, but we will still need staffing resources to enlist, train and manage them. When we have identified the resources needed, we set metrics and measure our progress toward achieving the desired level of resources.

A dashboard for measuring the results at all stages of the process over five years might look like the table shown in Figure 8 below:

Years	Resources		Inputs	Outputs		Outcomes
	Volun-teers	Staffing	Individual Parent Meetings	Number Of pledges	Average Pledges	TOTAL Parent Annual Giving
Baseline	0	1.5	0	500	$1,000	$500,000
Year 1	13	1.5	260	600	1,000	600,000
Year 2	26	1.5	480	700	1,050	735,000
Year 3	32	1.5	640	750	950	712,500
Year 4	44	2.0	880	850	1,050	892,500
Year 5	50	2.0	1,000	910	1,100	1,000,000
Goals	50		1,000	910	$1,100	$1,000,000

Figure 8: Annual Giving Dashboard

Although this is a highly simplified model, it suggests some management directions for development. In Years 1 and 2 we seem to be on track toward our goal. But then in Year 3 we take a backward step in total parent annual giving. To find out why, we look up the chart, moving upstream in the process, as it were, to find where the breakdown occurred. We notice that our average gift slipped significantly. This recognition will send us hunting for reasons. Was there an issue in the general economy? Was there an adverse event in the school? Was there a change in the way we trained our askers? Was it that in increasing our participation rate we brought in pledges from people of lesser means, which lowered our average? Even the simple numbers on this dashboard give some clues as to where to look for root causes. Looking further up the chart to resources, we can see what happened with volunteers. We needed to recruit at least 36 to stay on track, but we only had 32. When we look at the staff to support the volunteers, the numbers suggest that the existing 1.5 FTE was able to manage effectively through Year 2, when we had 26 volunteers, but was not able to support the Year 3 goals. Using this information, we now decide to add another half FTE to staff, which, as the numbers suggest, will get us back on track toward our goals.

There are three advantages to this approach for setting performance metrics for the development office. The first is that it uses a long-term view. In the example above, we set an ambitious target but gave ourselves five years to achieve it. While the first year in itself is not a spectacular achievement, it can be celebrated by the development staff and the community as a step toward the bigger goal.

Second, this approach allows us to do root cause analysis. We don't just stare at the bottom line figure and wonder what went wrong or right. We can look at the metrics for the intermediate steps of the process and make adjustments accordingly. This is analogous to the difference between a summative assessment and a formative assessment. Having a metric only for the total dollars raised is helpful for evaluating what was accomplished, but it doesn't point the direction toward improvement. For that you need the intermediate metrics.

The third advantage of this system is that it can be used to incentivize the development staff. As discussed previously, development is like sales. Development staff are paid to get results, which has caused many to suggest that they should be paid according to the results they get, similar to the way sales people are paid on commission. This approach causes other problems, however. It can over-incentivize the staff, who quickly realize that each call they make will impact their own pocketbook. The school needs them to be working toward the long-term needs of the institution and the donor rather than just for the short-term impact on themselves or the school. The development profession recognizes this challenge through such organizations as the Association of Fundraising Professionals, whose member guidelines prohibit them from being compensated by a percentage of contributions. These guidelines do allow for bonus programs consistent with local professional practice[xi]. By basing bonuses not only on bottom line results but also on various input factors that should lead to those results (such as number of calls made, volunteers recruited, etc) we can incentivize development staff not only to aim for the bottom line, but also to sharpen those skills that lead to long-term success in increasing the resources available to the school.

F. Employee Recruitment

The last major area of the school supported by the marketing plan is the recruitment of employees. How this should be approached has already been discussed in Chapter IV. The point that needs to be made here is that, although marketing for employees generally isn't as urgent as marketing for mission, for students and for donations, it is critical to the long-term effectiveness of the school. Thought needs to be given in the beginning stages of crafting the marketing plan to how it will touch the people we want to attract to the team. How will they perceive the school's identity through its logo and core messages? We can't develop a special logo just for prospective employees, and even the messages we put in our job ads have to be consistent with the core messages we send to our potential school families and potential donors. If we are doing our job with these latter two groups, our identity and messages should be pervasive enough that they appear on the radar screens of potential employees. And it's not just potential employees we should be thinking about. What about our current employees? We need to make sure they also understand our identity and are continually motivated by our core messages to not only remain with the school, but continue to recommit themselves to its mission.

Making sure the marketing plan, and particularly our branding and core messages, speaks to current and potential employees is an important exercise in consistency. When I see an ad claiming that every employee of a certain company is committed to giving me a good experience, I wonder whether the employees would recognize the spirit the ad so attractively depicts. There was one a few years ago that showed an airline employee running through crowds and vaulting over seats to give a customer a bag they'd left behind. Since this wasn't my own experience with the airline, I wondered how the employees saw that ad. Did they say, "Yeah, that's us!"? Did they even say, "That could be us."? Or did they say, "Who the heck are they talking about?" In the case of this airline, I'll bet the ad bred cynicism because it did not reflect who the company really was. When ads like this come out of nowhere and then disappear, I assume they are fantasies that aren't based on actual experience. That's a good test for us. If we can craft a brand and core messages that our own employees can identify with, it will ring true for others we are drawing into the circle. And as they draw closer, the perception we engendered in them will be reinforced rather than contradicted.

G. Financial Management

As discussed earlier in this chapter, finance is as essential to the business model, and therefore to the apostolic, pedagogical and community models, as electricity is to the proper functioning of a home. Most of us don't give a lot of thought to how we manage the electricity that comes into our home. But if we lived in a less developed country, or on a small island like my friend, thinking about managing electricity would become a major part of our lives. As non-profit organizations in a challenging business environment, I think our financial needs are more akin to being on a resource-scarce island than on a grid with plentiful, cheap electricity. Not everyone on the island recognizes this fact, however, which means we need to be clear about what financial management is and why we need it.

Three Tasks of the Finance Office

The finance office in a school has three main functions: financial controls, financial reporting and financial management.

1. Financial controls

Financial controls refer to those policies and procedures that safeguard corporate assets. Controls fall into two categories: Internal controls and compliance. Internal controls are policies that reduce the risk of intentional or unintentional misuse of corporate assets by employees. An example would be the purchasing system and the need to make sure that any purchase has been approved by someone with the proper authority, that the price is legitimate and that the goods or services have actually been received before payment is made. An absence of controls in any one of these steps could mean an unnecessary loss of the school's resources, sometimes unintentionally, and sometimes by people taking advantage of inadequate precautions. Other examples include policies that specify how cash is counted, reconciled and deposited; who is authorized to issue checks or make withdrawals from school accounts; how employee hours and leave time are recorded; and how purchases are charged to departments. Sometimes employees get impatient with these controls. They seem like unnecessary paperwork, or a sign that the school doesn't trust them. "We needed money for a new fresnel spot," the drama director might say. "So we just took some cash from our ticket sales and purchased it. What's wrong with that?" In most cases, probably nothing, at least nothing with criminal intent. But if people are dipping into gate receipts for legitimate purposes it creates the possibility of skimming for non-legitimate purposes. For controls to work, they have to be applied consistently. We can't make only careless or dishonest people comply with the controls. If we knew who the dishonest and careless people would be, we wouldn't give them any responsibility to begin with. And if the honest ones don't follow the controls, they create a cover for dishonest people who either set out to cheat the school or get snagged by temptation. The classic embezzler is the "honest" person who gets into a financial predicament (often because of his addiction or someone else's). He sees an opportunity and tells himself that he'll pay it back when he's out of the predicament, which just never seems to happen.

Compliance refers to policies that assure the school is conducting business in accordance with laws and regulations from outside authorities. These include paying taxes, filing reports and assuring that the school is following laws and regulations so as not to incur financial penalties or burdensome operating restrictions. The list of laws and regulations schools or any business need to comply with has burgeoned over the years. We may be tempted to bury our heads in the sand and ignore them as much as possible. The real solution is to identify what the compliance issues are and try to routinize them to reduce the burden on staff. In many cases it will be advisable to outsource compliance issues (for instance, as part of payroll) to vendors who make a business of dealing with them.

2. Financial Reporting

The second function of the finance office is financial reporting. In today's world, knowing your financial position can be complicated. There was a bumper sticker that read, "I can't be overdrawn. I still have checks in my checkbook." It is only slightly less silly to say, "Of course we can hire that extra administrator, we have a positive cash balance." Comptrollers, CFO's, business managers or whatever schools call their financial administrators, have mastered a set of tools for stating the school's financial position in ways that will alert the leadership to any concerns, hopefully in time to address them.

The finance office will produce three basic statements, which should be annually audited by an accounting firm to assure that they are in accordance with "Generally Accepted Accounting Principles" or GAAP. These are the balance sheet, income statement and cash flow statement. The balance sheet (which in fund accounting is more precisely referred to as a *statement of financial position*) is a snapshot of the school's assets, liabilities and fund balances at a particular point in time. It is called a balance sheet because the total assets must always equal the total liabilities plus the total fund balances. It is a snapshot because these figures are changing constantly. Any time a piece of capital equipment is purchased it will cause a shift on the balance sheet. If it is purchased with cash it will increase fixed assets and lower cash assets. If it is purchased on credit, it will increase fixed assets, with a balancing increase in liabilities. The changes can happen on a daily basis, so we should take the snapshot on a monthly basis and produce an audited balance sheet once a year, at the end of the year. We then can compare our assets, liabilities and fund balances to the previous period to identify whether any important changes in our financial position have taken place over that time. What it doesn't tell us is what happened between those two snapshots, which is where the other two statements are helpful.

The income statement (in fund accounting called a *statement of activities*) shows the revenues coming in over a given period of time, as well as the expenses incurred, in order to show the net surplus or loss from operations. The net surplus or loss for the period from the income statement will equal the change in net assets shown on the balance sheet for that period. The balance sheet will show where the surplus or loss appears in the assets, liabilities and fund balances and the income statement will show where those changes came from. So if the school's revenues from tuition, fundraising and other sources exceeded the amount it had to pay out in salaries and other costs, the difference would add to the assets on the balance sheet. The surplus may show up as an increase in cash assets, or if it is used to purchase a new computer lab, it would cause an increase in fixed assets. The income statement and the balance sheet give part of the story of a school's financial position, but an important part still needs to be told.

The cash flow statement, also known as the *statement of sources and uses of funds*, provides another important lens for the school's financial position. Cash is the actual electricity that keeps the operations of the school moving. It is possible to have a growing fund balance on the balance sheet and to show surpluses on the income statement, and still be running out of cash. Here's how that could happen. A school raises its tuition but the actual tuition payments start to slow down, either because of economic conditions or a change in the school's collection procedures. The accounts receivable, which are considered an asset, have grown, but the cash received has declined. As the year rolls on, there isn't enough cash in the system to pay bills or make payroll. This can be addressed by borrowing money against assets, like accounts receivable, thus turning them into cash. But if the trends persist, the school might exhaust its credit or lose the ability to service the debt. Even though its income statement shows it is in the black, the school is in a financial bind. The cash flow statement isolates what is happening with cash in operations, so the school can make adjustments to assure there is enough available.

3. Financial management

The balance sheet, income statement and cash flow statement are the basic statements of financial condition, but the finance office really shows its value in the task of financial management. To make this point, I need to switch metaphors from electricity to blood. The finances of an institution are its lifeblood. Of course, what happens in our classrooms, chapel and fields is how we actually accomplish our mission, but unless the blood brings vital oxygen and nutrients to the muscles, brain and other organs, they will fail. Financial management keeps that blood flowing as it should, identifies openings that cause blood loss, eliminates blockages, and prevents pooling. But the circulation system also carries with it a lot of information about how the body is operating. I learned this once when I was exercising so vigorously (for a man my age) that I got faint and thought I might have had a heart attack. When I went to the hospital, they could tell from analyzing my blood that I hadn't. Blood can tell the story of how my organs are functioning, whether I have too much cholesterol, whether I'm a diabetic and many other things about me. Just so, skilled financial managers can analyze an institution's financial circulation system and shed helpful light on various aspects of operations. They can see when too much money is being invested in development for the results we're getting. Or too little. They can see when energy costs are drawing off disproportionate resources, and suggest an evaluation of mechanical systems. They can see where personnel costs are disproportionately high, which might indicate management issues. Increased medical insurance utilization may suggest that a wellness program is needed or that employees are experiencing too much stress.

I wish I could say that such financial management is happening in all our schools. To some extent it is, but to get the full benefit of the CFO's ability to analyze our bloodstream requires both time and creativity. Just as some doctors are just too busy or not imaginative enough to diagnose people beyond the obvious symptoms, it takes time and creativity to get the most out of financial management. It also takes good tools.

Budgeting

One tool used by every school is the yearly operating budget, which projects where resources will come from and what resources will need to be used. It's amazing when you think about it, because a budget is an attempt to bring order out of chaos. Meeting revenue projections depends on independent decisions being made by thousands of people, from eighth graders doing well enough in school to qualify for admission, to parents budgeting money for tuition, to alumni answering the phone during the phonathon, to foundations picking our proposal from a flood of requests. On the expense side, think of all the people empowered to make decisions that will commit the school to expending resources. Looked at in terms of the sheer number of independent decisions that have to be made, any of which could easily go a different way, it's remarkable that schools can function at all. But they do. We have learned how to project reliably, based on data available to us, how many people will choose to send their children, how many donors will respond favorably to our requests, and what departments will need to spend to do their work. We're so good at it, that it is a matter of some concern when our projections are off. If the auction comes in below expectations, we ask ourselves and the person in charge what went wrong. If a department head overspends her budget, she may have a serious discussion with the principal. The fact is, despite the chaos at the foundations of the budgeting process, we're pretty good at it. We are able to identify what needs to happen and we're pretty good at projecting what's likely to happen. A budget can also be a tool for shaping what we want to happen. Let's look at three unlikely metaphors that may help us to see the role of the budget in a different light.

When I was little, I remember hearing about paint-by-numbers kits. As someone lacking any apparent artistic talent, I thought this was pretty cool. All I had to do was choose the paint that corresponded with the number in each spot on the picture, and voila! I could produce something I never thought myself capable of. Today,

I am more gratified by painting an artistically challenged picture of my own than executing someone else's vision. After all, that person had all the fun of actually conceiving what the work of art would be. He just translated it into numbers so that I could execute it for him. That's how a budget should work. We start with a vision, and then translate that into numbers so that independent decision-makers can add the color they need to to produce our collective work of art – a coherent and effective response to our mission. I like to keep this in mind when I work on a budget. I try to look beyond the seeming necessity of the individual numbers to ask what picture they paint of who we are. Is that really how little we want to spend on fostering diversity? Or the formation or professional development of our faculty? Or is it just that that's all the money we have left after budgeting the same amounts we've always budgeted for our various programs. In one year, we had to increase our financial aid by 25% because of severe economic circumstances. It wreaked havoc on the budget, but the picture it painted of who we are was compelling. A school may have a beautifully written mission statement and vision, but that isn't who you really are until it is painted through the numbers of the budget.

A budget is also like a script, because it orchestrates the many independent decisions into a coherent whole. If our organizations were simpler, we could be like my son's two-man comedy team and just improvise. We wouldn't need to follow any script. But imagine going to a performance of *The Importance of Being Ernest* in which none of the actors bothered to read the script or memorize their lines. If the actors were talented they could still create some entertaining moments, but the overall production would lack the crispness and preposterousness Oscar Wilde intended and audiences have enjoyed. Just so in our schools. If the admissions director targets an entering class of 120, and the AVP is building a schedule for a class of 100, and the cafeteria is staffing for 150, and the campus minister is scheduling enough homeroom retreats for 80, each of them may be doing good work and we could probably still get through the school year, but it would be messy and frustrating for us and the people we serve. The budget is the tool through which all these elements are thought through and crafted into a coherent story. That's straightforward enough. But then reality happens. Maybe we all agreed on a freshman class of 120, but only 100 end up coming.

I remember producing a stage adaptation of *Casablanca* in college. On the morning of opening night, the man who played Victor Laszlo suddenly wasn't available. This was a big production. The director had adapted the screenplay himself and had talked Yves Saint Laurent into providing designer originals for costumes. As producer, I had gone to most of the rehearsals and I was the only one who had any chance of learning the lines by that evening. Even with that, it required the other actors to cover for all the blocking and cues that I would not be able to master in time.

Reality happens. While actors prepare to perform the show in its ideal form, they also know the overall plot well enough that they can deal with inevitable miscues. It's not good enough for the people in our schools to know their own budget parameters. They need to understand how they fit into a bigger picture. They will be more motivated to play their part when they know how it contributes to the overall success of the school year. But they will also be better prepared to adapt when something else in the school doesn't go as planned. If fundraising is suffering, the CFO can decide that this may not be the year to ramp down the endowment payout rate as planned. If admission yields jump for some reason, the principal makes arrangements for more sections and more teachers. If financial aid costs jump, all departments may be asked to hold expenditures to last year's levels. Like actors, we do our best work when we have a good script to follow and we know it well enough to make adjustments as necessary.

Finally, if you'll bear with one more analogy, a budget can be compared to a set of GPS waypoints. A hiker may be unfamiliar with the route that leads to where she is going. When she loads the waypoints into her GPS, she knows that all she has to do is find each waypoint and she will reach her destination safely. So it is for a school. There are many things we don't know about the year ahead. But budget numbers can give us a set of targets. We know that if we meet the individual targets we will reach our goals at the end of the year. Taking a larger task and breaking it down to smaller targets is an effective motivational tool. A backpacker might not know how she will lug 50 pounds 10 miles while gaining 4,000 feet, but she knows she can make it to the next waypoint. Similarly, if the athletic director has to cut 10% from his overall budget, it may seem impossible until he builds it into the individual budgets for coaches, travel, officials and so forth. He and his coaches now have waypoints to shoot for that will bring them to the overall goal.

Long-range Financial Planning.

Up to this point, I have been talking about the annual budget. But the reality is that it's difficult to use an annual budget to do much reshaping of the school's vision. It tends to be more descriptive than prescriptive. Meaningful change just doesn't happen in a one-year window (especially if a year is only ten months long). To get across the river generally requires stepping across a series of stones. It doesn't do any good to get only halfway across. But many changes we'd like to make in our schools can't be accomplished in a year. If we are focused only on annual budgets, we will avoid bigger, more strategic changes because the annual budget can only bring us part way across the river. If we have a multi-year vision in mind, but we can only capture the first step in the budget, we can't sustain the change effort because the rest of the team doesn't know why the step is there. Even if they do, they may not be committed to the necessary follow-up because they don't know where it leads. So when the next annual budget is prepared, people focus on the exigencies of the moment, unaware of the longer-term picture. An example might be a decision to eliminate ancillary fees and roll them into tuition so parents can more clearly understand the true costs of attending the school. To cushion the financial impact this might be rolled in over five years. But if people are only looking at this one year at a time, other pressures, like keeping tuition increases down, can easily trump the original plan. If we are doing long-range strategic planning, as discussed in the next chapter, we will uncover a number of potent opportunities that can be accomplished over a series of years. This is where a multi-year financial plan can help.

A multi-year financial plan is a series of annual budgets for a number of years into the future. It incorporates assumptions from the strategic planning process both for what is beyond our control and what is within our control. This multi-year budget is also called a *pro forma*, a Latin word meaning "according to form." I prefer to have the pro forma cover a 10-year period because there are important factors that can be seen only at this scale. The first three years tend to be the most accurate because they are based on current experience. After that, projections become markedly less precise, but valuable nonetheless for alerting the school to trends that need to be watched. As each year of the pro forma is completed, the assumptions for future years are adjusted based on actual results and the school's strategic plan, and another year is added. This is called a rolling pro forma, which allows the school at any time to look ahead ten years to understand the impact of trends and the choices it intends to make.

The pro forma is an important tool for the success of the long-range strategic plan. It captures the assumptions of that plan and shows the financial impacts of the strategic choices being made. Conversely, it is nearly impossible to create a multi-year financial plan without a strategic plan in place to provide the assumptions.

The model for the pro forma is generally built on a spreadsheet, where the "workbook" (to use Microsoft Office terminology) comprises the total pro forma and each "worksheet" comprises a budget year. This allows assumptions to be linked in such a way that changes made to one budget area in one year will cause automatic revisions to other budget items and other years. If the spreadsheet is well-constructed, it can allow the school to look quickly at different scenarios based on different assumptions, and then choose the one that is most salient. It is also important to construct the model in such a way that it is easy to identify what the major assumptions are, for instance by listing them in cells in a special assumptions worksheet.

As the multi-year financial planning process becomes more refined, schools will find it easier to prepare their annual budgets. Each year using this discipline will bring greater accuracy to assumptions, which means the next year in the pro forma will just need some verification to be adopted as next year's budget.

The greatest utility of the pro forma is that it allows schools to identify multi-year trends and explore different scenarios for responding to them. It's like going from driving a car looking through a porthole to having a full windshield. The pro forma isn't just a tool for making better decisions; it also helps to communicate the *whats* and *whys* of the decisions to the whole team. All the actors can read the script, understand the plot and know what they need to do to play their part.

Asset management

To be successful, schools need to manage their assets carefully in light of their mission and strategic goals. This has increasingly become the responsibility of the school's financial officer. While a university or other large organization would have specialists in place to manage each kind of asset, in a secondary school the task must fall to the CFO, assisted by her staff, volunteers and outside consultants. Let's look at the major classes of assets and how they should be approached.

1. Cash

We have used the metaphors of both electricity and blood to talk about the role of cash in the institution. Cash is the medium that makes a business—any business—work, and Jesuit schools are no exception. It must be carefully managed. Cash is a component of working capital. As opposed to capital tied up in long-term assets, cash consists of liquid assets that can be used to deal with immediate needs. Cash can take several forms, including actual bills and coins in a petty cash drawer, deposits in checking and savings accounts, even stocks or mutual fund shares. In general any asset that can be quickly sold to pay for other things is considered cash or a cash equivalent.

Having idle cash can be wasteful because the cash isn't producing a return. It may be sitting in a checking account earning no interest or in a savings account earning very little interest. It only becomes productive when it is committed to some use, either within the school, like purchasing new, more cost-effective buses, or outside the school, like investing in long-term CD's. Generally, though there are many exceptions, the longer you can tie up your money, the greater return you can expect. And we want our cash to be productive. Cash isn't productive until it's committed to some productive use and when it is, it's no longer cash.

But having too little cash on hand can be risky. A school could tie up all its cash in capital investments, like buildings, equipment or long-term investments. These might promise a great return over the long-run, but if the school runs out of cash it could wipe out the returns quickly. For instance, if the school experiences a major roof failure and all its cash is tied up, it might have to go and borrow the money needed for repairs. The very fact that it has low working capital may affect its "quick ratio" (current assets divided by current liabilities) and cause the bank to charge a higher interest rate.

To strike the proper balance, the school will want to develop cash management policies that specify how much cash should be kept on hand and what kind of investments are appropriate while the cash waits to be used. A cash management policy will "ladder out" investments with a progressive series of maturities such that cash becomes available as it is needed. Banks have products and advice for doing this, but they may have to be asked specifically to provide them. They have to maintain cash management products, like cash sweeps which daily move excess cash to higher paying investments, to stay competitive. But if customers don't ask for them, they are content to have their customers' cash sitting in low-interest savings and checking accounts.

2. Investments

Any use of cash can be considered an investment, but in this case I am referring to investments in financial instruments. Some of these are the cash management instruments mentioned above, but the bulk of most schools' financial investments are held in endowment funds. Endowments are funds invested with the intention that the income from the investments, rather than the original gift, or corpus, will be used for the various needs of the school. True endowments are restricted by an outside party, generally the donor, so that the corpus cannot be "invaded." The school can access only the income from the investment of the corpus. Quasi-endowments are funds committed by the school with the intention of preserving the corpus, but the school retains the right to invade the corpus at its sole discretion in the future.

Endowments have been set up by schools in various ways. Some schools serve as trustees of the endowment funds themselves. They are thus owned by the school, but subject to the restrictions agreed to when the gifts were accepted from the donors. In other cases schools will set up separate foundations to serve as trustees. This has the advantage of separating the endowment's assets from the school's and offers possible protection in the event that the school is sued. It has the disadvantage of potential conflict between the school board and the foundation board, which has been known to happen. A third version is to have an independent trustee, like a bank, have trusteeship of the funds, but with clear investment and distribution policies. This has the advantage of separation from the school's other assets, is less likely to risk conflict between the trustee and the school, but has the disadvantage of less control than direct ownership provides.

Generally, assets are invested conservatively to provide for both income and stability of the underlying market value of the corpus. Risk is minimized by three basic means: weighting toward more conservative instruments, diversification and investing for the long term.

Especially in smaller endowments of up to $100 million, most of the funds, usually around 40%, are invested in debt instruments like bonds, which pay a fixed return. Because the return is fixed, bonds tend not to decline in value as much as the broader market does, and even when they do the school is assured of consistent income. But bonds also tend not to increase their value when the market for other investments rises. The major portion of most endowment funds is invested in "equity" instruments, like stocks, though this category also includes real estate and commodities. While debt instruments are loans by the endowment to the bond issuers at a fixed interest rate, equities give the endowment an actual ownership interest in a company or asset. In the case of stocks, there may be dividends, but these are at the discretion of the company. Generally the return on equities comes from increases in the value of the company or asset itself, which can fluctuate widely and often.

A second way of conserving the endowment's assets is diversification. If the assets are not concentrated in any one company, sector or type of investment, declines in one can be offset by gains in another. Some very large funds at major universities invest aggressively in high return but risky investments. They feel they can achieve stability of assets mainly through diversification. The theory is that the most any equity investment can lose is 100% of its value, but its return on the upside is virtually unlimited. So if you invested in a hundred high-growth companies and 15% went bankrupt, 20% lost value, 40% gained value and 15% more than doubled in value, you'd be doing well. You need a large endowment to make this work, however, more than most secondary schools are blessed with.

A third way of conserving value is setting a long-term investment horizon. There are arguments about whether stocks, despite their volatility, outperform bonds in the long run. If they do, then the longer you can hold stocks, the safer, more productive investment they become. If you have a short investment horizon, like someone drawing near to retirement age, you run too great a risk that when you need to cash out you'll catch the stock market at a low point. Endowments, especially if they are conservative on their distribution policies (for example, limiting themselves to 3-4% of the 5 year trailing average market value of the corpus) can stick with investments for a long time. Whether this is in itself a winning strategy can be argued, but one thing it will do is keep the endowment managers from timing the market.

Market timing is the practice of investing and divesting based on what you think the overall market is about to do. I'm not expert enough to argue for or against the efficacy of market timing, but I am quite sure that it is not a good idea for most endowments. It requires constant attention to the market and quick movement of cash in and out. Most endowment boards meet monthly or quarterly. Most of them know they shouldn't try to time the market. But the temptation to time the market is still seductive. When we see the market, or a sector, a money manager or even a particular stock declining, it means that other investors are losing confidence in it. What do they know that we don't know? We'll look foolish if we're the last ones to figure this out. So we pull out, more often than not about when the stock hits bottom. Then we see it rising, but based on recent history, we don't trust the increase to last. We wait until it seems like everyone has figured out that the stock truly has increased in value. Now we don't want to miss out again, and manage to buy in just as it's hitting its peak. Making money in the stock market requires buying low and sell high. Unskilled market timing leads us to do just the opposite. If a school's endowment committee can't spend the time to watch its stocks all day, every day—and they can't—they're better off identifying the diversity they want, invest with competent money managers who know those sectors and sit tight through the ups and downs.

3. Facilities

While the business office is not necessarily in charge of supervising facilities management, the CFO should help the school understand its physical plant as an asset. The CFO should periodically ask whether there are in place adequate controls, reporting and management processes to preserve the value of this asset. This will be discussed more in the section on facilities later in this chapter, but I bring it up here to underscore the role of the CFO in managing facilities assets. Facilities is generally considered a separate department from the business office, reporting to either the president or the principal. As a result there may be a hands-off partitioning in which the CFO doesn't feel responsible for or welcome to give input on the management of facilities as an asset. And yet physical plant is often the largest asset the school has, far greater than the supplies inventory, cash or endowment. Given that few facilities directors have financial management skills or training, it makes sense that they work closely with the business office to apply sound asset management principles.

4. Personnel

Because of their small size, few secondary schools have separate departments for human resources. Generally the functions that would be handled by an HR department in a larger organization— compliance, record-keeping, compensation, professional development, evaluation, recruitment, discipline and workplace climate—are distributed among various offices throughout the school. Because the business office handles payroll, it becomes responsible for many aspects of HR management, especially those that have high stakes, like compensation and compliance with government regulations. If the CFO has the skill and inclination, she is in a position to lead the school in reflecting on its management of human resources as an asset. That sounds a little cold, because "human resources" really means people. As was made clear in the chapter on the school's community model, employees should not be looked at as comparable to physical or financial assets. But by the same token, they should also not be treated as less valuable. It's easy to see that an investment in a new roof is a good use of the school's scarce resources if it prevents the deterioration of a whole building. It is more difficult to see that paying for additional in-service days at the beginning of school to better prepare teachers for the year ahead could prevent a deterioration in human capital that would be even more costly. These are difficult calculations to make with any certainty, but the CFO can help the school adopt asset management principles to make sure that investment in human resources is getting at least as much consideration. She can also review how the school is handling the HR functions listed above in light of best practices in other organizations to make sure that distributing these functions hasn't resulted in unintended gaps.

5. Risk Management

Managing all of the foregoing asset types—cash, investments, facilities and personnel—involves not only optimizing their value on the upside, but minimizing the chances of their losing value. All the downside possibilities can be aggregated under the heading of risk management. CFOs have a reputation for being conservative. This reputation is somewhat deserved because we need someone who can help us avoid untoward risk in our enthusiastic pursuit of our mission. Under-insuring buildings may seem like an attractive way to find money to fund a new and exciting program. For 19 out of 20 years this would seem like excellent use of resources. But in one of those 20 years there will likely be a disaster that could set the school back years, or send it over the brink. The CFO needs to make sure the school has adequate insurance not only for facilities, but also for possible lawsuits against teachers, administrators and staff. The school owes it to board members to have insurance to indemnify them should they be included in lawsuits against the school.

The CFO needs to pay close attention to what is being covered by insurance policies. Don't assume that earthquake, flood or wind damage is automatically included. And even if it is, the biggest risk may not be damage to facilities, but a business disruption that would turn off the flow of income to the school. Such disruption could come not only from natural disaster but from a pandemic, computer virus, or a protest action. Good financial management will tell us that these risks are part of the costs of doing business. If we are not funding the cost of these risks, we will be misstating our financial performance as surely as if we were disbursing cash from an account without recording it.

The way we fund the cost of risk is by budgeting payments into a fund capable of making us whole if and when the untoward event happens. If the chances of the event are small but the potential financial impact great, like a fire destroying a classroom building, we generally contribute to a fund shared by other organizations facing the same risk. We call this buying insurance. If occurrence of the adverse event is more likely and we are able to generate enough funds to cover the cost of the occurrence, we can budget a certain amount every year into a set-aside fund that we retain ourselves. This is called self-insurance. Buying insurance has the advantage of getting high coverage at low cost, but the disadvantage of not being able to re-coup any of the payments if we never have to draw on the fund. Self-insurance has the advantage of being able to sweep money back into the school once the fund has exceeded the amount at risk, but the disadvantage of not being able to generate much coverage for the amount budgeted. The CFO and a good insurance broker can help the school decide which method is appropriate for which circumstances.

Insurance is not the only way to manage risk. In fact, it's generally better and more cost-effective to reduce risk by improving operations. For instance, installing a better fire alarm system or automatic sprinklers can reduce the risk of loss in the case of a fire.

Or having better supervision can reduce the risk of a lawsuit for negligence. Often these operational changes are a good idea, regardless of their impact on a school's insurance costs, because they make people safer, improve overall quality and exemplify the mission of the school. But they often will lower insurance costs as well. This can happen in three ways: 1) if they lead to lower claims, the insurance companies will see that their risks are lower and will compete for your business by offering lower rates; 2) insurers will often give rate credits when certain safety features, like fire sprinklers, are present; and 3) insurers often offer consulting or classes on how to reduce risk in operations. Simply accepting this consulting and following the recommendations may lead to lower rate proposals from the insurer.

The goal should not be to eliminate or insure every risk. To do so would either so hamstring the school or be so expensive that it could not achieve its mission in any meaningful way. Running a school, especially a school where we want students to push themselves, where we want rich experiences on campus and off, and where we want students to have some sense of the world as it really is, involves risk. The point is that we want that risk to be at an acceptable level. What constitutes acceptable risk is a subjective question. Answering the question involves first acknowledging where a risk is present. The next step is assessing its likelihood and the impact on individuals and the school as a whole. And finally measure the likelihood and potential impact against what we hope to gain in terms of our mission. Doing the things we need to do to be a good school will always introduce some risk. But not accomplishing our mission, a mission people thought was so important that it was worth the sacrifice required to bring our school into being, would also be risky.

H. Facilities

Capital assets are an important part of most business models. Most businesses require physical space and equipment to produce their product. Although education's space needs and equipment, as well as the final product, are different than those of other businesses, our work is somewhat capital intensive. That may change over the next few decades, depending on what happens with technology and movements like home-schooling, but for now Jesuit education relies on classrooms, studios, courts and fields, libraries, chapels and theaters to deliver its product. Physical facilities are key not only to the school's pedagogical model, but to its apostolic and community models as well. We see bringing students together into a cooperative, and sometimes competitive, learning environment as indispensable to fostering openness, intellectual competence, authentic religiosity, love and justice in our students.

Facilities are important to the school's financial well-being. We have already discussed the importance of the physical plant as an asset. Like a car, our campus is necessary to get where we want to go. Even those of us who do not love cars enough to want to care for them for their own sake need to give them love and attention, or they will make our lives difficult. If we don't change our oil and air filter, replace the signal bulbs and get new tires occasionally, we're going to end up stuck someplace and frustrated. For some of us, investing in our physical plant is the last place we want to spend money. So we do it only because we recognize that scrimping money now will cost us more later. Consultants with Sightlines Inc, which specializes in management of school investments in facilities, estimate that every $1 of deferred maintenance will eventually cost $2-3 in catch-up costs. Old lighting, old heating and cooling systems and fragile infrastructure can quickly suck away dollars from other school needs. We all know this, but it is difficult to make choices between replacing roofs that aren't leaking yet and hiring a learning specialist. How do we even know how much we need to invest in plant, let alone what kind of return we can expect?

Facilities are important to the school's program. Facilities should be shaped by program, but it is also true that facilities will shape program. It is more difficult to have a serious drama program without a theater. Maintaining high levels of participation in athletics requires a broad range of sports and different levels of teams for each, all of which require access to fields or courts. And while it doesn't necessarily follow that better facilities mean better programs, they are certainly an important ingredient. Batting cages will improve a baseball team's batting average. Better acoustics in the music room will help instrumentalists hear what notes they are actually producing. Larger classrooms support cooperative learning.

Facilities are important to attitude. It's difficult to convince a student that learning is important if the environment says it isn't. Conversely, replacing dilapidated facilities with new ones fosters pride in students and new respect for the work done in them. It says, "This is where the action is; be part of it." And it's not just about having shiny new buildings or equipment. I remember touring our campus with senior administration and having the vice president for development point to several areas of campus where we let things be broken, unpainted and cluttered with junk alongside newly renovated areas that we were proud of. She said, "Those areas just don't look loved." She was right. There are parts of our campus that look loved and parts that don't. They don't just look messy; they raise questions as to why we are willing to let these areas go to seed. If it's the maintenance shop, it seems to be saying that maintenance isn't that important. If it's around the readerboard, a little mess can send a message about a lack of love for our identity. Students pick up on this. Why be careful about litter in a space that is messy to begin with? Or next to an area that's messy? Disneyland understands this concept and has developed it into a science. They determined that if they put a certain amount of effort into cleaning up litter, especially near entrance areas, their patrons get the message that litter isn't appropriate in this place and they start taking responsibility for keeping it clean. How we shape the environment sends the most powerful message about what takes place in that environment. Unfortunately, the longer we live in that environment, the less we are aware of the messages it sends. So we need a way to see how it looks through fresh eyes.

Facilities are important to marketing. I remember visiting Harvard and walking across the Yard in late winter. The sky was overcast and slate gray with impending rain, the grass seemed non-existent after students playing ultimate frisbee all fall and winter, and the buildings were dark with the many years of service they had rendered to this country. I thought, "Good heavens! If I were a student from California visiting here on this day, I would never come to Harvard." Now that would be a decision made for the wrong reasons, because Harvard is of course a terrific university and few students wouldn't benefit from the opportunity of attending. But it made me aware of how powerful perception of a school campus can be to someone's attitude toward the school as a whole. So investing in physical plant is important to a school's health, if only because "curb appeal" is as important to selecting a school as it is to selecting a home.

Facilities departments are customer service organizations. This means that they measure their success by how well they have met the needs of their customers. The importance of this is that sometimes facilities departments can become self-referential. They can think that how a teacher or a student feels about the work they do has nothing to do with whether they get a paycheck or have a job. They will decide where they will put their energies and resources in ways that become disconnected from their customers. We've all experienced businesses or organizations where the people working with customers try hard to meet their needs and ones where they don't seem to care. Think of your recent experience with various airlines.

But the other side of customer service is that you can't please everyone, because you just don't have the time or resources to meet everyone's expectations. And if you try to, you end up pleasing no one. The muscles of the heart have to follow a sequence if the heart is to pump blood to the rest of the body. Simply firing muscles in response to immediate stimuli doesn't accomplish anything. We call this fibrillation. Like everything else in life, you have to prioritize. Sometimes to serve customers, you can't do what they want when they want it. So you have to manage their expectations. You listen to their needs and develop priorities and a plan for addressing the most important needs first, and you communicate back to them how you will meet their needs. To do this, the facilities department needs the support and guidance of the school administration, which can help them set priorities.

The facilities director can report to various people, most often the president or principal, but sometimes the CFO. Because facilities supports the whole school, I think it's important that the director report directly to the person who represents all the customer groups, the president. But when you look at where the demands on the department come from, it becomes clear that the main customer group is represented by the principal. The facilities director wants to make the president happy, but the president will be most concerned that the needs of the principal, or more accurately, of those departments that the principal leads, are being met. Unless the facilities department is responsive to those needs, the quality of education starts to erode, and along with it the apostolic model and the vibrancy of the community. If classrooms are not clean and ready, if gyms are not set up for assemblies, if the play director can't get into the theater for rehearsal, the school's performance grinds down to unacceptable levels.

Given the many and varied expectations placed on a facilities department, it's important for the president and the principal to help the facilities director identify and prioritize the key needs of the school. Once the community as a whole begins to understand what the priorities are, they can begin to put their own expectations into a bigger context. They can better understand why their personal priorities may have to be delayed in favor of critical institutional priorities. The facilities staff can concentrate on a finite set of important objectives and actually accomplish them, rather than being distracted by undifferentiated urgencies. The irony is that by lifting up some tasks as having higher priority than others, the staff will likely be more effective even with the lower priority needs. This comes about both because of greater focus and efficiency, but also because often the high priority tasks are ones that bring about systemic change. For example, replacing a malfunctioning electrical service can obviate the need for constantly resetting blown circuit breakers. I've seen this work and it makes a big difference.

Hand in hand with setting priorities based on customer needs is setting metrics to track how well the department is meeting those needs. If progress is slow, performance metrics can tell the department and school leadership that more effort or resources need to be applied. If progress is good, the metrics can stave off fibrillation by giving people something other than their latest experience to judge the department by. Just knowing the department is rigorously measuring its performance will increase the confidence of customers, which increases their patience and support, which in turn increases the effectiveness of the facilities staff.

Metrics for facilities are not easy to formulate. The business office can generate some financial measures, like cost of custodial and maintenance per square foot, or costs vs. budget. What would be helpful, though, is a measure of plant condition, both curb appeal and underlying integrity, as well as customer satisfaction.

Curb appeal can be difficult to measure because people become less conscious of campus appearance (though they are still affected by it) the more they are in the environment. Either surveys administered to people like visitors of relatively new students or parents, or proxies for school appearance (e.g. a measure of campus litter) could be used.

The underlying integrity of the plant can be measured and quantified, but it is a fairly time-consuming and sophisticated process. Colleges began doing this in the last decade and now some secondary schools have begun. They use a set of rubrics to audit the entire physical plant and measure the level of deferred maintenance. The urgency of certain conditions is categorized by how soon repairs will be needed, the costs of the repairs are estimated and the resulting numbers can be compared against benchmarks from peer institutions. Though the process is involved and will require investment in outside technical assistance, it gives a reliable picture of campus needs and so is worth the effort. Again, physical plant is the school's largest investment. It deserves to be managed accordingly.

Customer satisfaction can best be measured through a work-order system. An electronic work-order system is a great way to prioritize customer requests. It puts some responsibility on the customers, and is particularly burdensome for them as they are first learning how to place a work order. But like any new skill, it gets easier with practice. The information provided and the ability to gather work orders efficiently will repay the customer with better, more responsive service. The work order system can generate metrics for response time and, using simple surveys, customer satisfaction. The effects on the esprit, efficiency and performance of the facilities department will not be immediate, but eventually will be palpable.

I. Technology

What has been said for the management of facilities can also be applied to the management of technology in the school. Technology is an investment in an asset, it shapes and is shaped by program, it is important to marketing the school and it can inspire the community to a more serious commitment to learning. Technology departments also need to be customer service oriented, which includes managing customers' expectations. These expectations are driven by wide ranges of customer skill levels and perceptions of what other schools and businesses are doing. I discussed earlier my own experience of organizational fibrillation as the growth in technology overwhelmed our embryonic staff. The IT staff used customer service tools recommended above for facilities to bring order out of the chaos of varied expectations.

Technology is really part of a school's facilities and could theoretically be managed as part of the facilities. In the future, the lines between them will continue to be blurred. But for now, the level of sophistication and specific technical knowledge required by IT suggests that it needs to be a separate department. Because IT serves the whole school, the director should report to the president, but because the majority of customers is represented by the principal, the principal must be seen as the IT director's primary client. In some cases it may be appropriate simply to have the IT director report to the principal, who must then make sure IT is serving the needs of other departments like development and the business office.

Despite its similarity to facilities, IT has some special issues. The first is the speed of change. Intel co-founder Gordon Moore predicted this rate of change in what became known as Moore's Law, which states that the number of transistors that can be fit onto an integrated circuit doubles every two years and will continue to do so well into this century. The significance of this is that more and more functions can be performed, in more accessible devices, at lower cost. The functionality of electronic devices has far outstripped our ability to use it. How often are we aware that we have in our pocket a computer more powerful than the main-frames which made IBM the world's largest corporation? This explosion of technological potential has created a wide variation in the competence of people using it. Because new knowledge in this field is so quickly making old knowledge obsolete, it has also created the inversion described earlier in which students are the most knowledgeable, teachers less, and administrators the least of all. This creates complications for the change management process for the IT department and the school.

The scene looks something like this: The IT team knows that there are powerful teaching tools available. They are so powerful that they don't just automate existing functions; they introduce new concepts in how teaching is done (for example Smartboard systems which allow automatic feedback to teachers during presentations). The IT department struggles even to explain the concepts to the teachers, let alone show them how to use them, and the teachers resist learning about them because of the time involved and the lack of understanding of what they could do. Students are frustrated because teachers hold them back out of fear of technology they don't understand. Administrators know something needs to happen with technology, but never having used it when they were in the classroom, aren't sure what. And, even if they don't admit it, they are a little suspicious of technology, not knowing how to tell the useful from the merely flashy. And it's all expensive. Even if schools get grants to cover the initial costs, they have to commit themselves to the high recurring costs of keeping the equipment updated. A school could invest hundreds of thousands of dollars in equipment that could become obsolete in just a few years.

Another complexity introduced by technology is the additional security concerns. As data is taken out of paper files and put on computers connected to the school's local network and to the internet, it becomes more accessible. For the most part, this is a good thing. It means that all those who need access to information can easily have it, even if they are not on campus. It means that the same information doesn't have to be typed up over and over again and reams of paper don't have to be stored in bulky file cabinets. But it also becomes harder to control who has access to the information.

My experience is that we generally expand access first and worry about security second, sometimes not until there has been an actual breach. No part of IT is more boring or under-appreciated than security. It frustrates us when we have to come up with complicated passwords and change them every three months, when SPAM filters catch needed email, when we can't access a website because of filters in place for students or have to continually make adjustments to our settings for the "Big Brother" security software. We may not even be aware of the "firewalls" IT has to maintain, or back-up and off-site storage procedures, issues with clean power and power interruption protections, software license monitoring or compliance with PCC-DSS (Payment Card Industry Data Security Standard) and HIPPA (Health Insurance Portability and Accountability Act).

Technology is a great blessing for the process of teaching and learning, but like a classroom full of energetic freshmen it has to be managed into something coherent and useful. The only way to navigate the management challenges brought on by technology is to set clear goals. One of the things we decided early on at my school is that we would not be on the cutting edge. We saw other schools getting publicity for innovation and we felt pangs of envy. But we learned that in many cases these schools were finding out for the rest of us what works and what doesn't. We decided our role would be to let others be the pioneers and we would avoid the pitfalls by learning from their experience. This choice alone brought some clarity to IT's mandate. Then we decided that "Job One" was to build a reliable network. Nothing fancy, just a good solid backbone that would help teachers feel confident as they began to experiment with technology. In the early days we determined that getting email to work reliably, which meant effective SPAM filters, was an important goal. By building consensus around goals like these, we were able to distill out of the chaos of technology possibilities some clear directions which could not only move us forward, but could be sustained.

One of the early goals that we found most problematic was defining and implementing minimum competencies for the faculty. Our thought was that it would be fruitless to invest in technology capabilities if our teachers and staff didn't know how to use them.

But we found it difficult to define just what those minimum competencies should be, and we encountered resistance at all levels as we pushed everyone toward them. One of the things our IT director realized is that the more we stressed the importance of technology competencies, the more some employees resisted and tried to opt out. He shifted instead to just-in-time strategies. He made the assumption that every teacher will at some point be pushed, by a student, a parent, colleague or administrator, to try some new technology. He then structured the work of his department to have the training available, putting some training online in distance learning modules, setting up a drop-in center three days a week in the faculty room, and offering either periodic or on-demand training sessions. In addition, he began developing a way to publicly recognize those who had acquired competencies both as a way to reward their efforts and to let others know who they might get help from if they need it. While some in-servicing was still done, it was minimized in favor of the just-in-time approaches. The success of this approach was evident in the number of requests the IT department received for software and hardware to use technology applications. Competency was growing, while the sense of technology demands hanging over everyone's head seemed to diminish. In some cases, people may not even have realized they were being trained in minimum competencies. This approach might not work in all situations. We were blessed with an exceptional IT director who had skills as a teacher, engineer and change leader.

J. Conclusion of Business Model Discussion

A healthy business model is not a sufficient condition for a healthy school. But it is a necessary condition. No school can accomplish its apostolic, pedagogical or community goals unless the business model is sound, and no school can accomplish them well unless the business model is shaped specifically to support the other three models. Every business needs to have a product, customers, a way to charge for its product and a way to make its product known. In a Jesuit school these fundamentals take on a special meaning because the product is what we foster in our students, the customers are the people Jesus himself calls us to serve, the charge is a tuition/ financial aid structure which must account for "the least among us," and the promotion of this product is part of our teaching and evangelizing mission. For this reason, the school's business model can't be the concern of just the business office, the development office, the president or the board. It must be understood, at least in its basic elements, by all who depend on it to carry out their work. The irony is that ignoring the business model will only make it more important and more problematic. As with Freud's notion of the return of repressed memories in the unconscious, if you pretend the business model isn't there, it will hurt you; if you learn how to embrace it, it will bring you great strength.

Chapter VI:
Strategic Planning

The preceding chapters have looked at four models: the apostolic model, the pedagogical model, the community model and the business model. For the Jesuit school to flourish, each must be functional in itself and must support the others. One of the challenges of managing a school is that each model is complex enough that those of us who work in the schools tend to focus on one, or maybe two. People get uncomfortable and sometimes even suspicious when they are asked to deal with issues outside their normal field of operation. Teachers rarely sit on development committees; coaches don't usually read audits; business managers are usually happy not to grapple with discipline issues; development directors often rely on someone else to lead the prayer. We need a process that will focus all the leaders and participants in these multifaceted organizations toward a common vision of where the school is headed, what might prevent it from getting there, and how the school will overcome these obstacles. This is what strategic planning can do, and given the complexity of our four models, it must do it well.

A. The Role of Strategic Planning

We all know we're supposed to be doing strategic planning, but not everyone knows exactly why, or what strategic planning really means. Strategic plans have a way of emerging at various points in a school's history and then fading into the background. Like fireworks, they produce a brilliant light when they are first set off, but they too rarely provide the steady light needed to guide the school for the long-term. I have learned from my own experience and observing others that it's vexingly difficult to formulate a plan that will continue to guide school decision-making for more than a couple of years. But I also know it can be done.

What is a strategic plan? Let me rather address the question, what is strategic planning? --since the process is more important than the document it produces. Strategic planning is the process of identifying and aligning all the significant factors within an organization's control to accomplish its mission more effectively in the face of environmental factors that are not within its control. The word "strategic" implies that the plan produced must be:

Comprehensive. The strategic plan must strengthen all four functional models in the school. It can't just focus on one aspect of the organization, say, the curriculum or the business model. The organization as a whole must be understood and aligned. Not only must we identify all the major pieces, but we must understand how they interact.

Significant. It must focus on the big factors, the big ideas, the big trends, the ones we consider strategic because they will make a difference to the school's mission-effectiveness as a whole. These are game-changers for the school.

Forward-looking. Wayne Gretzky's response when asked the reason for his success as a hockey player captures the essence of strategic planning: He explained that he doesn't skate to where the puck is. He skates to where it's going to be. And so must we. The strategic planning process must identify the trajectory of trends in our environment and guide changes in the organization so that it can thrive in a new reality.

Broadly owned, so that the people who implement it are invested in its success.

Coherent, meaning that it can't just be a hodge-podge of good ideas that don't support or may in fact contradict each other.

Focused. We don't want to attack on many fronts. We want to find a few key beachheads on the way to our desired future and concentrate our forces there.

Accurate. We have to accurately assess our current situation and make intelligent assumptions about future trends. If these assumptions are sloppy or wrong, the plan will steer us off course.

Timely. The plan must respond to external trends soon enough, but not too soon. The prioritization of the plan goals must reflect the inherent timing of the issues the plan addresses. Hopefully, the planning process will assure that it does, but what is accurate and timely when the plan is written may change, especially if the plan horizon is 10 years.

Flexible. In a dynamic environment, the plan must be able to adapt to changing circumstances. One way to be flexible is to be vague. Not good. A better way to achieve flexibility is with an annual process for revising the plan, which will be discussed later in this chapter.

Why is such planning important? This is a crucial question. One board chair I have worked with always says, "If you don't know where you're going, any road will do." We all know that we're supposed to have strategic plans, but they take a lot of institutional energy to produce. When faced with the demands of the process, we are tempted to ask if it's really worth it. I think Jesuit schools have a special vulnerability here because they generally have the reputations, balance sheets and waiting lists that put them among the top schools in their catchment areas. This looks a lot like success. So if we are so successful, why should we put the whole operation at risk by fixing what ain't broke? Why, in any event, should we divert precious resources into a complex process, when to our intuitive judgments as experienced administrators things seem to be working so well? Life has enough problems without going to look for them.

To move beyond this thinking, I would offer both a *carrot* and a *stick*. The *carrot* is that even if we are already good, we can be better. I remember listening to a hospital administrator tell about his career. His first major administrative post was as a vice president in a suburban medical center in North Carolina. He knew he was an effective administrator because the hospital's profit margin, payer mix and daily census were in the top percentile of hospitals nationally. With this confidence, he applied for the CEO position at an urban hospital in Chicago and was hired. He quickly realized that his success at his former employer was a product, not of his or his colleagues' management skill, but of their location in an area where patients were affluent. In a more challenging inner-city environment, he quickly realized that he would have to learn true management skills if he and the hospital were to survive. It took him a few years, but to his credit he dedicated himself to improving his management skills and was able to turn that hospital around.

Jesuit schools have inherited a vital spirituality, effective pedagogy, great reputation and deep loyalty of successful alumni that often place them at the top of the heap in the cities where they operate. The patrimony which so richly blesses our institutions can lead us to complacency. We can easily make comparisons that persuade us that the job we are doing is plenty good enough.

But as Jesuit schools, we have a responsibility to be continually better. We call this the *magis*. We all contribute to the coming of Jesus' Kingdom by continuing to improve and grow into the people God created us to be. There is nothing more life-giving, once we get past our initial reticence, than seeing just how much we can do with the gifts God has given us. This is exactly what we expect from our students. Getting a comfortable A in trigonometry isn't good enough for a student who can cut her teeth on AP Calculus. In a world with too much hunger, destitution, violence and despair, schools, just like their students, have to keep getting better.

The *stick* is the fact that schools, even Jesuit schools, can cease to exist. Commercial enterprises are keenly aware of the precariousness of their existence. Blockbuster Video opened its first store in Dallas, Texas, in 1985. Taking advantage of new technologies and negotiating deals with the film industry, it grew within a few years to become a cultural staple of American life, with thousands of stores around the country and new ones opening every 17 hours. In 1995 it was purchased by Viacom for $8.4 billion. By 2002, however, it was losing money, and 25 years after it started it was in bankruptcy and being liquidated.[7] What happened? There were probably many miscalculations in an extraordinarily dynamic industry, including growing too fast and losing control of its cost structure. But one factor was how quickly its business model was superseded by Netflix. Blockbuster made the transition from VHS cassettes to DVD's in their stores, but since DVD's were much smaller and cheaper to manufacture, they could be mailed inexpensively. Capitalizing on this fact, Netflix stole Blockbuster's market in the span of a few years by building a clever distribution system without costly stores. It used the Post Office as its distribution system and let subscribers keep a DVD as long as they wanted, until they sent it back for another. Lower overhead and more convenience for the customer. That's strategic.

The technology-driven home viewing industry is at the opposite end of the spectrum from the famously stable education "industry." Education hasn't changed in 500 years as much as the video rental industry changed in ten. Why would I even bring it up for comparison? Because in education our very assumption of permanence puts us at risk. The story of the frog in the pot of water on the stove is instructive here. He notices the water getting warmer, but while he has the ability to leap out, he doesn't feel he needs to. When the water starts boiling, it is too late. Even education, even Jesuit education, is vulnerable to the changing world around it. If we don't anticipate the trends before they become full-grown realities, our response will come too late.

In the mid-1960s there were 5.5 million students enrolled in American Catholic schools. Today those numbers have declined to 2.1 million. During that time 8 Jesuit schools have either gone out of existence or morphed into something else.[8]

Why? Because there are fewer Catholics? Because Catholic schools aren't effective? Because public schools have gotten so good? Because the Catholic community has fewer resources than it used to? The demonstrable answer to each of these questions is "No." While many factors that engendered Catholic schools have changed or disappeared, there are still sufficient conditions to support their viability. Their decline, in general, has come about because they either failed to apprehend the changes in external factors, which were beyond their control, or failed to address them appropriately by re-aligning the internal factors, which were within their control. This is, by definition, a failure of strategic planning.

I am not arguing that keeping these schools open would have been easy, or even that it is always possible to see the trends or know how to adjust. Not all of us are Wayne Gretskys and even he probably misjudged from time to time where the puck would be. But unless strategic planning becomes an integral part of our modus operandi, we will leave ourselves and our schools entirely at the mercy of changes in the environment.

By systematically assessing our environment, we can begin to see the range of possibilities for where the puck will be. We can narrow down those possibilities to the ones we feel are most likely. And we can think about what responses within our control might prepare us for these possible futures. If changes in the future threaten us, strategic planning may be the key to survival. If changes in the future offer new opportunities to accomplish our mission more effectively, strategic planning will move us toward our institution's *magis*.

B. The Steps of Strategic Planning

There are many ways to do strategic planning. The following is intended to outline the most important steps in the order that I find generally makes sense. But there may be good reasons for skipping a step, adding one, or changing the order. In offering this list, I'm hoping to give readers a starting point from which they can determine their own process. [To get a more detailed treatment of the process see *Contact the Author* at the end of the book.]

Confirmation of the Mission Statement.

Since the strategic plan's purpose is to support the school's mission, the formulation or major revision of the plan is a good time to revisit the school's mission statement to see whether it still articulates what the school is about.

The mission is the reason the school came into being and remains in being. It should be possible to state the mission simply. When I first began working with our school's planning process in the early 1980's, our mission statement was four paragraphs long. We thought it was fairly succinct compared to the two-page "Philosophy Statement" that we drew from. But it sat on a shelf and was difficult to remember or even reference in going about our work. In the 1990's I decided it needed to be boiled down and proposed the following to the board, which they approved: "Our mission is to proclaim the Gospel message within an educational community and to graduate students who are leaders in action, modeled on Christ, and committed to the transformation he envisions for the world." This was a statement someone could memorize and slip into speeches and articles, put on signs, or use as a lens when considering a particular decision. And to my knowledge only one person actually did memorize it—me. So in the 2000's we came up with a one-word version of the mission: "Transformation." We were in the business of transforming students along the lines of the Gospel and having them become transformational people in the world. It didn't make our school unique, because many institutions share that mission. But it did capture why we were in business. No transformation, no reason to exist. Successful transformation, successful school.

Examine Assumptions.

1. Formulating Plan Assumptions

In many ways this is the most ambiguous part of the strategic planning process, because it involves assessing what may happen in the future. We often find that the possibilities are so numerous, as are the factors that determine which might become reality, that it seems futile trying to predict where the puck will be. And yet if we don't have some method for handicapping future trends the way a bettor at the track does before the horse race begins, we will be at their mercy. And there is little solace in looking back later and realizing that we had the tools to deal with the situation if we had seen it coming.

One of the factors that make formulating assumptions about the future so difficult is that there is no shortage of data. That is in great part the challenge of strategic planning, and a good place to begin to address it is the SWOT analysis.

2. SWOT Analysis

SWOT is an acronym for Strengths, Weaknesses, Opportunities and Threats. It is a simple structure for looking at both the external challenges facing a school and its internal resources. In the following explanations I have changed the order to address the external factors first, because the internal ones should respond to them.

Threats. Threats are those factors in the external environment that could make it more difficult to accomplish our mission. Examples could be higher costs of energy, fewer Catholic feeder schools and fewer students of high school age in our catchment area. These would be trends we cannot change, we can only respond to.

Opportunities. Opportunities are those factors which could give momentum to accomplishing our mission. Examples might be declining quality of public schools, lower cost and increased functionality of technology, hunger for spirituality in a secular society. Again, we couldn't create these opportunities if we wanted to, but all the same, there they are. Interestingly, some trends could be seen as both threats and opportunities. For instance, would the establishment of a new Catholic high school in one's catchment area be a threat because it would be competing for students or an opportunity because the public's awareness of Catholic education will be increased? It could also be an opportunity because competition motivates us to raise our game to a higher level.

Weaknesses. These are internal pieces that are missing or deficient within our institutions. Examples might be high operating costs, an aging facility, or not enough room in the schedule for electives. These are things we could change, though we haven't done so yet because it would be difficult or have consequences we'd rather not deal with.

Strengths. These are internal elements that we're good at, that give us leverage in accomplishing our mission. Examples might be an experienced, well-educated faculty, a beautiful, functional physical plant or a unique and highly regarded service program. The thing to watch with both strengths and weaknesses is that they must be seen as such in terms of the mission. For instance, a school that has a population with enough affluence that it doesn't need to spend much money on financial aid could see this as a strength or a weakness, depending on how it understands its mission.

After conducting and discussing the SWOT analysis, the school would then gather pertinent data relating to the key assumptions that emerge. For instance, an external assumption might be that the feeder schools will be graduating fewer students in the next ten years. An analysis of enrollment in the lower grades would be important data to have. Using the collected data to verify the assumptions that emerged from the SWOT analysis, the school will then finalize the assumptions that will shape the strategic planning process.

Setting Goals

Once assumptions about the future have been clarified—which means the school has identified the biggest and most likely threats, the opportunities it wants to capitalize on, the strengths it has that will help it do that and the weaknesses it will have to shore up to be ready—the school can set specific, strategic goals designed to bring it to where the puck will be.

Strategic goals are major initiatives the school must undertake to better accomplish its mission. By saying "major," we mean that they are beyond the incremental improvements you expect in the normal course of business. Strategic goals are therefore, by definition, disruptive, challenging, time- and energy-consuming and generally not attractive to folks who are just fine with the way things are. We begin to realize this as the process unfolds. There is an unconscious, sometimes conscious, tendency to water down the goals so they keep us well within our safety zone.

The most likely way for strategic goals to lose their potency is by becoming too broad and vague. I've been down that road. These are goals like, "The school will substantially improve the annual giving program." This is a good goal in the sense that it's probably important to do. But imagine trying to determine five years later what progress you've made on it. What qualifies as a substantial improvement? $5,000, $100,000, $1,000,000? While you might not think a $5,000 increase met the goal's intention, someone else might. Who's to say whose interpretation of this goal is valid?

Another problem with this goal is that it can be evaluated in terms of inputs rather than outcomes. Someone could hire a consultant to upgrade the solicitation materials and claim they have substantially improved the Annual Giving program. Nor does the goal tell us when the improvement was to take place, nor who would be responsible for it. This is how strategic plans become dust collectors. Even if they give expression to our hopes for the school, if we don't agree on what specifically we will see when the goal is achieved, if we don't know what mission-related outcomes it will produce, or when it will produce them or who will be responsible, such strategic goals will be of little use in managing change at the school. For the plan to have value one, three, five and ten years from now, we need to push ourselves to make sure the goals are complete. A moat does not protect the castle unless its circle is complete. Going only ¾ of the way around does no good. To help us remember the four characteristics of complete goals, think of them as a **MOAT** protecting the goals' integrity, with each letter from this word representing one of the characteristics: **M**easurable, **O**utcome-based, **A**ssigned, **T**imed.

1. First MOAT Characteristic: Measurable

The first MOAT characteristic which a strategic goal requires is a measurable result. Whether we acknowledge it or not, we rely on some form of evidence to tell us whether we are moving toward our aspirations or not. If a school says its goal is to prepare students to succeed in college, it can point to its use of best practices in developing a superb college prep curriculum; it can cite the example of several graduates and their success in college; or it can look at college graduation rates. Whatever progress or lack thereof the evidence indicates will decide what changes, if any, it makes to its program. So it is important that the evidence be reliable.

Essentially, we have three kinds of evidence on which we base our decisions: intuitive, anecdotal and statistical. Each has its strengths and weaknesses and none is reliable by itself.

All three of these forms of evidence are important in the management of a school. Measurable results for a goal should be a statistic that indicates whether the desired outcomes are being achieved across the board, but they should be verified and challenged by both anecdotal and intuitive evidence. Anecdotal evidence is especially helpful in pointing to where the statistics chosen may not be telling the whole story. Intuitive evidence is indispensable in developing process steps that lead to better results. The point is that while statistical evidence is the main tool for gauging progress on the strategic plan, it must also be interpreted in light of anecdotal and intuitive evidence for the three-legged stool to stand. [To get more information on using the three types of evidence to build better metrics see *Contact the Author* at the end of the book.]

The first MOAT characteristic of a strategic goal is a measurable result. Without a measurable result, we can't tell if we are making progress. If we can't measure our progress, we can't adjust our processes and see which adjustments positively impact results

2. Second MOAT Characteristic: Outcome-based

Unless we define the ultimate results we want, it will be unclear whether our solutions are accomplishing them. We must work backwards from ends to means, from *outcome* to *output* to *input* to *resources*. To understand this backward design, let's say you are concerned about an increase in student attrition, which could eventually threaten enrollment levels. You decide that an important strategic goal would be to reduce attrition by 50%. This is your *outcome*. You determine that most of your attrition is due to academic issues and particularly freshmen not being prepared for the increased demands of high school. You want to address this by ensuring that every freshman understands how to use time-management skills by the end of the first 6 weeks of school. This is your *output*. To accomplish this, the school introduces lesson plans on time-management into every freshman English class. This is an input. To accomplish this, the school provides in-service training, and purchases a time-management workbook, which are resources. The *resources, inputs* and *outputs* should all lead to the *outcomes*, and outcomes should be defined in the goals of the strategic plan.

3. Third MOAT Characteristic: Assigned

To be successful, strategic goals need champions. The school must know who is responsible for leading the implementation of each goal. Sometimes the goal will correspond neatly with an administrative position. For example, "Increase the endowment by 30% between years 2 and 7 of the plan," would probably be led by the director of development. At other times it is clear that someone on staff has a passion and talent for leading a certain process. For example, "Increase parent support of the formational goals of the school by 25%," might be managed by a teacher who has a special talent for and interest in adult education. Generally, the more accountability required from more school departments, the higher up the administrative ladder leadership must come.

Regardless of who provides the ongoing leadership for a strategic goal, accountability must clearly tie into the governance and administrative structure of the school. The board and its committees must have ownership, oversight and appropriate involvement in the strategic goals.

Regardless of the accountability structure, the strategic plan must make clear to those responsible for goals and to everybody else, who is leading the charge.

4. Fourth MOAT Characteristic: Timed

Imagine yourself evaluating progress on one of your strategic goals five years from now. You know the measurable outcome of the goal and who was responsible for leading its achievement. But when did it need to be achieved? Are you behind schedule? Ahead? If this goal was important enough for you to include in the strategic plan, you must have had some sense of when you wanted to accomplish it. Finishing a 10K run is nice, but it's not an accomplishment unless you do it in a meaningful timeframe.

I propose that early on in the formulation of the goal you start writing down time-line expectations. They are almost certain to be inaccurate. That's okay. It is better to have an inaccurate completion target than no target at all. With no target, everyone is working on their own time-line. With even an inaccurate target, people start communicating with one another about whether there is some way to achieve it and how it might be done.

What would a time-line for a strategic goal look like? The time-line sets out the date by which the measurable outcome will be achieved by those to whom it is assigned. This deadline has to be within the time horizon of the overall plan. So if it's a ten-year plan, the goal has to be achieved in no later than 10 years. It must be achieved even sooner if some other strategic goal depends on its earlier completion. In some cases, what can be accomplished within the horizon of the strategic plan is not what is ultimately envisioned for this goal. For instance, let's say the vision for the school is that the entire campus be retrofitted to the highest LEED environmental standards. This may take 30 years to accomplish. So the goal for a 10-year strategic plan might reference the school's ultimate vision but commit the school to retrofitting one third of the campus within the ten-year horizon of the current plan.

The goal should also contain some milestone time-lines to allow progress checking during implementation of the plan. The strategic plan shouldn't be weighed down with tactical information, but a mid-term target would be helpful. An appendix accompanying the strategic plan can contain more information about implementation milestones.

C. Coordination and Leadership of the Strategic Planning Process

For the board, the strategic plan is a tool for providing governance-level guidance to the administration. Using the strategic plan, the board can discharge its main responsibility of assuring that the administration is pursuing the mission faithfully and effectively, without drawing itself into implementation. For the administration, the strategic plan is a way of confirming direction with the board. As long as the board has approved the plan, based on their thorough understanding of the goals, the administration need not fear that major strategic initiatives will be second-guessed by the board.

For the school president, the strategic plan is the primary management tool. It gives the president his leadership agenda. Because it is his leadership agenda, the president's job is to lead the formulation of the plan and then lead its overall implementation. The president must see that the board, administration and any other key leaders in the school are educated about the planning process, understand its importance and are ready to incorporate it into their priorities. The president must see that the strategic planning process is well-designed and disciplined. The president must see that people are encouraged to participate in the planning process, and reminded of the vision, both for the planning process and for the school. And the president must make sure the activities of the various leaders of the plan's goals are coordinated and receive the resources needed.

D. Participation and Ownership

If the president leads and coordinates the process for the strategic plan, who actually creates it? The simple answer is, "The people who will be needed to implement it." I remember early in my career visiting an attorney at his office to ask him for a pledge to our capital campaign. I showed him a summary of the long-range plan that I had authored for the school and, asking if he had seen it yet, was surprised to hear him say, "I wrote that." Fortunately I suppressed my pride of authorship long enough to learn that he had been on a committee that put together a philosophy statement upon which the plan would ultimately be based, so in a sense he did write it. Of course he made a pledge to the campaign because he saw it as implementing a vision he had helped create. This is a lesson I have learned over and over again. The difference between a good plan and a bad plan is that a good plan is one that people make work. And people tend to make work those plans that they have helped create.

So answering the question of who needs to be involved in shaping the plan means answering the question of who you will need to make this plan succeed. Of course, you'll need the board. If they don't see this as their plan, then their attention and governance directives will be leading the school elsewhere, or generating a lot of work extraneous to the strategic plan. If the board has a strong committee structure, then by extension the committees will need to be involved as well.

The administration, and not just the president, will need to see it as their plan. The principal is crucial, because the plan begins and ends with improving the educational program. The CFO will need to develop and monitor financial projections. The development director will have to shape how the fundraised resources will be achieved. The facilities director and the IT director will almost certainly have to give input to and help with implementation of components of the plan. The vice-principals and all those administrators responsible for curricular and extra-curricular program will be key to "operationalizing," since they shape the schedules and priorities of the faculty and students. I've seen schools err on both sides of administrative inclusion. Some don't involve the administration at all because they are "too busy" to take on the extra work involved. So the board or a group of well-meaning volunteers does the work for them, with the consequence that the administrators feel free to ignore it as something someone else came up with. Other schools don't involve anyone besides administration because of concerns that a bunch of non-experts will complicate administrative work by bringing in initiatives from left field. Both extremes should be avoided.

Without faculty input and support, the plan will fight a constant current of push-back. Not only will teachers be heavily involved in implementation, but it is hard to imagine others supporting a plan that the people at the center of the education process don't understand and support. Since a strategic plan requires fundraised dollars to implement, benefactors like the attorney in my story above, and particularly the school's alumni, will need to support it. If the first opportunity they have to be part of the plan is when they're asked for money, it's not likely they will. And finally other organizations that have authority or otherwise exert influence over the school should be brought into the planning process so that their support can be counted on during implementation. These include the Province leadership, the local diocese, local school district, media and local opinion leaders.

This is starting to sound like a pretty big committee. How do we get the input and ownership of all these stakeholders without creating an unwieldy process? The key is to develop a variety of vehicles of involvement and use them to maximize participation by these different groups.

Avenues of Involvement in Strategic Planning:

Steering Committee. This is a small committee that will guide the overall planning process on behalf of the board. It should include key representatives from the board, faculty, administration, parents, alumni, benefactors, sponsoring agencies and possibly a student. Of course some members may represent more than one category. For instance, a board member may also be an alum and a major benefactor. (8-12 total participants)

Topic Teams. Committees of 10-15 members who will meet 2-4 times to focus on and develop recommendations for specific areas of the plan (e.g.: academics, facilities, etc.). (80-120 total participants)

Plenary Planning Meeting. All constituents can be invited to an evening or weekend session, or a series of sessions, to kick-off the planning process. Often these meetings have a presentation about the process and some of the key issues facing the school. Then participants are invited to sit in on sessions on various topics that will become the focus of the Topic Teams. (100-300 total participants)

The process can also broaden its outreach with **special presentations** to groups like parents' clubs and the alumni association (100-500 total participants); **focus groups** (30- 60 total participants); and **surveys** (500-2,000 total participants).

Looking at all these different vehicles (and there are other variations as well) it's conceivable that the school could involve over 400 people directly in shaping the plan, and another 2,500 giving input that will be used in formulating it, with everyone else at least having been given the opportunity. Imagine all these people not only sharing their insights, perceptions and hopes, but also learning more about the school and its needs and beginning to see themselves as part of the team that will address those needs. The power of this involvement for the ultimate success of the plan should not be underestimated.

Rolling up all the Input into a Plan

The participative process described above will secure broad ownership, but how will we be able to take the hundreds of ideas and forge them into a coherent and focused plan? To do this, we use a *funneling* process. Funneling is the process of narrowing or distilling a large number of recommendations into a strategic few. As recommendations are funneled up from broad-based participation vehicles, like public meetings and topic teams, toward a steering committee which formulates the overall strategic plan, they are often consolidated, eliminated or changed to produce a focused and coherent set of strategic goals. To accomplish this, it is important that participants understand how their input will be molded into a focused plan. This should be built into the process from the beginning. [To get more information on the funneling process, see *Contact the Author* at the end of the book.]

E. Time Horizon for the Strategic Plan

One of the first questions to come up in strategic planning is, "What should the time horizon of the plan be?" Some organizations find it appropriate to plan 25, 50 or even 100 years into the future. Others in fast-changing industries, like our example Blockbuster, have trouble planning beyond two or three years. In our own industry, education, there are three factors that influence how we approach the planning horizon issue. The first is what I call the "Ground Hog Day Effect." This is based on the movie of the same title, starring Bill Murray. Through most of the movie Murray's character is condemned to reliving the same Ground Hog Day over and over again. He wakes up each morning only to find that this day will go the same as the day before, and the day before that. The nine-month school year can have that same effect. Research has shown how much students forget during summer vacation. But so do institutions. Most of people working at a school will be gone for one to three months in the summer. Like the students, they will leave school thoughts as far behind as possible. They will work on re-charging their batteries and on personal and professional development. September will be Ground Hog Day, when everyone wakes up and goes through the cycle again. Administrators know this cycle and how difficult it is to engineer change that doesn't fit easily into it. The Ground Hog Day Effect makes big-picture thinking difficult and big-picture implementation nearly impossible. The strategic planning process is a way to get beyond this, but only if done thoughtfully.

The second factor influencing the planning horizon for schools is that education is conservative. Despite an uncountable number of reform initiatives, it has changed little since the Renaissance compared to just about every other industry. And because it hasn't changed, we have come to believe that it won't change. Many educators simply don't believe Harvard researcher Clayton Christiansen, author of *Disrupting Class*, when he predicts that over half of all high-school classes will be delivered on-line by 2019. Technology is not the only disruptive force. The fact is that 19.7% of Catholic schools in the US in 2000 were closed or consolidated by 2010. The Archdiocese of Detroit closed all 7 of its Catholic high schools in one year, 2005.[9] Are these just wave patterns, or early warnings of a sea-change?

The final factor influencing the school's planning horizon is how communitarian we are. Research has shown that the biggest factor leading to the success of Catholic schools is our abundant social capital. This concept, introduced by researcher James S. Coleman in the 1980's, refers to the community that surrounds the school. Teachers, parents, volunteers and benefactors comprise a village that supports each student. A strategic plan is a key tool for fostering that community around the school. But it takes a lot of time to receive the input of a broad community, and that itself will influence the time horizon of the plan.

So what do these three factors tell us about the time horizon of our strategic plan? 1) It has to be long enough to spread the implementation beyond the confines of what can be accomplished in one hectic nine-month cycle, yet short enough that people can see results from the extra, strategic work that's been added to their plate; 2) it must take into account just how fast the environment around could change, or already is changing; and 3) it must allow for the participative process described earlier to gather input from its support community and roll it up into the plan.

Each school must decide based on its own circumstances how to weigh these factors, but based on my own work, which includes four strategic planning cycles at one school and assistance at others, a ten-year time horizon seems to work best. The biggest driver of this is setting up the participative process. It takes about three years to build that participation. Ideally, by year 8 of the current plan, we need to start educating people, particularly the board and administration, about the planning process. In year 9, the board must evaluate the current plan, set parameters for the process and appoint a steering committee, and the administration must start gathering data. In year 10 the topic teams make their recommendations to the steering committee, which then finalizes the next strategic plan and presents it to the board for approval. It takes a lot of energy for the school community to give the kind of input and provide the broad ownership needed.

F. Format of the Strategic Plan Document

Once the steering committee has finalized the goals for the long-range strategic plan, it must now decide how to communicate them to the school's stakeholders. This will be done by a number of means, but anchoring all the communications about the strategic plan will be a document, referred to as the Long-range Strategic Plan, which captures the essentials in a readable format. To decide on the format, it is important to understand what you want the document to accomplish.

First, you want to **inform**. Anyone reading the document should have a clear understanding of what the school intends to accomplish over the time-frame of the plan and why.

Secondly, you want to **inspire**. Anyone reading the plan document is likely to be involved in some element of the plan implementation. This is your chance to touch their imaginations and their hearts, to help them see a vision of what the school could be if they would help it accomplish its strategic goals.

Thirdly, you want it to be **read**. Unless the document is actually read, and referred to, it can neither inform nor inspire. To accomplish this, it must be attractive, well-written and, most important, brief.

If the funneling process is used rigorously to focus the plan, the actual document should be short. As with the mission statement, the shorter the document, the more likely it will be read, remembered and referred to. Brevity competes with completeness, however. Readers must be given enough context that they understand the reasons that major, strategic goals are being proposed for the school. The goals must have enough specificity that readers will be able to picture what they mean and what the school will look like when they are accomplished. Much of the detail about metrics, implementation, assignments, time-lines and data which drive the goals can be included in appendices so the plan itself can be as streamlined as possible.

G. Annual Implementation Planning (AIP)

The way to achieve flexibility and maintain accuracy and correct timing is by building Annual Implementation Plans (AIP's) every year. Essentially, this involves the administration each year reviewing the goals of the long-range strategic plan, assessing the school's progress and deciding next steps.

As stated earlier, the long-range strategic plan won't go into detail about implementation or intermediate targets on the way to the strategic goals. These should be left to the AIP. Using the long-range plan as a guide, the administration, collaborating with faculty, board, parents and others as appropriate, outlines the steps it will take in a given year to move toward attainment of the school's long-range strategic goals. This is how schools overcome the "Ground Hog Day Effect." The school focuses on what can be done within the nine-month window, because that's what schools do. But thanks to the long-range plan, it is able to set targets for those nine months that feed into a larger, multi-year cycle that leads to significant improvements.

The most difficult AIP to formulate will be the first. In order to decide on the steps to be taken the first year, the school needs to have a sense of what steps will be required in future AIP's. If you've ever crossed a stream by stepping from stone to stone, you know that you have to choose a first stone that you can reach and that will be secure. But you also have to glance across the stream to your destination and trace back a plausible series of stones that connect with the first stone. You don't evaluate future stones as carefully as you evaluate the one you are about to take, but you have to at least know that the first one will give you good options ahead. Once on the first stone you can then take a closer look at your options for the next step, again glancing ahead, and so on till you cross the stream. In formulating the first year's AIP you will already be shaping future implementation steps.

I won't go into detail here on the how and who of formulating implementation steps, but it will be helpful to look at the general approach. In general, the process is similar to the "backward design" of a curriculum, developed in the work of Grant Wiggins and Jay McTighe. You start with the outcomes you want and work backward through the steps required to achieve those outcomes. This is your glance across the stream. One way to do this is by building a *Process Chain*. The essential idea is to have the administrative team identify, in a visual way, all the links in a causal chain needed to achieve a plan goal so that it can build implementation steps around each link. [To get more information on process chains see *Contact the Author* at the end of the book.]

Formulating the Annual Implementation Plan

The foregoing can be a time-consuming and mentally challenging process. It requires busy administrators who have many demands pressing on them throughout the school year to somehow carve out time in their week to do some proactive thinking. But it has to be done if the school is to continue to improve, and no one else can do it other than the administrators who are at the front-lines, who are experts in their area and who will have to lead their colleagues in implementing the plan. Once they have formulated the objectives in this way, the following years require far less planning and can focus on execution. If everyone has done their job in the design phase, implementation should actually give back more energy than it takes and should be enjoyable.

The process for finalizing the AIP involves another funneling process. Even though the results of the process chain were funneled, there will still be too many objectives to focus on in one year. And achieving strategic objectives, especially in an environment where people have a lot of daily demands, requires focusing on the most important strategies. The administrative team reviews the objectives written up by the managers and puts them into four categories:

1. Objectives that have implementation steps which are major and critical to do this year

2. Objectives that have implementation steps that are minor but still critical to do this year

3. Objectives to defer because they aren't priorities and won't fit on this year's plate

4. Objectives to defer because prerequisites need to occur first

The first category, those objectives which have major steps to be done this year, constitute the core of the AIP. These might be items like "Complete construction of the new library," or "Have all faculty meet minimum technology competencies." You may not be able to accomplish everything you want to this year, but you need to accomplish these. The AIP must be formatted in a way that everyone who reads it—administration, board, faculty and staff—know that these are the must-do's. For this reason, when they are presented in the plan, they must be presented with all the MOAT characteristics: the **M**etric, the downstream **O**utcome it is measuring, who is **A**ssigned as manager and the **T**ime-frame for achieving the objective.

The AIP may also include objectives from the second category, those which have only minor steps but which are critical to accomplish this year. These might include: "Budget money for a marketing plan to be done in year 2," or "Establish a metric and base-line measure for the new formation program to be implemented in year 3." If they are included, they should be presented in abbreviated form at the end of the AIP, so as not to distract from the importance of the Category 1 items. The president and key administrators need to follow up on them, but they won't want to waste precious attention span by highlighting them in the plan. Resist the temptation of turning the AIP into a grab-bag of things it would be nice to do if you had the time. The AIP should consist only of those objectives the school leadership simply must make the time to accomplish. This is why funneling is so important. The funneling process can be painful, but it is the key to making meaningful change without burning everybody out.

Categories 3 and 4, objectives that can't fit on the plate or require a prerequisite, will be queued up for future years and considered for future AIP's. An example of Category 3 might be "Begin construction of the new theater" when you have to finish the library and can't do both at once. An example of a Category 4 might be "Implement a distance learning component in all courses," when this would require all faculty to attain certain technological competencies first. The current AIP should not contain any Category 3 or 4 items.

The annual implementation plan is then presented to the board for approval, ideally at the end of the prior school year, but no later than the first meeting of the year covered by the AIP. The AIP is a key tool for the board to verify the administration's understanding of priorities, and bless or redirect them. For the administration, it is a tool for getting the board's concurrence and relieving the concern that during implementation the board will be surprised and unsupportive of the direction the administration is taking. In short, it allows the board to give governance-level guidance without being drawn into micro-managing.

[To receive an example of an annual implementation plan see *Contact the Author* at the end of the book.]

H. Common Pitfalls to Strategic Planning

In the foregoing description of the strategic planning process, I have tried to identify those elements that will lead to an effective plan. I want to take a moment to look at planning from the other perspective and address the forces that can undermine or simply dilute the planning process. I have myself fallen into each of these pits at various times. We have to resist them vigorously if the plan is to succeed.

Pitfall 1: **Apple Pie and Motherhood**. It is emotionally difficult to choose between good ideas that have passionate people advocating them. But the funneling process required to produce a plan that is focused enough to be truly strategic means saying no to some good ideas along the way. To avoid the pain of disappointing people, we have a tendency to just make the plan bigger and make sure no good idea is lost. I've done this. I've presided over the formulation of a plan that is more an inventory of everybody's ideas than anything strategic. An inventory of everybody's ideas or of every department's needs isn't a bad thing to have, but it is bad if you call it your strategic plan. Because it throws all ideas, strategic or not, into one big-grab bag, this is as sure a way of killing strategic decision-making as having no plan at all.

Pitfall 2: **A big target**. One way to hit the bulls-eye is to become an expert marksman. The other way is just to make the target very big. An example would be a goal like "We will improve our AP test scores." For the goal to be strategic, however, we have to challenge ourselves, say precisely what we hope for, what will really make a difference to the school. This pushes us out of our comfort zone, but I would rather articulate a goal, fail to meet it and learn why, than put forth a goal that I can't miss and doesn't challenge me to look at what I'm doing. Another variation on making the target bigger is just moving it closer. This can be done by focusing measures on inputs rather than outcomes, saying something like, "We will increase the number of AP offerings by 5 courses." By focusing more on means than ends, we bring it more under our control, and in the process avoid the possibility of having to make unanticipated changes to how we do things in order to achieve specific results. This may seem attractive but it reduces the probability of achieving meaningful outcomes, because we haven't described precisely what they would be.

Pitfall 3: **Kicking the Can Down the road**. The most common example of this is the goal that begins with, "Develop a plan to..." or "Determine whether such and so needs to be done..." I find myself gravitating toward this approach when the planning process is up against time constraints and we're having trouble getting consensus about a trend or what we want to do about it. So we make a plan to make a plan. There may be cases where this is all you can do, but it's just too easy and not very strategic. Imagine Gretzky saying, "I think I'll just watch a while and see where the puck goes." Strategic planning is skating to where we think the puck will be, not forever chasing it. It is better to be bold, start skating. Even if we're wrong, we're in the flow of the game and can more readily make adjustments.

Pitfall 4: **Shooting the moon**. For 15 years I have tutored first graders who have trouble learning to read, and I notice they tend to "shoot the moon." They pick books beyond their level so they have a good justification when they find they can't read them. I have to patiently direct them back to goals which challenge them to the next level, but are reasonable steps along that path. In strategic planning, the same principle applies. The difference between a challenging goal and shooting the moon is that, with the former, you are prepared to make the sacrifices that will get you there. With the latter, you don't give much thought to methods because you're basically relying on luck. And that doesn't take a lot of planning.

Pitfall 5: **The sky is falling**. The whole point of long-range planning is to take big goals and break them down into doable steps that can be worked into the 9 month cycles of a school. But if people aren't used to breaking big goals into smaller steps, or if they've worked in a culture where they are not given the opportunity and tools to do that, the goals themselves will induce anxiety. They can even run around like Chicken Little, crying out that the sky is falling. I experience something similar every time I scramble up one of the beautiful mountains in the region where I live. Sometimes the summit, if I can even see it, is so far away it makes me laugh. It generally feels impossible for me to reach that summit and return in a day. But I can get to that ridge to the northwest in two hours and from that ridge angle north to that gully in maybe another hour and a half. From there it's just another 1,000 feet up a talus slope to the top. Rare are the times when I haven't made the goal, but if I let my initial anxiety about the overall goal prevent me from breaking it down into the doable stages, I would never take the first step.

Pitfall 6: **Red Herrings**. With strategic planning we can establish the track that leads us to our desired future. But as we follow the true scent, other possibilities are dragged across the trail that can divert us from where we really need to go. Maybe it's a new foundation-funded program that offers the prospect of more dollars, or a new sport that has a strong constituency of parents or students behind it, or a building that isn't in your top five priorities, but there is a benefactor ready to fund 20% of it right now. Unless the call of the strategic plan is firmly planted in people's hearts and minds, other inevitable attractions and urgencies will divert us from our resolve.

How do we overcome these various pitfalls? The most important defense is to know that they will be there. As with any pit, once you know it's there you're much less likely to fall into it. They are all natural human inclinations. Knowing this can help the leaders of the school to be more patient and understanding, but also to be firm and not let these distractions from the true course rule the day. In his book *Good to Great*, Jim Collins talks about the flywheel effect. From his research of companies that have made the transition from being good firms to great ones, he learned that they generally went through an early period of little perceptible progress, mostly because the people who had to implement change were resistant to it. This early stage looks a lot like failure, and inexperienced administrators will conclude that they need to change course. But like a flywheel, strategic changes gain momentum if the leadership is persistent. People learn new skills, learn new ways of viewing obstacles, and soon what was very difficult just becomes the new normal. If you can recall learning to ride a bike, you will surely remember that it seemed impossible. The only reason you didn't give up is that all the kids before you managed to do it. The leader of strategic change must not let people back down before they begin to feel the flywheel move, and the more he can articulate the vision and make the desired future palpable in the present, the more he can increase persistence in the culture of his school.

Chapter VII: Governance

This book is about management, which in a school is primarily the domain of the administration. We have defined management as the direction leaders give to align the decisions and actions of all participants toward desired organizational outcomes. Governance addresses how those desired organizational outcomes get defined. Governance is a term most often associated with non-profit organizations, which exist to serve society according to their mission. Missions are open to interpretation and sometimes even need to be revised. A governance structure is intended to be a human link between an organization and the community it serves. It is intended to interpret and steward the organization's mission on behalf of the community. It holds the organization accountable on behalf of the community and encourages the community's support of the organization. Sometimes a governance structure can feel like a burden to an organization, just another layer of expectations and constraints. But it can also be a resource and a source of great strength. Like the business model, it is problematic if you try to ignore it and helpful if you embrace it.

For many non-profits, the governance structure is synonymous with the board. For Jesuit schools, the governance picture is more complex because our accountability structure is more complex. In the first place, like all non-profits, we are accountable to the community around us, and especially the members of that community we serve directly as students and school families. Then, because our schools were founded by the Jesuits and remain part of their ministry, even if we have few or no Jesuits working in them, we are accountable to the Society of Jesus. At one point all of our schools were owned by the Society of Jesus and little effort was made to distinguish between the school, the local Jesuit community and the province. Over time, the schools became separate corporations, though the boards, as well as the administrations, generally consisted entirely of Jesuits. Eventually Jesuit teachers and even administrators were succeeded by lay people, and in most cases predominantly lay boards were established to govern the schools. Today there are a variety of board structures at Jesuit schools. In some cases, the governing board of the schools is entirely or predominantly Jesuit, often with an additional predominantly lay board with limited or only advisory authority. Whatever the structure is, its purpose is to provide both a personal connection and accountability to the surrounding community and to the mission of the Jesuits.

While the governance of Jesuit schools most prominently reflects their accountability to the community and the Jesuits, they are also accountable to other authorities. In the revision to the Code of Canon Law, approved in 1983, the Church gave greater responsibility to the local bishop for supervising schools which called themselves Catholic. Before, the Catholic identity of an order-sponsored school came almost exclusively through the order. The new Canons 804-806 give the local bishop greater authority over the schools' programs of religious formation and those who deliver religious instruction. While they call for respecting autonomy for the internal direction of order schools, there is an ambiguous suggestion of authority for the general regulation of the schools as well. Individual bishops are given wide latitude in how these Canons are promulgated, but school administrators should be alert to their potential impact on school governance. The other Canons they need to be aware of are 116 to 118, which deal with "public juridic persons." Every Catholic institution must have a person or group of persons with direct accountability to the Church hierarchy. This makes sense when you think about it. If I decided to start a school and call it Catholic, I might think it enough to follow Church teaching to achieve recognition as such by the local church. If this were all that was required, it could lead to a proliferation of institutions with no way to assure their continued fidelity to the Church. Jesuit provinces are increasingly relying on a formalized sponsorship process as the means of assuring continued fidelity. But the Church has been more comfortable having a person or group of persons (such as a local Jesuit community) as the official link for Catholic identity. So while Fr. General may say that the president is the "director of the work" and the local superior along with the local Jesuit community are "animators of the work," Canon Law would consider the local superior and/or community as the public juridic person responsible to the Church for the institution's Catholicity.

As if that weren't complex enough, the governance structure also must address government authority over the Jesuit schools. This varies greatly from state to state, but the trend has been toward more influence exerted by state offices of public instruction over who is offering education in their state and what standards they should meet.

Finally, some Jesuit schools, notably Cristo Rey and Nativity schools, belong to networks that have another set of requirements they must meet in order to claim those additional identities.

Though the characteristics may vary, for most Jesuit schools governance is primarily invested in a board, known either as a board of trustees or a board of directors. The names suggest the two prime attributes of the boards. They hold the school in trust for the community and sponsoring entities named above, and they have a responsibility at a high level to direct the schools. In practice, however, the terms trustee and director are synonymous.

A. Role of the Board

In a Jesuit school the board has a responsibility to care for the apostolate as a whole. The Jesuit phrase for this is *cura apostolica*. Holding the administration and other employees accountable is part of that care, but only part of it. The board also works to make sure the institution has the resources and public support it needs to carry out its mission. Board members serve as ambassadors to the community and channels of communication from the community back to the school. They help with fundraising by linking the school to potential philanthropists in the community and, when appropriate, by asking for donations themselves. They set an example to the community by their personal gifts of time, talent and treasure commensurate with their capacity. As they seek the community's support they learn more about its needs and its expectations of the school. Sometimes they surface issues which the school is not aware of that could erode the support and confidence of the community. They can then carry what they learn back to their work on the board or share it with administrators to help them in their work. If they do their job well, the community will have a stronger understanding and appreciation of the school, and the school will be more in touch with the community's needs.

Cura apostolica also means overseeing the stewardship of the school's resources. Board members generally bring skills, especially in finance, law and organizational management, that augment the skills of the administration. By overseeing the budget, asset management and personnel policies, they are able to assure the soundness of the business model. Although board members usually have less expertise in the areas of the apostolic and pedagogical models, their very need to have these explained by the school administration provides an important form of guidance. Administrators can be too close to a situation. As a rule of thumb, if they can explain their decisions and strategies to persons of intelligence and broad experience, even though the issues are outside their area of expertise, the decision is probably a good one. Conversely, if there are gaps or unsound assumptions at play, these will come out.

In addition to care for the institution, boards of Jesuit schools have a responsibility to care for persons, referred to as *cura personalis*. *Cura personalis* is a core value for the Jesuits and Jesuit institutions. It goes back to St Ignatius himself, who early on resolved that he wanted to care for souls. We often think of the Jesuits, and Ignatius himself, as great organizers and builders of institutions. But their more important focus has been on individual people and their spiritual and material well-being. Ignatius and his early companions cared for the outcasts, for prostitutes and orphans, as well as for the wealthy and powerful, meeting the contrasting needs of each.

Cura personalis in our schools is centered on our students. If we love and care for our students, individually and unconditionally, they will experience the loving, creative presence of God in their life. They will feel empowered to learn, to grow and to become part of God's loving, creative presence for those around them. This is our mission, of course, and *cura personalis* is at the center of it. It begins with the care shown by the teacher for her individual students. But it is difficult for her to show this care if she herself does not experience it in the way she is treated. The teacher must experience *cura personalis* from her administrators, as well as her colleagues. But the administrator must in turn draw on his experience of care from his superiors, all the way up to the president. And the president must know that the board cares for her well-being. What we have in Jesuit schools is a chain of care which actually starts from Jesus himself, given to the Church, which is given to the Society. The Society, in the person of the provincial, communicates that unconditional love to the board and the president, who also give the same love and support to each other. This chain continues down to the principal, vice principals, departments heads and faculty and finally to the student. If you have experienced this chain, both when it is intact and when it is broken, you will understand how powerful it is. It is perhaps the best thing we do.

Each of us can experience a similar chain of care on a personal level. When I anticipate a particularly difficult day, my morning prayer often includes this meditation: If God can be gentle with me I can be gentle with myself. If I can be gentle with myself I can be gentle with others. If I can be gentle with others they can be gentle with themselves. If they can be gentle with themselves they can be gentle with me. If they can be gentle with me I can be gentle with myself. If I can be gentle with myself I can let God be gentle with me. I have found that I can start a chain reaction of *cura personalis* that comes back to me. Try it.

One of the main ways the board does its work is by setting policies. A policy is a principle to be followed in decision-making or a parameter limiting the range of decision options for those to whom authority has been entrusted. The board uses policies to give direction to the school both in its own work and in the work of the administration. For instance, the board may adopt a policy related to the school budget. The policy might direct the administration to prepare a budget that maximizes quality of program without increasing costs to a point where certain socio-economic groups are denied access. It might give further parameters for that budget, such as seeing that the employees receive a wage increase equal to the cost of living adjustment, or that tuition not increase by more than 5%. After specifying these general principles and additional parameters, it then leaves it to the administration to work out the details. In many cases the administration submits an entire budget for approval by the board, complete with budgets for individual departments. Generally, however, the board is concerned with only a few major assumptions of the budget and the administration is empowered to make adjustments that don't affect those assumptions without returning to the board for approval.

A key challenge for boards is discerning the line between its role (governance) and that of the administration (operations). While the board has authority over all aspects of the school, it has entrusted operational responsibility and authority to the president. The president in turn delegates authority to the rest of the administration. The administration exercises its authority following the guidelines and within the parameters set by board policy, and only in exceptional circumstances does the board directly exercise authority that has been delegated to the administration. The danger of the board exercising authority in areas delegated to the president is twofold. First, the board generally lacks the expertise and sufficient knowledge of the circumstances to make the best decision. And second, if this becomes a pattern, the president or other staff will stop making decisions and defer more and more to the board. Since the board consists of volunteers who meet only periodically, they cannot handle such a decision-making load and the school begins to experience either erratic decision-making or overall stagnation. This same principle should be followed by the president, who should not be pulling back authority proper to the principal, who in turn should not be making decisions proper to his reports. In Catholic social teaching, this is known as the principle of subsidiarity.

In formulating policies, the board of a Jesuit school uses a particular mode of decision-making which goes back to Ignatius and the early Jesuits. This Ignatian discernment process is described in Chapter IV on the community model. It differs from the decision-making model in most contemporary organizations in that it is not about simply finding out the will of those who wield the most power, or even the will of the majority. It's about figuring out what God's will is, and sometimes that can be revealed in unexpected ways. During a deliberation I have a tendency to marshal my arguments and be preparing my next one as someone else is speaking. This is not helpful to discernment, which calls us to listen deeply to others, open to how God may be speaking through them. In discernment I need to listen to my own feelings, acknowledge the ways that I may not be free to accept another point of view and pray for the grace to let go of my position. It also means I need to engage in loving conflict with people of other viewpoints. When new board members are first exposed to these ways of approaching contested issues they often seem bizarre, but they soon grow to appreciate the efficacy of what is happening. I especially like to watch the reactions of new board members when Jesuits skilled in honest dialog challenge each other. Lay people are often shocked to hear them not observing the normal politeness that tiptoes around differences of viewpoint. But they eventually perceive the deeper love and trust beneath the tension and can even begin emulating it in their own engagement of issues.

The other major responsibility of the board, or at least most boards, is the hiring, evaluation and, when necessary, termination of the president. In the past this may have been the responsibility of the provincial superior, but for most schools now this responsibility has been entrusted to the local board. The board must exercise great care in hiring the president, and in those times when transitions occur, board members need to be prepared to invest significant time into the process. Hiring is a difficult process and most people don't find it much fun. But anyone who doesn't find hiring fun should remember what terminating someone is like. It will encourage them to put much effort into the front end of the process, to avoid the problems of the back end.

Evaluation is the point where *cura apostolica* and *cura personalis* come together. The board has the responsibility to evaluate the president every year, not just when things seem to be going sideways. The evaluation should be supportive but honest. I favor the inclusion of a "360°" survey of the school's constituencies, including all board members, direct reports and a sampling of other administrators, faculty, staff, parents, alumni and benefactors. Students may also be included, though most won't have a clue about what the president is supposed to be doing. Then a small evaluation committee (such as the chair, vice chair and, if he is on the board, the superior of the Jesuit community) meets with the president to review the year. At the meeting, the evaluation committee reviews the president's performance on a set of agreed upon goals from the prior year's evaluation, reviews the ratings and comments from the 360° survey, perhaps reviews the progress on strategic plan goals and/ or the president's performance against her job description. It is important in reviewing the 360° ratings and comments that the committee not treat them as the evaluation itself. For instance, several faculty may rate the president poorly and make negative comments about a decision made during the year. What's important is whether the board thought it was a good decision or not. While it's helpful to both the board and the president to know what employees think, only the board has the authority to set evaluation criteria. Two products should come out of the review: a report to the broader board on the committee's evaluation and a set of goals for the following year. If the committee has identified serious issues in the president's performance, the goals should reflect steps to correct the deficiencies. The goals are approved by the committee, and the entire board if it wishes. Based on the evaluation report, the board must decide whether the president's contract will be renewed once the current term is completed.

B. Board Function

A board is made up of volunteers, generally busy individuals who have achieved success through their competence and leadership in fields other than education. They convene on a periodic basis (at most monthly) and collectively share ultimate responsibility for the apostolic, pedagogical, community and financial health of a complex organization comprising hundreds of students, faculty and other employees. On the face of it, this doesn't sound like a very promising arrangement. If we didn't know better, we might assume that they would be prone to either exert too little influence over the school or too much, to indulge in benign neglect or make decisions that disrupt the work of the full-time professionals who manage the school. Sometimes those excesses do happen, but for the most part boards provide wisdom, encouragement and leadership to the institutions they govern. The extent to which they do so depends on three main ingredients: who is on the board, how the board is structured, and how the board is staffed.

C. Board Membership

When I led a discussion at the JSEA Presidents' Conference in 2011, these are some of the characteristics the presidents from schools around the country mentioned as important for members of their boards:

Wisdom in deliberation and policy formation
Commitment to and understanding of Jesuit education and spirituality
Stature and leadership in the community
Philanthropy, the ability to give and/or draw out the support of others
Expertise for and willingness to serve on an appropriate board committee
Leadership potential at both the board and committee level
Balance in gender, ethnicity, profession and geography

Religious diversity, while assuring enough Catholic members to assist the board in its responsibility to support the school's Catholic mission

Of these, the first two would hopefully be characteristics of all board members. The others need to be present in the board as a whole. Some presidents liked having faculty members on the board and others said they'd had bad experiences with it. The latter were concerned about the conflict of interest when it comes to budgeting and setting salary levels (although when you think about it, parents would also have a comparable conflict of interest when it comes to setting tuition levels). I have worked with about 15 faculty members who have served on the board and have found every one to be a valuable voice for faculty concerns while still understanding that their job as a board member was to discern the interests of the school as a whole. They helped break down adversarial relationships and increased confidence in the board and its processes. As one president at the conference remarked, much depends on how they are prepared for the job.

It is also important to have Jesuit members on the board. Even in a two-tiered structure with a Jesuit board and a "lay" board, the collaboration in discernment is critical to the lay members' understanding of how Jesuit principles are applied. The presidents I spoke with suggested other types of people to consider as well: someone who has influence with the board, but not too much influence; certain families who are perennial pillars of the school's mission; younger Jesuits; someone from the local public schools; and someone who can be a dissonant voice to spur discussion.

Recruiting the right board members is only part of the equation. They also need to be oriented, trained and supported in their learning and growth. They will bring in their experiences from other boards, which will be a great help. But they will also need to learn how Jesuit schools are different from other organizations. The Ignatian discernment process is often counter-intuitive for people used to more conventional decision-making models. Board members are often hungry for greater understanding of Ignatian spirituality and know instinctively that it is important to their work as board members. But their time is limited, so we need to be thoughtful in using their time, and ours, strategically to give them what they want and need. And since board members are at different points in their terms, what they need will vary from person to person. Some training and formation can be given to the board as a whole during meetings and retreats, but some must be sequenced, based on the board member's time into his term.

D. Board Structure

Somehow boards have to set directions for the school and monitor its progress without becoming enmeshed in operations. How the board is structured is crucial to being able to accomplish this. One of the first questions is how big the board needs to be. For-profit businesses tend to have small boards of 5-8, but it is difficult for this to work for non-profits because of the need to draw key stakeholders and stakeholder groups into the tent. 15-25 tends to be the range.

The most critical element in the board's ability to provide appropriate oversight is its committee structure. Through its committees the board can gain a deeper understanding of the various areas of the school while conserving precious time in board meetings. A friend of mine told me that when he was in high school the police force of Mascoutah, Illinois, consisted of four officers and one squad car. Because there was only one car, they all had to ride on patrol together. Not a good use of their time. The committee structure allows the board to deploy its members across the range of issues, and then bring reports and recommendations back to the board. For this to work, the board has to trust the work of the committees. If it has to review all the data and recreate all the deliberations of the committees, they are all piling into the same squad car again. Some board members find it frustrating to receive high-level reports from the committees, and trusting them so much feels like rubber-stamping, but this is the only way a board can realistically provide the oversight required of it.

The next question is what committees the board needs. The list of possible arenas that might need a board committee can be quite long and include:

Academics
Formation
Student life
Sports and activities
Personnel
Development
Finance/ budget
Facilities
Technology
Strategic planning
Ignatian identity
Board development/ membership

Reviewing this list, it is clear that the board could be overwhelmed with committee work. It can realistically only manage 5-8 standing committees, and 8 would be pushing the limit. Let's say the Board feels it can handle six. It then has to decide which ones really need to be standing committees, then roll some of the others into these six, or address those issues with ad hoc committees on an as-needed basis.

Then it has to figure out how to populate the committees. If the board has 20 members and six committees that means that it can have about three members per committee. It can require board members to double or triple up on committees, but this starts to look like that Mascoutah squad car again, and if board members are the busy people we try to recruit, this can result in shallow participation on each committee as they try to spread limited time between them. In order to address this many organizations have extended committee membership to people who are not on the board per se but sit with board members on the various committees. These can be given official status as associate directors or associate trustees and can have deliberative power along with the trustees at the committee level. Thus a finance committee might have three board members who form the link back to the board, but they are joined by four to seven associate members who bring more expertise and breadth of perspective to the financial issues facing the school. This approach has the added advantage of identifying and forming a pool of potential candidates for the board itself. Our school reached a point where we rarely brought members onto the board who did not have two or more years of experience as associate directors. This not only helped them to understand the school, its mission and governance structure, but it allowed the board to gauge their effectiveness and commitment.

The role of board committees, especially committees with associate members on them, can be confusing at times. There is a tendency to think of board committees as similar to those formed within an organization to accomplish some task. Such committees are what organizational change authors John Kotter and Dan S. Cohen would call "guiding teams." Their role is to identify and lead change in an organization. So when someone is asked to serve on a facilities committee, he may assume that his role is to guide change in the school's facilities department. But this is not their role. If it were it would mean that the facilities director now has two bosses, the administrator she reports to and the facilities committee. Management is the responsibility of the administration, and ultimate accountability to the board must find its way through that structure. Board committees essentially have three roles:

1. *To help the board monitor mission-effectiveness in their area and recommend board level policies when necessary.* For instance, the board has a responsibility to assure that the school is managing its human resources effectively and in a way consistent with the mission. Since it cannot, as a whole board, monitor the personnel issues, it delegates this function to a personnel committee. The personnel committee receives reports from the administration on their personnel-related activities and raises questions to clarify how those activities are supporting the mission. At times a board-level policy may be needed to ensure that human resources are serving the mission. For example, the school may need to update its benefits package to meet certain criteria important to the school's mission. The committee could recommend this to the board and, if the recommendation were approved, the board would require the administration to update the

school's benefits package accordingly. The committee would not directly exercise authority over the administration to update the benefits. Rather, the policy would be approved by the board at the committee's recommendation and then be given as a parameter to the president.

2. *To serve as a sounding board for the administration.* While the committees do not exercise direct authority over the administration, in practice they provide invaluable consultation. The administrator whose responsibilities correspond to a given committee's area would do well to bring questions and concerns to the committee to help her discern a course of action. And the committees may alert administrators to issues they might not be aware of. For instance, an outside educator on an academic committee might be aware of new state curriculum standards and suggest that the principal review the curriculum in light of them. The principal might in turn ask the committee to help him formulate a response to the new standards.

3. *Provide hands-on support when appropriate.* Because of their expertise and their commitment to the school, committees are a good source of volunteers for helping with work in their area. An attorney on the personnel committee might draft a harassment policy that complies with current laws, development committee members might serve as solicitors for the annual giving campaign or the formation committee might organize and direct the board retreat. Such hands-on involvement not only avails the school of valuable volunteer assistance but helps the committee members get on-the-ground experience that helps them in their committee deliberation.

These three roles are listed in order of priority. Those listed lower should not interfere with those listed higher. The most important job is being the eyes and ears of the board and helping it formulate policies when necessary (which isn't very often). If consulting with the administration or doing hands-on volunteering interferes with that job the committee must pull itself back and refocus on its primary responsibility.

E. Board Staffing

In my experience, the structure described above works well to incorporate quality board members into the school's governance and allows them to provide appropriate guidance. But it has a cost. It takes a lot of effort to maintain. It means recruiting board members, but also associate board members with the skills and diversity that they can bring with them if they eventually join the board itself; it means recruiting not only committed, qualified officers for the board, but chairs for each of the committees; it means developing agendas with those chairs that give meaningful work to the committees, preparing timely reports, scheduling meetings, preparing minutes and dealing with committee members who don't understand their role or turn out not to be sufficiently committed. This is a lot of front-end investment to make the system work. I believe it pays off in sound governance of the school, but I can understand why some schools focus on a simpler structure and improvise additional structure as the needs arise.

I would suggest two approaches that can help busy boards and administrators manage this challenge. The first relates to how the committees are staffed. The president has the primary responsibility of providing the staff support needed by the board. This is a major part of the president's role, but she cannot do it alone. At the committee level, other administrators should provide the staffing support. So the CFO should be the primary liaison with the finance committee, the development director with the development committee and so forth. For some committees, like personnel, or an Ignation formation committee, who the appropriate liaison would be is not as obvious. The assignment will depend on how responsibilities are distributed among the school's administration.

Serving as a liaison can be seen as a great opportunity by some administrators and a distraction from the demanding job of running a school by others. Some may have great skills for the give and take of supporting and being supported by a committee of outsiders, and others may not. But if schools are to achieve their full potential, all administrators need to step up to this role. Not only will it provide depth to the board's governance of the school, it will provide a crucial professional growth opportunity for administrators. It is incumbent on the president to make these expectations clear and to provide guidance and support for administrators stepping into an unfamiliar role.

The other key to managing the time it takes to maintain a healthy governance structure is to "hard-wire" the activities required. Work out a calendar in advance so that the proper time is allocated. This means not only scheduling board and committee meetings a year in advance, but having an internal calendar for all the background processes, like sending out meeting reminders and materials, scheduling meeting spaces and preparing reports. Recurring activities should not surprise us. Use templates to keep from reinventing the wheel: templates for agendas, for reports and presentations, for evaluations. The more things become routine, the less time they take. The other side of the coin is that routine can prevent us from being creative. We need to be open to rescheduling meetings and re-thinking the agenda as new circumstances arise. But most of what we do is routine, or can be. Most things don't need to be re-invented every time we do them. And having a backbone of routine in place can actually allow us to be more flexible, like an actor who can improvise when necessary because he knows his lines and blocking so well.

Boards of Jesuit schools continue to evolve as the Society of Jesus redefines its own role in light of the last few General Congregations' call for greater collaboration in Jesuit ministries. More and more the Society is looking to local boards comprised mainly of lay people to assure the fidelity of the Jesuit school not only to its mission of service to the local community, but also to the common mission of the Society and its ministries. It can be a sobering experience for a board to realize that it is no longer just an appendage helping Father run the local Jesuit school, but a team of people actually entrusted with stewarding this great legacy they have inherited. There is wisdom in the Society's trust in local lay boards to carry on the tradition of Jesuit education. This act of trust is not unlike the trust God gives to all of us to carry on His work on earth. Boards need good processes and support from the school administration and the Jesuits of their Province, but what they bring to the table can ensure that the richness of Jesuit education will serve their community for years to come.

Conclusion: One Model

We have been studying four different models—apostoic, pedagogical, community and business— that must be healthy and functioning within Jesuit schools in order for them to achieve their mission.. Even though our discussions have not exhausted all the elements of these models, it is clear that they are complex in themselves. Considered together, as components of one model, the complexity only increases. This book has been an attempt to bring them all together and I have tried to suggest how they interact at various points. As we conclude, it will be helpful to fly to a higher level to see in general terms how the four models function together as one. To do this, I want to take four values that have been woven throughout this book. While these four values are clearly important, arguments could be made that others are equally critical. But these four will at least suggest the continuities that must be achieved in the model that unites all our work in a Jesuit school. The four values are: *purpose, freedom, growth* and *trust*.

A. Purpose

St. Ignatius begins the first week of the *Spiritual Exercises* with what he calls the *Principle and Foundation*. The whole of what is to follow in the *Exercises* is predicated on the notion that our lives have a *purpose*, which is to praise, reverence and serve God, both in this life and the next. Our schools also have a purpose, which we articulate as our mission. Many organizations have mission statements, but more often than not, they sound like afterthoughts, something to give a positive spin to organizational activity which is really just about making a profit. For us, the purpose must be the starting place. Taking what Ignatius says is the purpose of every human life, the purpose of a Jesuit education is to help students experience the loving presence of God in their lives and choose to become part of that loving presence. Clearly, this is the purpose of the apostolic model of the school. But it is also the purpose of its pedagogical model. Our curriculum is not centered on getting kids into college or even on learning for its own sake, as valuable as that is. It is centered on helping students become the persons God created them to be. Our community model isn't centered on providing a safe or comfortable place for our employees, or even for our students, as important as that is. It is centered on providing experiences of God's loving presence in students' relationships with each other and with the adults responsible for helping them grow into the people God created them to be. And our business model isn't centered on making money or even having enough resources to assure our success as a school, as critical as that is. It is centered on inviting and involving people to form that vital, broad community which can support students in becoming the people God created them to be. Our lives have a purpose, our school has a purpose, each of the models has a purpose, and that purpose should center everything we do.

One of the ways we stay centered is by continually asking what the outcomes are that we seek. There is a human tendency to begin with what we know how to do and then determine what purpose that can serve. But we must begin as Ignatius did, with our deepest desire and work backward to the decisions that will lead us to it. This is the principle of "backward design," and it doesn't apply just to curriculum. We must focus on ultimate outcomes in every area of the school, and then order the programs and methods to those outcomes, be they fundraising, faculty professional development, athletics, liturgies or management of the endowment. All these processes, Ignatius would say, are useful only insofar as they help us toward the end for which we were created. The strategic planning process plays a key role here. It must articulate the outcomes for each of the four models in terms of how they support the mission, and it must show how activities within the four models converge to support the mission as a whole. It should challenge individuals to move beyond narrow horizons, beyond old habits and beyond departmentalized thinking. This means moving into uncharted territory. This is why measurable goals are so important. When we don't have a clear vision of what our goal is we cling to our methods. What castaway would ever swim from the plank he is clinging to if he doesn't see the shore? When we know what the goal is we are free to use the best methods to achieve it. Setting measurable goals and measuring our progress isn't helpful just for students in the classroom, it's helpful for teachers too. It's important to measure whether the development office is meeting the annual giving targets, but it's also important to measure whether the formation programs are helping students encounter and develop a deeper relationship with Jesus.

In 2010, Fr. General Adolfo Nicolás told the representatives from Jesuit higher education assembled in Mexico City, "Jesuits are very good at thinking. They want to do things. They are very generous. But the challenge is to be realistic and to be able to follow up our work with some form of measurement ~ which is not mechanical measuring. It's always human and often spiritual fruits that we have to measure. Whether our students are being transformed ~ this also has to be evaluated. How do they perform later? Not only if they keep praising the Jesuits, but do they collaborate when we get involved with faith and justice? Do they collaborate when some of the issues in which we are involved bring conflict with the government, when this might bring some weakening in the profits they make in companies?"[10] Pursuing the *magis* means knowing what our purpose is and being creative in measuring how much progress we are making.

B. Freedom

The second value that must be applied to all four models is *freedom*. God knew what would happen if Adam and Eve ate of the fruit of the tree in the center of the garden. And He warned Adam and Eve not to eat of it. But He didn't put a fence around it. For me this is emblematic of the value God places on human freedom. I wish God would just prevent me from doing bad things or stupid things, but He has given me free will and seems reluctant to constrain it in any way. Somehow our choices, as flawed as they may be, are important. Because we operate in God's world, we simply have to acknowledge the principle of freedom in our work with other people. We know that when we are working in our apostolic model we cannot force students to choose God or embrace the Catholic faith. But the principle of freedom applies to the other three models as well. We cannot force students in geometry to gain an insight, we cannot force students to let go of stereotypes about their classmates' backgrounds, and we cannot force alumni to make a pledge to the school that propelled them to the success they enjoy. The best we can do is invite them into these better places by drawing them in their door, so that they may come out the door we desire for them.

This is *marketing*, and we have to do it well for each of the four models to function. When a development officer is trying to coax a pledge from a financially capable school parent, she probably wishes she could just make him give. But she can't. She has to go through the marketing process: identify the parent's "door," make the best case that it is in the parent's interest (even if just his enlightened self-interest) to give. And then she has to let go. Sometimes people respond and sometimes they don't. The campus minister experiences something similar trying to invite the brainy student atheist to consider faith in God. He will try to find the door that will bring her to God, use every argument and inducement likely to speak to this student, and then let go. It is similar for the teacher trying to coax a student to make the extra effort to master a new concept, or the dean trying to convince seniors not to harass the sophomores. Or the administrator getting faculty to respond to parent emails. All of them have to follow the iron law of marketing: we can't *make* people do what we want them to. Yes, we can punish people who don't cooperate, but this is just a negative incentive and only temporarily effective at best. It won't work unless they see it as worth their while to cooperate. The best we can do is to see what it looks like from their angle and explain in as compelling a way as possible, with incentives and inducements as appropriate, how to get from where they are to where they really need to be.

Rather than fighting the reality of human freedom, we would do well to learn the principles of marketing, an authentic marketing which encourages people to use their freedom responsibly, and apply them to all areas of the school where we are helping people transform their behavior or their beliefs.

C. Growth

The third value to be applied across all four models is *growth*. "Openness to Growth" is the first of the five characteristics of the *Grad at Grad*, presumably because it is the prerequisite for the others. If people are open to growth they can become intellectually competent, religious, loving and committed to justice. If they are not open to growth, they will not make progress in any of the other characteristics. In the world as God has created it, we are either growing or dying. This principle is closely related to the previous one, freedom. We can't force people to grow. But we can create an environment where growth becomes possible and where it is encouraged. In the apostolic model we can present the Gospel as a message of life, as something that will bring peace and happiness. In the pedagogical model we can help students see that what they learn can strengthen them and broaden their possibilities. In the community model we can improve communications, give people the time and space to strengthen relationships and foster an environment of safety and freedom that encourages individuals and community to grow. In the business model we can set goals for growth that are challenging yet realistic and explain to people what achieving these goals will mean for the accomplishment of the school's mission and their own deepest desires.

The Ignatian Pedagogical Paradigm describes the natural dynamic of human development. By attending to each step of the IPP we can foster healthy growth in our students and the school. It should be used as a guide in the development and strengthening of each of the four models. In the apostolic model we can ask: have we given students the *context* that shows why Church doctrine has developed as it has? In the pedagogical model, have we let physics students *experience* how mass and weight are distinct concepts? In the community model, have we given faculty time for *reflection* on how a new schedule is changing the way they teach? In the business model, are we making changes to get different results, moving ahead with *action* even if we can't be sure of what the results will be? And in every model, are we disciplining ourselves to set measurable goals for *evaluation* of those areas we say are key to our mission? Any one of the steps of the IPP can point us to opportunities for growth in any one of the models.

Growth implies change and change takes a lot of energy. This is why it is difficult to sustain. It is even more difficult if new ways of doing things have to be re-created every time we do them. One of the disciplines that can help sustain change is hardwiring new approaches once they are proven. Examples would be developing on-line courses to train teachers in new procedures, maintaining knowledge-bases of helpful approaches to various challenges, developing checklists for new procedures until they become second nature, and delegating procedures to support personnel whose skills are geared to carrying them out. Developing performance metrics is a good example. Some metrics can be difficult to formulate. But once they are formulated the measuring process should be made as automatic as possible. So if taking the JSEA Student Profile Survey is important for measuring progress on the *Grad at Grad*, the principal shouldn't have to set up meetings each year to schedule administration of the survey. It should be a regular feature of the school schedule and included in the job expectations of those responsible for conducting it. All of our models should be encouraging growth, and that encouragement should be built in to our yearly routines.

D. Trust

Underlying all these values and making them possible is *trust*. In the first place we must trust God. Ignatius is often quoted as saying, "Pray as if everything depends on God; act as if everything depends on you." A number of years ago, I heard that he was being misquoted. What he actually said is, "Pray as if everything depends on you; act as if everything depends on God." I'm not sure which he said, but my experience has led me to believe there should be a third version: "Pray as if everything depends on God; act as if everything depends on God." Because, after all, everything does depend on God. If we act on a different assumption, if we ignore this fundamental reality, our results will be distorted. Trust in God should be the foundation of the Jesuit school and each of its models. It is God who evangelizes, it is God who gives us understanding, it is God who draws us together and it is God who provides the resources we need.

By and large, God does all this through people. So trusting God means trusting other people. Trusting students in the often circuitous ways they pursue the good, trusting administrators who want to make adjustments to the curriculum, trusting a co-worker who says something inflammatory in an email and trusting a parent who fills out a form asking for financial aid. Generally, we require our trust in people to be earned. Sometimes we are willing to give them the benefit of the doubt but we are quick to withdraw it at the first sign of slippage. It is difficult to maintain the trust needed for the four models to function when this is the case.

As people managing for mission, we must emulate Jesus and initiate that trust, even when it hasn't been earned. Even when it has been betrayed. *Cura personalis*, what I have described as the *chain of care*, goes through us. We are always a link in that chain, both receiving love and giving it. We are also a link in the chain of trust. If the links on either side of us are weak, if a teacher is wary of a change being proposed, or a board member doubts that a program is where it needs to be, we need to demonstrate and ask for trust. We need to encourage it by the way we manage. We need to increase collaboration rather than decrease it; we need to take more time for discernment, not less; we need to share more information, not less; we need to be more honest and transparent, not less; we need to practice the *Presupposition*, even if those around us do not.

Managing for mission in a Jesuit school is not a path of least resistance. It is challenging, and at times heroic, even when it does not appear so to anyone else. Sometimes what we must do is counter-intuitive, but it is not mysterious. The *magis* for Jesuit schools is not a place we arrive at; it is an ever-ascending path. By incorporating sound management principles, proven in our schools and in other successful organizations, we can give the gift of the *magis* to our students, our colleagues and the world.

Notes:

1. Address to the Pontifical Council for Interreligious Dialogue, June 7, 2010

2. *Shared Vision*, The Institute of Jesuit Sources, 1995

3. *The Great Game of Business*, Jack Stack and Bo Burlingame, Doubleday, 1992, p71

4. *Economics*, Paul Samuelson, McGraw Hill, Eighth Edition 1970, p.11

5. NPR *Fresh Air*, February 16, 2011

6. "Education Pays: The Benefits of Higher Education for Individuals and Society," Sandy Baum and Jennifer Ma, The College Board, 2007, p. 9. http://www.collegeboard.com/prod_downloads/about/news_info/trends/ed_pays_2007.pdf

7. For a more detailed look at the Blockbuster story, see "On Sparring with an Activist Shareholder," by Blockbuster's former CEO, John Antioco, Harvard Business Review, April 2011, p39

8. Jesuit HS, Shreveport LA, 1928; Cranwell Preparatory School, Lenox MA, 1975; Brooklyn Preparatory School, Brooklyn NY, 1972; Marquette H S, Yakima WA, 1968; Campion HS, Prairie du Chien WI, 1975; Jesuit HS, El Paso TX, 1972; Bishop's Latin School, Pittsburgh PA; 1973; Loyola High School, Missoula MT, 1974. http://en.wikipedia.org/wiki/List_of_former_Jesuit_secondary_schools_in_the_United_States

9. http://www.ncea.org/news/annualdatareport.asp

10. "Networking Jesuit Higher Education: Shaping the Future for a Humane, Just, Sustainable Globe." Presentation by Fr. Adolfo Nicolás SJ, Superior General of the Society of Jesus, Mexico City, April 23, 2010

11. See guidelines 21 & 22, http://www.afpnet.org/Ethics/EnforcementDetail.cfm?ItemNumber=3261

Glossary

Accountability: How we assure that individual members of the community do what is necessary for the community as a whole to succeed in its mission.

Admissions recruiting: The process of attracting, selecting and enrolling students in the school.

Anecdotal evidence: The observation of conditions within a group when such observations are not frequent enough to generalize about the pervasiveness of those conditions.

Annual giving: Donations about which the donor decides on a yearly basis, generally given for operations and often unrestricted.

Annual Implementation Plan (AIP): A plan which outlines the steps for a given year to be taken toward accomplishing the goals of the long-range strategic plan. An AIP is prepared prior to each year and should spell out the most important 4-8 objectives to be accomplished that year.

Apostolate: An active work or ministry that carries on the mission of Jesus, entrusted to his apostles, and through a chain of discipleship to those engaged in this ministry today.

Apostolic model: The assumptions, components, and interactions of a ministry's system for responding to Jesus' command to spread the Gospel to all people.

Ask: The process of motivating and requesting a decision about a proposed gift or transaction.

Backward design: A way of formulating a process by beginning with the ultimate outcomes and organizing in reverse succession the components that will lead to those outcomes.

Balance sheet: (statement of financial position) A snapshot of a school's assets, liabilities and fund balances at a particular point in time. Total assets will always equal the total liabilities plus the total fund balances.

Baseline: Beginning level of performance against which progress will be measured. The baseline period (e.g. year) is the timeframe when the baseline measure is taken.

Benchmark: A standard derived from the performance of similar institutions, useful in setting measurable goals that are challenging but realistic.

Benefit: A consequence from buying a product, which a customer finds valuable.

Brand: The identity of an organization in the mind of its publics that gives a clear and accurate, if not detailed, impression of who the organization is and what it does.

Budget: A projection of revenues and authorization of expenses for a given period of time.

Business model: The assumptions, components and interactions of an enterprise's system of producing and exchanging products for sufficient financial return to accomplish the enterprise's mission.

Call-reluctance: The anxiety about potential disappointment that prevents a solicitor from initiating a call on a potential donor.

Capital campaign: A fundraising effort of limited duration with a goal to provide funding for specific long-term assets needed by a school, though it may also incorporate gifts to annual giving.

Capital intensive: Requiring a significant investment in fixed assets, like plant or technology, to accomplish the goals of the business model.

Cascading: The process of having the institution's strategic goals shape decisions, activities and resource usage at all levels of the organization.

Case: A term of art in development referring to the compelling reasons the community should support a particular project, need or set of needs identified by a non-profit organization.

Cash flow statement: (statement of the sources and uses of funds) A report showing where cash added to the balance sheet during a certain period came from and what cash that was subtracted from the balance sheet was used for in that same period.

Catechesis: The process of acquiring or teaching knowledge of the faith.

Collaboration: Several people working together to produce a common result or product.

Communications (in marketing): The way we transmit information about ourselves and our products to our current and potential customers.

Community model: The assumptions, components and interactions of an institution's system of relationships which supports the people involved, both individually and as a group, in their own well-being and in accomplishing the institution's mission.

Consultative decision-making model: A method of organizational discernment in which authority and responsibility for making decisions on behalf of the organization are vested in certain individuals or groups, with the requirement that they listen to and take into account the experience, insight and needs of those being affected by their decisions.

Consultors: As part of Jesuit governance and its consultative decision-making model, those appointed to serve as advisors to a superior, who is under obligation to consider, though not bound to follow, their advice in important matters.

Cura Apostolica: Care for the apostolate or institution as a whole.

Cura Personalis: Care for the person as an individual.

Curriculum: A course of studies spanning multiple learning experiences, that leads a student to attain specific outcomes for knowledge, skills and understanding.

Customer: The person or entity that makes a decision to purchase and has the ability to authorize payment for a product. In the case of a Catholic school, this could be the parent of a student or a donor.

Dashboard: A one-page chart used for tracking key performance measures for an organization.

Debt instruments: Investments (such as bonds) by which a business borrows money from investors with a promise to return their original investment plus interest, generally after a set period of time.

Because the investor is a lender, his return is limited to the agreed upon interest rate, but his investment is not affected by a decline in the business's value unless the decline is so severe that the business defaults.

Development Pyramid: A visual representation of the four categories of development activity showing the range from most to least broad-based, but also from least dollar value per gift to most. At the bottom of this pyramid are special events, with annual giving above that, followed by major gifts and finally planned giving at the top.

Development: The process of securing resources for an organization from people for whom at least some portion of the benefit is realizing their aspirations for the organization and its work rather than for themselves directly.

Discernment: The process of making better judgments by considering more than immediate data or desires and exploring ever deeper levels of meaning for the issues about which judgments are made.

Diversification: The practice of distributing investments among different categories, strategies, sectors, industries and issuers, to avoid the risk of exposure to a significant decline in one of these that is not experienced by the market in general.

Donative intent: The desire to give to an organization that goes beyond the value of any goods or services the donor receives in return.

Donor-centric: Built around a prospective donor's desires and needs rather than the institution's, as in a gift request which is formulated to meet the four rights about the donor (the right person asking, the right amount, the right purpose and the right timing).

Donor: A person or funding organization which has made a gift to an organization, the value of which exceeds any goods or services received in return.

Endowment: Funds invested with the intention that the income from the investment, and not the corpus, will be used for the various needs of the school.

Equities: Investments (such as common stocks) that provide the investor with an ownership position in a business. Because of the ownership position, the investor benefits from any increases in the value of the business, but is also exposed to any decreases in value.

Evaluation: Determining the value of someone's work in relation to the needs of an organization as defined by a supervisor's expectations, a written set of job expectations and/or the organization's mission and goals.

Evangelization: The process of spreading the Good News of the Gospel, by teaching, exhorting, modeling and inspiring, which leads to a conversion to faith in Jesus and the Gospel.

Fallacy of composition: A logical error resulting from the assumption that what is true of part is also true of the whole, or the assumption that what is true of the whole is also true of its parts.

Feature: The characteristic of a product that can produce a benefit for a customer.

Feel-felt-found: A method for handling objections by 1) acknowledging and verifying what the customer feels, 2) explaining how you have had a similar feeling, and 3) sharing what you found when you looked into the issue further. The approach can also be used to deal with disgruntled parents, employees or students when we don't want their concerns to cause them to disengage.

Financial controls: Internal procedures which reduce the risk of intentional or unintentional loss of assets in the course of school operations, as well as regulations from external authorities with which the organization is required to comply.

Financial management: The processes and procedures for protecting and maximizing the value of an organization's assets.

Financial reporting: Presentations of the financial condition of an organization for a given period of time using generally accepted accounting principles (GAAP). The reporting includes the balance sheet, income statement and cash flow statement, as well as other statements and notes as appropriate. Reports should be prepared monthly, and at least annually.

Formation: A course of experiences and reflection that leads students to grow into the form that best expresses their full potential as children of God grounded in faith, hope and love.

Formative evaluations: Assessments intended to provide feedback that leads to improvement during a process.

Free will: The ability to choose the good, but also to choose its negation. More precisely, the presence of the conditions that allow persons to choose to actuate their potential and the absence of conditions that prevent them from choosing to actuate their potential, along with the conditions that allow them to choose the negation of their potential and the absence of conditions that prevent them from choosing to negate their potential.

Funneling: The process of narrowing or distilling a large number of recommendations into a strategic few. As recommendations are funneled up from broad-based participation vehicles, like public meetings and topic teams, toward the steering committee formulating the overall strategic plan, they are often consolidated, eliminated or changed to produce a focused and coherent set of strategic goals.

Goal: The endpoint for a series of actions which has crucial significance to the overall mission. Goals align factors within the institution's control to adapt to factors not within the institution's control to produce a desired reality. Goals are the building blocks of the strategic plan and are in turn achieved by a series of intermediate, tactical objectives.

Grad at Grad: The Profile of a Jesuit High School Graduate at Graduation. A document first formulated by the Jesuit Secondary Education Association (JSEA) in 1981, which describes five fundamental characteristics that Jesuit schools foster in their students by the time they graduate. They are to be: open to growth, intellectually competent, religious, loving and committed to justice. Also known as the Profile, or the Characteristics.

Growth: The process of becoming more; moving toward one's full potential and away from the negation of one's being.

Hardwiring: Building proven approaches into organizational behavior and process so that they can be repeated with sustained effectiveness.

Ignatian discernment model: A model for making decisions that uncovers God's desires for us as well as our deepest desires for ourselves, both individually and as organizations.

Ignatian Pedagogical Paradigm (IPP): A description of the learning process based on the spirituality of Ignatius of Loyola which identifies five key steps in coming to understanding: context, experience, reflection, action and evaluation. The IPP makes the assumption that effective teaching must adequately address each of these steps.

Incentive: A reward based on meeting or exceeding previously set performance standards.

Income statement: (statement of activities) A report showing an organization's revenues coming in over a given period of time, as well as the expenses incurred, in order to show the net surplus or loss from operations for that period.

Inputs: Processes which are used to produce a desired output or outcome.

Intuitive evidence: Deductions about whether outcomes have occurred or will occur under certain conditions based on experience with similar conditions.

Magis: Latin for "the more," referring especially to quality versus quantity, as in non multa, sed multum: "Not many, but much."

Major gifts: The development category in which donors are asked to make gifts which are large in proportion to the school's overall fundraising goal.

Management: The direction leaders give to align the decisions and actions of all participants toward desired organizational outcomes.

Market timing: An investment strategy that tries to maximize return by buying investments in anticipation of a general market increase and selling investments in anticipation of a general market decline, based on formulae or indicators believed to be predictive of market behavior.

Marketing: The process of connecting products and customers. It involves identifying what people need (Research); producing it (Product); presenting it to them in a compelling way (Promotion); and asking them for their commitment to purchase it (Sales).

Metric: A quantitative measure which can be used to establish a baseline, measurable goals and progress made in the performance of a process. Could consist of a statistical measure or a truth statement about whether a product or condition does or does not exist.

Mission: The purpose for which an organization exists. This purpose is expected to remain substantially the same throughout the life of the organization. If it remains, the organization remains, even though its name, personnel and physical assets may change. If it changes, even if these others remain, it can be argued that there is now a new organization.

Model: A distilled representation of a system showing assumptions, main components and how they interact to achieve their purpose, so that the system can be preserved, changed or replicated, as needed.

Objections: Voiced or unvoiced reasons why a customer does not want to buy a product, based on what she understands about the product and its costs and benefits to her.

Objectives: Intermediate targets which lead to the accomplishment of goals. Objectives are targets at the tactical level, as opposed to goals which are targets at the strategic level.

Open-book management: A practice in which employees are given the critical information about an organization's performance, are trained in how to use that information, and know what contributions they can make to improve that performance.

Outcome: The ultimate result of a plan or process, which is valued as an end in itself rather than as a means to another result.

Outputs: The product of a process or action which can in turn be an input toward an ultimate outcome.

Pedagogical model: The assumptions, components, and interactions of a school's system for producing growth in the skills, knowledge and understanding desired for its students.

Pedagogy: The art and method of guiding and assisting students in gaining knowledge, skills and understanding.

Plan horizon: The furthest point in time envisioned by a plan. All plan goals will be accomplished and all activities planned will take place within this horizon. If the plan is a 10-year plan, then the plan horizon is ten years.

Planned giving: The development category in which donors are encouraged to make gifts to the school as part of the strategic disposition of their estate (e.g. through their will, life insurance, a trust or interest in a home).

Policy: A principle to be followed in decision-making or a parameter limiting the range of decision options for those to whom authority has been entrusted.

Presupposition: (from the *Spiritual Exercises* of St. Ignatius Loyola, Annotation 22) "That both the giver and the maker of the *Spiritual Exercises* may be of greater help and benefit to each other, it should be presupposed that every good Christian ought to be more eager to put a good interpretation to a neighbor's statement than to condemn it. Further, if one cannot interpret it favorably, one should ask how the other means it. If that meaning is wrong, one should correct the person with love; and if that is not enough, one should search out every appropriate means through which, by understanding the statement in a good way, it may be saved." (Translation by George Ganss SJ.)

Principle and Foundation: (From the *Spiritual Exercises* of St Ignatius Loyola, Annotation 23) "Human beings are created to praise, reverence and serve God our Lord, and by means of doing this to save their souls. The other things on the face of the earth are created for the human beings, to help them in the pursuit of the end for which they are created. From this it follows that we ought to use these things to the extent that they help us toward our end, and free ourselves from them to the extent that they hinder us from it. To attain this it is necessary to make ourselves indifferent to all created things, in regard to everything which is left to our free will and is not forbidden. Consequently, on our own part we ought not to seek health rather than sickness, wealth rather than poverty, honor rather than dishonor, a long life rather than a short one, and so on in all other matters. Rather, we ought to desire and choose only that which is more conducive to the end for which we are created." (Translation by George Ganss SJ.)

Pro forma: A multi-year financial plan showing what budgets will be, based on assumptions about trends beyond the school's control and choices within the school's control.

Process chain: A tool for visually representing all the steps necessary to accomplishing a given outcome. The process begins with the outcome, then moves backward to the most proximate causal link necessary for that outcome, then to the most proximate causal link for that, and so on until all the links are visually represented. This is a form of backward design.

Product: What an organization produces and sells to generate the revenue needed in its business model.

Promotion: Fostering an environment of understanding and favorable perception of a product by an organization's publics.

Prospect pipeline: The continuum of necessary steps for suspects to become prospects and eventually donors.

Prospect: A suspect for whom sufficient information on capacity and relationship has been gathered to justify an ask at a specific level.

Purpose: The reason for which something exists seen in terms of its contribution to a larger whole.

Quasi-endowment: Funds committed by the school with the intention of preserving the corpus, but the school retains the right to invade the corpus at its sole discretion in the future.

Resource: Raw material, including time, money and people power, inputted to a process to produce a desired output or outcome.

Sales force: The people who help potential customers see the benefits of an organization's product and, if they see these benefits, to follow through on a decision to purchase it. All stakeholders of an organization who come in contact with customers are potential members of the sales force.

Sales: The process of helping a potential customer come to a decision about buying a product.

Self-insurance: A risk-management practice in which an organization accepts the risk of its own potential losses, rather than pooling risk with other organizations. The organization may set aside money to fund the anticipated risk or assume it can cover the loss out of other assets or income.

Special events: The development category in which funds are raised by activities where the participant receives a high proportion of goods and services in exchange and has low donative intent.

Spiritual Exercises: A manual written by St. Ignatius of Loyola, which can be used by a retreat director to lead an exercitant (the person making the *Exercises*) to a deeper relationship with God, by discerning, as Ignatius did, how the Spirit is at work in one's own life. Ignatius proposed the *Exercises* as a way for us to free ourselves from excessive attachments so that we can find the will of God and thereby order our lives to the salvation of our souls. He was able to use these *Exercises* to effect remarkable conversion of heart in the people whom he convinced to take them, and they can have this same effect for us today.

Stakeholder: A person who realizes the benefits, either directly or indirectly, from the activities of an organization, and desires to preserve those benefits.

Statistical evidence: Data that indicate the frequency with which certain conditions exist in group.

Strategic Plan: A document or other presentation that defines how an organization will align its resources and activities to achieve its desired reality in light of its mission and the influence of external factors.

Strategic planning: The process of identifying and aligning all the significant factors within an organization's control in order to more effectively accomplish its mission in the face of environmental factors that are not within its control.

Strategic: Having significant impact on the institution's ability to accomplish its mission.

Subsidiarity: The principle that "each person or group should properly exercise the responsibility and authority of her/ his/ their office, but should not interfere in the office of another—either that of a superior, a subordinate or a peer....[T]rue subsidiarity is rooted in our faith that the Spirit of God is at work in all members of the community, who have been called into their positions of responsibility—it is presumed—through discernment....True subsidiarity relies upon the mutual trust of the parties involved, and so demands the cultivation of that trust through consistent and conscientious practices of dialogue and mutual understanding." (John Whitney SJ)

Summative evaluations: Assessments designed to measure outcomes. Although summative evaluations can also be used to improve processes, their primary purpose is to determine if an objective has been achieved. They foster improvement by holding participants accountable for the outcome.

Suspect: A person or funding organization who might have the interest and capacity to become a donor, but for whom interest and capacity have not been verified by adequate research.

Tactical: Relating to the intermediate steps to achieving a larger, strategic goal.

Technology: Any tools that extend human capability, especially those, such as computers, which can be programmed to augment the human intelligence needed in a process.

Topic teams: Ad hoc committees used in strategic planning to evaluate and offer recommendations for a particular strategic arena, like academics or facilities.

Transparency: The state of having all important facts available for view.

Trust: The willingness to place one's well-being in the hands of another.

Understanding: The apprehension of the intelligibility of an object, idea or person such that one can explain, interpret, apply, critique, appreciate, and reflect on it.

Value proposition: The justification for buying a product which demonstrates that benefits to the customer exceed costs. Benefits may include economic or emotional value. Costs may include the purchase price, time, risk and lost opportunity.

Vision statement: A statement which answers the question, "What will it look like when we get there?" Vision statements inspire an organization to sustain the effort needed to accomplish something its members believe is important. The vision statement paints a picture of the hoped-for outcome, to make it as compelling as the many immediacies that distract us from achieving that outcome.

Wiki: A tool or environment in which something can be created by a non-hierarchical group of participants.

Acknowledgments

As stated in the introduction, this book is the product of the insight and generosity of many people. In the category of insight and direct contributions to the manuscript, very special thanks to Dr. Michael Stebbins, Vice President for Mission at Avera Health System, for his editing of the entire manuscript; to Fr. Jim Stoeger SJ, President of JSEA, for his input and help tracking down research questions; to Al Falkner, president of Gonzaga Preparatory School, for his suggestions on a draft of an early portion of the manuscript; to Cindy Reopelle, Provincial Assistant for Secondary Education for the Oregon Province for her edits and suggestions; to Stephanie Cisakowski, the skilled and creative Chief Financial Officer for Bellarmine Preparatory School, for her editing and suggestions on the financial section; and to Bridget Nielsen, for her excellent book design.

In the category of generosity and general inspiration, my thanks to my wife Mary for her encouragement to undertake and persist with the project; to the late Fr. Dan Weber SJ, who mentored me and gave me a model of being president I could never completely emulate—a case where the student is indeed "not greater than his teacher" (Mt 10:24). To Chris Gavin, Principal of Bellarmine, who came to Bellarmine the same year I did, has served as its principal for over 25 years and has taught me lessons about leadership I could learn nowhere else; to Aaron Rogers, Bellarmine's ICT Director, an organizational and technology guru and a master educator of both adults and students; to my fellow presidents of Jesuit schools across the country who have always been ready to share their experiences and insights at conferences, or by email or phone. To the many Jesuits who have given me their spiritual gifts as well as their love and wisdom; and to all my colleagues at Bellarmine, both past and present, whose skill, commitment and generosity have made them the best teachers of management excellence a person could hope for.

About the Author

Jack Peterson has served as president of Bellarmine Preparatory School in Tacoma, Washington, since 1996. Prior to that he served as the school's vice president for development starting in 1981. He has his Masters in Pastoral Studies from Seattle University, and graduated from Yale University, and Seattle Preparatory School. He is a Senior Fellow of the American Leadership Forum and a member of the Yale Alumni Schools Committee. He serves as a board member and chair of the Strategic Planning Committee for Franciscan Health System, a $1.5 billion, five-hospital system in the Pacific Northwest. He has consulted with numerous schools and non-profits on mission, strategic planning, management, development and governance. He and his wife Mary have five grown children. His leisure activities include praying, hiking, backpacking, snowshoeing, running, native botany, digital photography, writing and reading.

Contact the Author

Managing for Mission was written as a way to share ideas and methods that have proven successful over three decades of managing a Jesuit school. The author has established a website and is hoping to share additional materials that he has been gathering to supplement what has been covered in this book. If you are interested in purchasing additional copies of this book, or receiving more detailed information on the topics indicated in the book, please contact Mr. Peterson via the website or email listed below. Mr. Peterson is also available for limited consulting engagements through his consulting firm, Managing for Mission.

Jack Peterson
www.managingformission.com
email: jackpeterson@managingformission.com